Love at Last Sight

Love at Last Sight

Dating, Intimacy, and Risk in Turn-of-the-Century Berlin

TYLER CARRINGTON

OXFORD
UNIVERSITY PRESS

OXFORD
UNIVERSITY PRESS

Oxford University Press is a department of the University of Oxford. It furthers
the University's objective of excellence in research, scholarship, and education
by publishing worldwide. Oxford is a registered trade mark of Oxford University
Press in the UK and certain other countries.

Published in the United States of America by Oxford University Press
198 Madison Avenue, New York, NY 10016, United States of America.

Library of Congress Cataloging-in-Publication Data
Names: Carrington, Tyler, author.
Title: Love at last sight : dating, intimacy, and risk in turn-of-the-century Berlin / Tyler Carrington.
Description: New York, NY : Oxford University Press, [2019] |
Includes bibliographical references and index.
Identifiers: LCCN 2018027024 (print) | LCCN 2018044299 (ebook) |
ISBN 9780190917777 (Updf) | ISBN 9780190917784 (Epub) |
ISBN 9780190917760 (hardcover : alk. paper)
Subjects: LCSH: Dating (Social customs)—Germany—Berlin—History—20th century. |
Single people—Germany—Berlin—Social conditions—20th century. |
Berlin (Germany)—Social life and customs—20th century. |
Sex customs—Germany—Berlin—History—20th century.
Classification: LCC HQ801 (ebook) | LCC HQ801 .C28515 2019 (print) |
DDC 306.730943/1550904—dc23
LC record available at https://lccn.loc.gov/2018027024

1 3 5 7 9 8 6 4 2
Printed by, Sheridan Books, Inc., United States of America

*For
Melissa, Lena,
and my parents*

Contents

Acknowledgments

THIS PROJECT BEGAN at the University of Illinois, where my mentor, Peter Fritzsche, directed me to Berlin's daily newspapers as the best source for turn-of-the-century urban life in Berlin. Peter then wisely counseled me to embed my burgeoning interest in the newspaper personal ads I found there in a larger investigation of love in the big city of Berlin, and I am thankful to him for his expert guidance in storytelling and historical analysis at every step along the way. Peter taught me that history is, at heart, about telling beautiful stories, and this advice has stuck with me perhaps more than anything else I have learned about being a historian.

I had the support of the entire history department throughout my time at Illinois, and immense thanks are due also to Mark Micale, Harry Liebersohn, and Mark Steinberg, who, together, made up my dissertation committee and made that initial project so much better. They recognized that I had first written a book, not a dissertation, and prefaced their requests for more dissertation-like theoretical and methodological content with the advice that I should save a copy of my manuscript, make the necessary additions to a separate document to use as the dissertation, and then return to the former. This book is so much more than that saved file, but they were absolutely right, and I am grateful to them for their friendship and training over the years.

In a (now) somewhat more distant but no less important way, I would also like to thank my academic mentors from graduate school and college, notably Clint Shaffer, who took me to Germany for the first time and inspired me to study German; Dean Rapp, from whom I took my first (and still favorite) history course; Rainer Nicolaysen and my cohort at Middlebury College, where I sharpened my German-language abilities; Suzanne Kaufman, David Dennis, and Timothy Gilfoyle, who gave me my first professional historical training; and Ute Frevert, who served as my adviser-away-from-home in Berlin and welcomed me into the fold at her fascinating History of Emotions institute.

For that matter, I first learned German from Margy Winkler and Heidi Galer at Iowa City West High School, and I do not see how I would have even come to this project in the first place without their excellent teaching and inspiration.

Numerous institutions and archives were critical to the development of this book, notably the Fulbright Commission, which funded a year of research in Berlin; the German Historical Institute, without whose training in reading the old German script I would have floundered in many of the archives I visited; and the Iowa City Noon Rotary Club and Doris G. Quinn Foundation, both of which provided important funding throughout the research and writing process. Archivists in Germany—especially the staff at the Landesarchiv Berlin, the Zentral- und Landesbibliothek Berlin, and the Deutsches Tagebucharchiv in Emmendingen—were also ever helpful and friendly to me as I came and went each day and made the research experience a degree less lonely and isolating.

Special thanks are due to Cornell College, where I teach and have been welcomed warmly by my colleagues in both History and Modern and Classical Languages, not to mention the entire college. The very first course I taught at Cornell was an upper-level German seminar on the history of Berlin, and that first class of five students was treated to some early material from this book. From the very beginning, then, my students have been wonderful and insightful interlocutors on the many themes and topics that make up this book.

I am thankful also to my editor, Susan Ferber, for taking such a keen interest in this book and shepherding it through to its completion, as well as to the anonymous reviewers of the manuscript, whose comments and critiques without question made this book better. My friend Suja Thomas also deserves many thanks for her creative ideas, advice, and friendship along the publishing road.

My gratitude to my family extends well beyond this book, but they of course helped in a variety of ways on this project, too. My father-in-law used countless frequent flyer miles to cover flights back and forth from Berlin so I could visit my wife back in Iowa during my year of research. My mother-in-law, too, provided critical support for us throughout the process. And my wife's great aunt, Dorothee, who lived in Munich until her death in 2014 at the age of ninety-three, was a dear friend and incisive historical interlocutor. My visits to her nursing home were always filled with much laughter and discussion about Germany, past and present, and I am sad that she is not here to see the finished product.

My mom and dad, brother and sister, grandparents, and wonderful in-laws have been enthusiastic supporters of this book project and were always eager to celebrate each milestone along the way. Special thanks are due to my mom and dad, who, among many, many other things, provided a most idyllic and nurturing upbringing and set me on a path for success and, more importantly, happiness. My siblings and their families have made every step along the way fun and memorable, and I am so very thankful to my grandpa and grandma for their innumerable kindnesses over the years.

This book is a history of love and dating, and it is dedicated to my own two loves: my wife, Melissa, and our daughter, Lena. Though she was not in Berlin with me when I made my archival discoveries, Melissa was the first to learn about each find, first to hear my ideas for weaving this story together, and always full of outstanding ideas for making it better. She has read, edited, and praised every part of this book, and it is infinitely better for it. And I am infinitely better because of her.

As for my daughter, I was editing portions of this manuscript as a week-old Lena lay sleeping in my arms, and I was sublimely happy. Lena will be just under a year old when the first copies of this book are printed, and while she is not yet old enough to read it, I hope and trust she will be proud of her dad when she is.

Love at Last Sight

Introduction

ON JUNE 17, 1914, a thirty-nine-year-old, single seamstress named Frieda Kliem left Berlin on a suburban commuter train to meet the man she had fallen in love with through a newspaper personal ad. What she found when she got there was not the wedding proposal she had hoped for or even the man she thought she knew. The man she met murdered her, stole her keys, and made off with the few valuables she had in her tiny Berlin apartment. When a forester found her body over a week later, the police launched an investigation into her upbringing, adult years, and love life that later made up the core of a highly publicized murder trial during World War I, one that pitted the full legal resources of the state against Berlin's most famous defense attorney, featured delays, false starts, and lengthy recesses, and produced more than one shocking twist. After the jury's verdict rang out in 1916, the case documents were placed back in their file folders, the evidence was sealed in green police envelopes, and the entire stack was filed away in the police archives, where it sat unused and unopened for the rest of the twentieth century.

On August 22, 2011, while searching through Berlin's state archive for material related to love at the turn of the century, I came across these files, the first of which detailed the police's frantic search for Frieda Kliem's murderer. As I worked my way through the file, opening green police envelopes of sealed evidence and hoping the archivists would not mind that I was ripping into previously unopened, century-old materials, I began to piece together the fascinating story of a poor, single Berlin seamstress who spent her life searching for love in the modern metropolis but found each effort to make connections and find intimacy thwarted. Here was a woman who, like hundreds of thousands of others, had arrived in Berlin at the moment of its metamorphosis into the most dynamic city in the world and then struggled to make her way without much in terms of family connections, employment prospects, or, crucially, money. It soon became clear that while Frieda Kliem was, paradoxically, totally unknown and, for a few weeks during 1914–1916, a sensation about whom every Berliner was talking, she was also the consummate turn-of-the-century Berliner. Apart from the fact that she was violently murdered, her concerns, her joys, and her everyday existence were shared by thousands upon thousands of other similarly ordinary Berliners whose lives were unremarkable enough that they have all but been forgotten.[1]

Love at Last Sight is about Frieda Kliem's world—more specifically, about the in-between people and places that held it all together. The turn-of-the-century city, indeed, the modern world it typified, was filled with the aspirations and anxieties of people like Frieda, people who were in a perpetual state of becoming.[2] For Frieda, as for so many Berliners at the time, "becoming" was all about becoming middle class, which stood above all for financial stability but also encompassed a set of social and cultural markers that conferred status and respectability. Frieda moved in and out of the middle class, but she spent most of her time somewhere between the working class and the lower middle class. Indeed, while her upbringing in a relatively prosperous rural family imbued her with some of the pretentions of the middle class, her independent spirit, her move to the big city of Berlin, and no doubt her gender seemed to set her back perpetually and leave her on the boundary of middle-classness, ever striving for a stable rung on which to plant her foot and move up the social ladder.

The historical questions Frieda Kliem's life raises are not new. Scholars have long sought to shed light on the complexities of class belonging and striving, on the tensions of urban life, and on the way intangible desires and emotions render each of these still more complicated and fraught. Yet employing Frieda as a prism for these topics—and focusing on love, intimacy, and dating—fractures many of the established ways of thinking about the city, the middle class, and modernity itself, and it reveals the mix of excitement and risk of trying to piece together modern love and middle-class respectability.

AT THE CENTER of this book is the middle class, or at least the dream of being middle class. Working- and lower-middle-class Berliners like Frieda were keenly aware of their city's hegemonic middle-class moral and cultural norms, and practically all men and women of these classes harbored not only the desire to achieve and adopt middle-classness for their own lives, but also the sense that it was possible and achievable, whether through hard work, craftiness, or sheer luck.³ *Bürgerlichkeit*, or middle-classness, thus in many ways extended beyond the very boundaries it defined and defended, and focusing on the margins of middle-classness opens a window onto the turn-of-the-century urban world.

But why was middle-classness so central to the way Berliners ordered their lives? Surely there was a degree of comfort associated with middle-class life. It was a cut above the gritty, tedious existence of peasants and workers. It also lacked the heavy baggage of the deeply patinated upper class. The middle class was in fact relatively new, the creation of the industrial age, and perhaps its newness made it seem a degree more attainable. But by the end of the nineteenth century, the middle class was confronting a threat it perceived in the social, cultural, and political aspirations of a rising working class.⁴ Fearing that its borders were becoming more porous, the middle class sought to immure itself by re-emphasizing the pristine moral, social, and heavily gendered qualities required to belong in its ranks.

But it had little to worry about, for the walls of the middle-class fortress were solid. Strict norms of respectable comportment ensured internal cohesion, and children of middle-class parents were generally careful to marry other middle-class men and women.⁵ Middle-class people were mostly uninterested in aping the styles of the upper class, and middle-classness, based as it was on this contentedness, in this way contained its own raison d'être.⁶ Theodor Mommsen put it succinctly in his 1899 diary with the aphorism, "[*Ich*] *wünschte ein Bürger zu sein*" ("If only I were middle class"). Mommsen's famous line may contain an underlying pessimism, but the self-legitimacy and desirability of middle-class status at the turn of the century is unmistakable.⁷ Indeed, middle-classness became at the end of the nineteenth century a sort of "religious mood" with its own sacralized tenets and values.⁸ Middle-classness, despite the usual handwringing, was thus still quite hegemonic, quite safe at the turn of the century.

If there were any cracks in the foundation, they were in the modern city and in the private and intimate aspects of men's and women's lives.⁹ The modern city and its manifold new lifestyle opportunities offered a chance at individualism and the cultivation of the modern self. But there was an inherent unorthodoxy to the modern self, and this created immense tensions for men and women on the margins of the middle class. As they moved from provincial towns to modern metropolises like Berlin, and as middle-class life became ever more fixed to urban centers, they were confronted with this tension between the opportunities for modern self-creation and the risk of losing the status and respectability of middle-classness.¹⁰ Sociologist Ulrich Beck calls this the tension of "individualization" in the modernized world. When the conditions of a more traditional, communal society melt away—as in the turn-of-the-century city—the individual becomes free to make her own way, free to forge her own self based on the opportunities of modern metropolitan life. But she also has no choice but to do so, and this produces tremendous anxiety.[11] In turn-of-the-century Berlin, men and women on the margins of the middle class also had to do this on their own, for the middle class lacked the solidarity of the working class and the built-in securities of the upper class. The risks of individualization were present in all aspects of life—work, leisure, dress—but especially so in intimate, private life.[12] As Beck writes, the private sphere was not immune to this modern conundrum; in fact, the tensions and anxieties of individualization were intensified in intimate matters, for here "the outside [was] turned inside and made private."[13] Love, marriage, and family, in other words, were in many ways thus the locus of this central tension of modern, urban, middle-class life.

THIS BOOK APPROACHES middle-classness in turn-of-the-century Berlin through the lens of love, marriage, dating, and intimate relationships because searching for and articulating love—indeed, navigating its compulsions, risks, and tensions—revealed the most foundational values of modern urban life.[14] Contemporary observers noticed as much: the pioneering sociologist Georg Simmel considered love "one of the great formative categories of existence," while Marianne Weber, another giant of sociology, recognized love as central to "matur[ing] to human wholeness."[15] Not everyone could speak so eloquently, but the changing dynamics of love and intimacy at the turn of the century nevertheless had people talking about them as never before.[16]

The modern metropolis presented men and women with the tools, ideas, and dreams for a different approach to love, intimacy, dating, and marriage. But it was not really the newness of these emerging approaches to love, nor frustrated marital dynamics, that occasioned so much talk and debate.[17] The debate was so fierce, rather, because love (and gender and sexuality, more generally) at the turn of the century was the site of a battle between a conservative middle-class orthodoxy and the bewildering and tantalizing explosion of new possibilities in the modern metropolis.[18] It was the thrilling but clearly transgressive possibility of women proposing to men, of meeting on the streetcar or through the newspapers, indeed, of marrying outside of the social circle deemed acceptable by family and friends. These were plainly off-limits for middle-class people, but the dynamics of the modern city were making these approaches nearly irresistible. The city was thus paradoxically both frustrating to those looking for love and, at the same time, the "place of the enlarged horizon of opportunities."[19]

The definition of love was itself also contested terrain, and these muddy conceptual waters raised the stakes even further. For the most part, middle-class society at the turn of the century approached love warily. Love marriages had famously been on the rise since the beginning of the nineteenth century, but strategic unions remained the favored middle-class means of connection. Casual sexual relationships were common enough but not acknowledged in public; nor were these allowed to count as "love." And love—where it was so named—was certainly always heterosexual for middle-class tastes.

For its part, the *Meyers* encyclopedia of 1905—a fixture of the respectable bourgeois home—defined love as "the irresistible impulse for union" and insisted somewhat provocatively that the purely physical nature of "sexual love" was something different altogether.[20] Other references saw in love the very "will of the 'race' for procreation and evolutionary betterment," while more cynical commentators, as historian Edward Ross Dickinson puts it, understood love as "really just the need for a highly desirable item of consumption—sex."[21]

In this book, love as a category of analysis extends beyond sex; indeed, it refers both to a discursive set of values and conventions, on one hand, and, on the other hand, to the totality or interwoven sum of affections, connections, desires, and tendernesses that were so magnetic and deeply meaningful for the men and women whose lives fill these pages. At the same time, the modern metropolis effectively decoupled love and sex more than ever before. Prostitution, fleeting liaisons, and pragmatic unions forged out of economic necessity (to able to afford an apartment, for example) all moved sex further away from "emotional unity" or something necessarily deeply meaningful. Even though love and sex surely continued to go hand in hand for some, the inverse was potentially true for a great many others. By that same token, intimacy, as in physical or emotional closeness, also acquired a new set of meanings in the city. Whether close, physical and emotional connection with others or mere companionship, intimacy is located somewhere between love and sex on a spectrum of emotions, though it is perhaps harder in the abstract to isolate intimacy from either love or sex. After all, one often found intimacy in loveless sex, and it is intriguing to consider the massive business of urban prostitution at the turn of the century as not just an economic exchange but also the search for physical and emotional intimacy.

Same-sex love was complex in an age when both sex and marriage were illegal and had to exist in a liminal, risky space outside the public eye. This book is keenly interested in the contours of same-sex love and intimacy in turn-of-the-century Berlin, as it was how a not insignificant portion of Berlin's residents found love in the city. Same-sex love also in many ways reflects doubly the problems, anxieties, strategies, and ambiguities of love, respectability, and risk at the turn of the century. After all, the city may have opened new horizons of opportunities for gays and lesbians when compared with smaller towns and villages, but it also proved especially isolating, alienating, and even dangerous for them, given deeply entrenched cultural biases and long-standing legal statutes with serious punishments.[22]

There is no chapter or section of this book dedicated to the men and women who navigated the tricky world of same-sex relationships; instead, their story is woven into the discussion of heterosexual love, as they illustrate common trends with particular clarity. Love and intimacy perhaps took on slightly different forms for same-sex lovers in some circumstances, but connection, closeness, belonging, and stability meant the same thing for straight and same-sex couples alike. Accordingly, this book seeks to unite gay history with straight history. The very real differences in gay and straight experiences must, of course, never be effaced, but insisting on a strict boundary between straight and same-sex histories merely reinforces the long-standing isolation of these experiences as mutually unintelligible. Exploring them together—and dissecting their similarities and differences—helps make sense of both experiences separately. The time has come to merge these stories.[23]

Love—whether straight or same sex—is in any case difficult to pin down in historical sources. Happy lovers often produce little by way of concrete evidence of their love. Unhappy lovers, on the other hand (not to mention the lovesick, broken-hearted, and vengeful), tend to leave behind an impressive trail of material. This book relies as much on sources that were produced in the absence of love as on texts composed in the delirium of found love. It also seeks out other registers of love: marriage, dating and courting, intimacy, sex, divorce, murder, crime, the law, and even death. The chapters of this story of love in turn-of-the-century Berlin approach love from different angles: loneliness and desire; dating and individualization; bachelorhood, spinsterhood, and "free love"; and newspaper personal ads. In doing so, this book attempts to portray the totality, complexities, and tensions of the search for love in Berlin around 1900.

A GREAT MANY of the stories and voices presented in this book come from the pages of Berlin's daily newspapers. Urban dailies like the *Berliner Morgenpost* and the *Berliner Lokal-Anzeiger* are indeed rich sources for turn-of-the-century urban life, and the newspaper has long been hailed as a critical feature and forum of intellectual exchange in modern life. In Berlin, specifically, reading newspapers was perhaps the most typical, emblematic turn-of-the-century activity. Day after day, edition after edition, newsprint shaped and transformed the way Berliners understood the city around them.[24]

But vibrant and important as they were and are, newspapers can also be deceiving. The stories and dramas pull one in, make one believe that each aged and brittle page (or, more commonly, microfilm reel) is a window through which the unmitigated past can be observed. But of course this is not the case. The Berlin that existed in the columns of the daily newspapers did not map perfectly onto the real Berlin in which people like Frieda Kliem worked and danced and moved about.[25] After all, it was a stylized, imagined, and emplotted city, one that registered the predilections of the writers and was marketed to its readers; one that was fit to deadlines and the moods of editors and squeezed into last bits of free space on a page. The newspaper formed a triangular relationship with the city insofar as it described, shaped, and was shaped by Berlin around 1900.[26]

Berliners talked about their city and about themselves, both the reality and the fantasy, and the text and discourse this created was a crucial part of what it meant to live in a city that was on the cutting edge of modernity. This was particularly true in matters of love and intimacy, for so much of a person's tastes, habits, ideals, norms, and practices was molded by the material she read and the fantasies she (or those around her) constructed for herself. Indeed, whether it was a news story about a personal ad swindling, an advice column about the propriety of bicycle riding, a readers' forum on making potentially intimate acquaintances on the street, a front-page column about men who avoided marriage and opted to extend their bachelorhood, or a serial novel about a workplace romance—all of which reflect to some degree how Berliners were living—these not only shaped the way Berliners thought about love and intimacy in their city but also influenced the way they looked for and reacted to love in their own lives. After all, they, too, were part of the city, and they made sense of their own lives according to urban narratives of love.

It is therefore important to hold newsprint narratives and social practices in tension when examining Berliners' lives at the turn of the century. When newspapers wrote about so-called eternal bachelors, for example, it was easy to believe that all Berliners had abandoned marriage for good. So, too, did columns about old maids, swindlers, modern girls, frustrated singles, and the disappearance of "mother's way" make it seem as if each of these trends was completely taking over the city. In reality, these were, for the most part, exceptional phenomena that were remarkable precisely because they were emerging but minority trends. They also made for fantastic copy. It was quite the same with the ubiquitous talk of newness, which was as much the reimagining of the old as new as it was actual revolutionary change. Finding love in the metropolis was a perplexing problem, but most Berliners ultimately did find love or at least got married and found some measure of intimacy. Statistics show that connection and marriage were not dying out but actually relatively healthy—evidence that Berlin was, strictly speaking, not the unassailable romantic antagonist it was often made out to be. With these caveats in mind, the problem of love and the rise of the new in the modern city were nevertheless exceedingly important narratives in turn-of-the-century Berlin. Even if most Berliners found spouses, the centrality of these discourses influenced the way Berliners lived their lives, raised their children, played matchmaker with their friends, and even understood their own relationships.[27]

Within these pages, newspaper tropes of love and modernity are situated against the many other sources of romantic discourse at the turn of the century, such as novels, plays, scientific articles, literary journals, diaries, memoirs, and police reports. However, daily newspapers do, in fact, offer the richest collection of evidence about everyday, ordinary lives from this era. The articles, columns, readers' letters, and serial novels that form the foundation of the following analysis are not the eccentric writings of anomalous, aberrant individuals; they are urban narratives that circulated by the millions throughout the city and formed the basis for many more conversations around dinner tables, in the seats of trams and buses, and at cafés and bars throughout the city. They also prompted responses, dialogues, and debates that found their way back into the newspaper, which allows for observation of how newspaper copy was digested, perceived, and measured against reality, even if features like letters to the editor were also shaped by editors.[28] And while Berlin's major newspapers generally catered to their predominantly working-class readership in a heavily working-class city, this is also what makes them such useful sources for the present study.[29] Indeed, in the stories they covered, the features they ran, and the viewpoints they presented, daily newspapers not only reinforced the allure of middle-classness but also seem to have addressed primarily those Berliners who were poised to achieve middle-class status or who teetered on the edge of losing it, people, in short, like Frieda Kliem.

THE BACKDROP OF the story of Frieda Kliem—the turn-of-the-century city—is more than window dressing or generic stage scenery. This book argues that the conditions and opportunities of the city created desires for, avenues to, and new risks of love and dating around 1900. The city, then, is itself an important cast member of this story. This book is set specifically in Berlin, not only because it is where Frieda Kliem lived, but also because Berlin at the turn of the century was regarded as the most electric, dynamic, and fluid city in all of Europe. But this book is also about more than a single city at the turn of the century. It is about urban environments and the way urbanites navigated them, how they interacted with each other, and how they narrated their experience.

But what was it about Berlin, specifically, that allows it to speak for other urban environments? It is certainly true that the evolving pressures and impulses of city life, the complicated relationship between twentieth-century Europeans and their nineteenth-century roots, and the always-tricky negotiation of class and gender norms were present in any number of turn-of-the-century cities.[30] Paris and London are also more famous as nineteenth-century capital cities.[31] But the characteristics that made twentieth-century cities distinct, whether the unprecedented intracity mobility, the lack of sustained connections to the surrounding countryside, or the self-consciously urban culture, were all present in Berlin in unique ways.[32] Berlin was unique in its rapid rate of growth, its overwhelmingly young, fluid, and unattached population base, and the fact that these new Berliners did not self-segregate into ethnic neighborhoods. These factors raised the stakes in the search for love and intimacy.

The fact that Berlin was the place of heightened romantic opportunity and risk was not lost on contemporary observers. Berlin attracted the attention of some of the most insightful urban sociologists, theorists, and philosophers of the early twentieth century, and its newspapers were filled with notes and travel reports by curious visitors from all over the world.[33] Regular people noticed it, too, and Berlin became one of the world's first destinations for sex tourism, as Berlin authorities noted nervously at the time.[34] Talk about Berlin ranged from concern to fascination, but nearly all voices concluded that the risks and rewards of modern dating were as clear to see in Berlin as anywhere else in the world.

The Berlin of this book is best understood as part of a larger typology, one that includes not only the standard list of great European cities but also a wide variety of urban contexts from Shanghai to Buenos Aires to Cracow.[35] To be modern, to be urban—these were about much more than growth or industrialism or technology or the western hemisphere; the modern metropolis engendered an aesthetic all its own: a quality of living, a pattern of expression, and a mode of interaction. Berlin cannot, of course, speak for the entire realm of meanings and methods of the modern world; but in exploring one aspect of turn-of-the-century urban life—love—this book aims to define some of the contours of this typology based on one of the most exemplary metropolitan environments.

The tensions between exceptional and representative, discourse and reality, and ordinary and celebrity are woven through each chapter of this book, and this fits perfectly with Frieda Kliem. Frieda was at once a celebrity and a totally unknown seamstress; her life was unquestionably—tragically—real, yet we know about it only in mediated, narrated, and emplotted forms. While Frieda's life was representative of the way Berliners lived and loved, her struggle to find love, not to mention her violent death at the hands of a personal ad killer, was absolutely exceptional.

The structure of the book harnesses the tensions embedded in Frieda's life in order to achieve a deeper, more nuanced analysis of the search for and navigation of love in turn-of-the-century Berlin. Each chapter opens with a period of Frieda's life and explores the themes with which that part of her life intersects. Chapter 1 begins with Frieda's arrival in Berlin and follows her as she struggles to fit herself to the urban environment, economy, and interpersonal dynamics. Chapter 2 sees Frieda finding her footing and stepping outside the lines of acceptable femininity and respectability as she pursued avant-garde paths toward intimacy that were more fleeting and individualistic than those of previous generations. Frieda's prospects for marriage—and its alternatives—form the beginning of chapter 3, which examines the debate sparked by the growing number of Berliners who sought to revise long-standing beliefs about marriage and adapt them to the modern world. Chapter 4 explores Frieda's use of newspaper personal ads and examines the matchmaking services and personal ads that represented revolutionary approaches to love and dating in the modern metropolis. Chapter 5, finally, delves into the trial of Frieda Kliem's murderer. After analyzing the legal strategy of the defense attorney, courtroom exchanges between judge and defendant, and the trial's dramatic ending, it concludes by considering the risks and rewards of love in the modern metropolis.

I

Romantic Fantasies in the Big City

SUNDAY, APRIL 13 was Berlin's first truly springlike day of 1902, and with the pleasant weather, Berliners spread out all over the city. The *Berliner Lokal-Anzeiger* newspaper reported that nearly 1.2 million people used public transit that day, making it one of the heavier travel days it could remember.[1] The city was alive again after a cold winter, and many of those 1.2 million commuters had, no doubt, taken the opportunity to head to the Grunewald forest in the western suburbs. Others perhaps went southwest to the Wannsee lake, though it would have been far too cold for swimming. Still others might simply have taken a pleasure ride on the elevated "ring" train that offered a bird's-eye view of the city below.

Some of those on public transit that day were arriving in Berlin for the very first time, and one of them may have been Frieda Kliem, arriving from the Brandenburg town of Wilsnack some seventy-five miles northwest of Berlin. Frieda was twenty-seven years old, and her arrival in Berlin in 1902 was a kind of homecoming. After all, she had been born in the Berlin suburb of Pankow and had spent her first fourteen years in the city. Her parents ran a large and successful nursery in Pankow, and if only Frieda had kept herself out of trouble, she probably could have stayed there and enjoyed a rather comfortable middle-class existence. But Frieda apparently tried her parents' patience, so she spent her teenage years bouncing around between the homes and shops of various relatives. Her parents finally decided to send the teenager to live with her grandparents. The walk to school, they had said, was too far and allowed her to get into too much trouble.[2]

So Frieda moved in with her grandparents in the sleepy Prussian town of Wilsnack and eventually went to work in her aunt Marie's sewing shop. At some point, Frieda proved too troublesome for even her aunt, and both decided it was best for Frieda to move back to Berlin once she was in her twenties. This no doubt appealed to Frieda, who, in her aunt's words, had always wanted to live in the city. So Frieda quit her job in Wilsnack and in 1902 joined the thousands of men and women who left the provinces and sought work and opportunity in the rapidly expanding metropolis.[3]

Frieda's first step was to look for an apartment and work. It is not clear in what order she found them, but she eventually moved into an apartment at Graunstrasse 72 in the working-class neighborhood of Wedding.[4] The fact that she was not registered with the city until 1905—a full three years after her arrival—suggests that she may have bounced around from apartment to apartment, living with distant relatives or in semilegal, short-term arrangements that did not occasion a listing in the Berlin phone book.[5] It is possible that Frieda moved to Graunstrasse 72 to be near her work, though it is equally likely that she found her first job precisely because she lived near her future employer. In any case, Frieda took a job working for a woman named Hedwig Rohls, a seamstress who lived just a few buildings away at Graunstrasse 42 and also ran a clothing store out of her apartment.[6] Frieda thus found her first job in Berlin doing what she learned from her aunt Marie and knew best: sewing.[7] Frieda and Hedwig became close friends—close enough that, when Frieda's parents passed away in 1903 or 1904, she asked for a lump-sum payout of her inheritance so that she could help Hedwig out with a loan. Indeed, she ended up loaning her well over DM 1,000 (around $7,000 in today's money).[8] Their friendship and partnership was cut short, however, when Hedwig, a widow, was shot and killed by her lover in 1906. Frieda never recovered the loan and found herself without work, too.[9]

Facing yet again the uncertainty of getting by on her own and surviving the "struggle for existence," as it was called, Frieda decided she would open her own clothing store. This move in many ways made sense, for she had seen Hedwig—also a single woman—run her own shop for a few years, and she still had a little bit left of the DM 5,000 (approximately $35,000) lump-sum inheritance she had received from her parents. So in 1906, Frieda left Graunstrasse 72 and moved to Demminerstrasse 12, a few blocks south, and started her own business. But this, too, proved short-lived, as Frieda was unable to make ends meet in a competitive market and had to close her shop.[10]

Frieda's plight—no savings, hardly any income—was the plight of many single, working women in Berlin at the turn of the century. She no doubt reflected, in her rather destitute and precarious position, that she had fallen a good distance from her comfortable, lower-middle-class upbringing. Indeed, this is an important tension in her story, to wit, the lifestyle she knew and wanted and the all-too-real economic and employment obstacles that stood in her way. But there was a way out. Marriage, a long-standing cornerstone of middle-class life and stability, offered a solution to her situation, and, at this point in her life, Frieda turned to this possibility that was, she knew, shrinking with each year as she entered her thirties. Frieda may not have known the precise statistic—85 percent of women married in their twenties—but she surely felt that her chance at the stability of married life was dwindling as she grew older.[11] Her interest in marriage was not only about money, but, having tasted the independence—and risk—of owning her own business, Frieda was perhaps ready to trade in her freedom for companionship or at least security, for the peace of mind that came with being taken care of, and for the respectability that middle-class marriage brought. Frieda does not appear to have expressed any interest in marriage at the age when most teenage girls and young women did; the tiny hamlet of Wilsnack likely offered her few options and, as a known problem child in a small town, Frieda might not have had too many suitors. Moving to Berlin no doubt brought many new opportunities for love and marriage, but Frieda was perhaps more concerned in those first few years with establishing herself. When she failed at this, she appears to have turned to the idea of marriage in earnest.

Frieda was not completely alone in Berlin or her search for a spouse. She had a friend, Anna Seibeke, who had also worked for Hedwig Rohls. Frieda watched as Anna got married and either found other work or perhaps stopped working altogether, and this may have increased her desire to find a husband of her own. Anna and her husband, Oskar, felt sorry for Frieda, who had no money and, as they later remembered, was extremely eager to get married. In fact, she talked about it all the time, telling Anna about the kind of man she wanted. There was one important stipulation: "Frieda's wish," Anna told the police in 1914, "was to marry a civil servant," someone who would have a stable position and handsome income. Despite her meager income and savings, Frieda was still a middle-class woman who, it seems, was set on maintaining certain markers of bourgeois status. She had, for example, bits of the family silver, and her tiny living room was dominated by an upright piano.[12] What these treasures lacked in quantity they no doubt made up for in symbolic quality. The silver was surely out of place in Frieda's otherwise plain apartment, and it is hard to imagine that she had much use for it. None of Frieda's friends or family members mentioned that she knew how to play the piano, so it may have served as an elaborate mantel for displaying photographs. And yet there are scarcely two better totems of the middle-class home than family silver and a piano.[13] Frieda went to the trouble of moving the piano with her from apartment to apartment, not to mention perhaps polishing the silver from time to time and refusing to sell them when she most definitely could have used the money. This speaks to Frieda's tenacious grip on the idea of middle-classness.

When Anna and Oskar tried to set up Frieda with a man from the provincial town of Altlandsberg, located just outside of Berlin, Frieda turned the offer down, telling Anna that the man was not good enough for her. Oskar remembered the same: "[It] failed because Kliem only wanted to marry a civil servant."[14]

Frieda's life up to this point can hardly be described as ideal, though there were certainly women who were worse off. This fact was surely of little comfort to her, though. As Ottilie Baader, one of Frieda's fellow seamstresses, described in her memoir, this kind of life weighed heavily on a person:

> I can't say that I was always very happy. I'd hoped for something else out of life. Sometimes I was just sick of life: Sitting year after year at the sewing machine, always the collars and cuffs before me, one dozen after another; there was no value to life, I was just a work machine with no hope for the future. I saw and heard nothing of all the beautiful things in the world; I was simply excluded from all that.[15]

For her part, Frieda's failed business marked the beginning of her problems with money, and while she did continue to receive the monthly interest on her remaining inheritance, she was constantly plagued by financial anxiety. This can be seen most poignantly in the handful of poems she cut out and collected from magazines and quote-of-the-day calendars over the years, most of which were quite doleful and melancholy:

> *A person does not know how much he can suffer*
> *until necessity forces him to learn.*
>
> *When a heart turns coldly from you*
> *One that you truly and deeply loved*
> *Plant a little cross on the place*
> *That once saw you so happily in love;*
> *Pass by it often in your sorrow,*
> *For there the lost one is close to you!*
>
> *God alone can protect you from sorrow*
> *you might as well spare yourself the resentment.*
>
> *The nightingale only sings in the dark. In this way, we*
> *discover the heavenly melody of a noble heart only when*
> *it grieves.*[16]

FIGURE 1.1 Calendar clippings found in Frieda's apartment

Source: Landesarchiv Berlin A Pr. Br. Rep. 030-03, Nr. 1425, Bl. 95.

FIGURE 1.2 Calendar clippings found in Frieda's apartment, reverse side

Source: Landesarchiv Berlin A Pr. Br. Rep. 030-03, Nr. 1425, Bl. 95.

Every friend and acquaintance interviewed after her death noted that
Frieda always complained about her financial situation and that she had to
live extremely sparingly.[17] This, along with her desire to get married, was what
her friends remembered most about her.[18]

Sociologists Ulrich Beck and Elisabeth Beck-Gernsheim recently referred to
the complex marriage calculus of migrating women as a "passage to hope."
Rather than characterize the attachments made by low-income, single women
as either "pure" (based on romantic love) or instrumental (so-called marriages
of convenience), they argue that these relationships involve a "complex interplay of motives in which hopes, emotions, and dreams of a noninstrumental
kind play a part."[19] In this framework, the search for emotional connection
and the desire for economic stability are part of the same process of selecting
a mate. A match ostensibly based on romance might well be rejected because
of certain instrumental considerations (e.g., finances, social standing), but so
might one seemingly founded on practical matters for a variety of romantic or
noninstrumental reasons (e.g., appearance).[20]

This may help contextualize Frieda's arrival in Berlin and approach to
marriage. Frieda no doubt felt the allure of financial stability, as well as a
desire for connection. More importantly, she clearly had a strong emotional
stake in being "middle class."[21] Lest we dismiss Frieda as a money-grubbing
opportunist or conclude that she was obsessed with money or only interested in marriage for the windfall or stability it might occasion, we would
do well to remember her struggle to make ends meet as a single woman in
the modern metropolis. Unlike the image of independent women spending
income on personal pleasures, Frieda's was, in fact, the most common urban
experience of all.[22] For all of the opportunity and sheer lifestyle vibrancy
of the modern city, its crowds, commotion, and dynamics created a host
of problems for the men and women who lived there. Chief among these
problems were how to get by and pay for food and rent, as well as how to
find someone in a city of three million people.[23] Of course, "getting by" and
finding a mate have never been easy, but what was new at the turn of the
century was the metropolis.

The social and material conditions of urban life at the turn of the century threw into question traditional beliefs about, and paths to, love, and
they led Berliners to put their faith in fate and fortuitous encounters that
might create shortcuts to love, even if this faith was rarely rewarded. City

life opened the door to new forms of love and intimacy, and this chapter focuses on Berliners getting to the point where they could imagine—and risk—embracing them.

BERLIN IN THE mid-nineteenth century might best have been described as a "swampy backwater."[24] Mark Twain remarked in 1891 that Berlin had not so long ago been "a dingy city in a marsh, with rough streets, muddy and lantern-lighted."[25] Yet with the Industrial Revolution, the invention of the railroad, and the building of factories around newly forming rail hubs, cities like Berlin were transformed. "That Berlin has disappeared," Twain continued in the *Chicago Daily Tribune* piece he penned upon returning from a half-year stay in Berlin. "It is a new city; the newest I have ever seen."[26] By the end of the century, urban centers like Berlin had blossomed into truly massive metropolises. Berlin's population between 1800 and 1850 grew from 172,000 to 419,000, but between 1850 and 1900, it exploded to 1.89 million residents. The 351 percent increase in Berlin's population in the second half of the nineteenth century made it the fastest-growing major European capital in the nineteenth century.[27] Berlin's rate of growth, as compared to Paris, Vienna, and London, is even more impressive considering that most of their growth came over the long course of the nineteenth century, whereas Berlin doubled in size in just the last quarter of the century.

Like most cities during industrialization, Berlin's growth came primarily from the migration of rural people to the metropolis, and the constant influx of new people gave it a uniquely chaotic dynamic. Berlin's dynamism played out in more than just the influx of provincials into the giant Friedrichstrasse train station, however. Its residents were in perpetual motion: half of all Berliners were said to have moved from one apartment to another within the city every six months.[28] Early sociological studies of the city's widespread housing squalor confirm this, as does anecdotal evidence from pastors like Eugen Baumann, who complained that half of his parishioners changed their addresses each year.[29] It amounted to almost constant movement and chaos. As the *Berliner Morgenpost* reported of moving day at the end of September, "Everywhere the streets are filled with yellow or green monsters, the moving trucks, crammed full, swaying dangerously back and forth, blocking the tracks of the Electric [the streetcars] and loathed by the taxis."[30]

Toting boxes and bed frames was, by no means, the only thing that had Berliners on the move throughout the city, for work and leisure kept city people on the move day and night. No city in Europe could claim the nonstop

FIGURE 1.3 View onto the bustling Potsdamer Platz from Café Josty, 1914
Source: Landesarchiv Berlin F Rep. 290 (01), Nr. OO72473.

commotion and energy of Berlin, and journalists, eager to show off their city's activity, penned stories that described "Berlin at night" in all of its frenetic splendor. The *Berliner Morgenpost*, for example, took readers on an hour-by-hour tour through the night, starting—perhaps tellingly—at 10:00 p.m. Only around three in the morning was Berlin relatively quiet, and at four "the cycle of Berlin life starts anew."[31]

During the day, people, goods, and vehicles whizzed through streets and across busy and often dangerous intersections. It is indeed fitting that the world's first traffic light was installed on Berlin's busiest square, Potsdamer Platz. An article in the *Berliner Zeitung* from 1905 describes a normal day on Potsdamer Platz. The author perched himself at the famous Café Josty and counted the vehicles moving by in the span of one hour: "416 streetcars, 146 omnibuses, 564 taxis and cars ... and 118 three-wheelers. Together that makes in one hour 1,836 vehicles, in one day—based on an eighteen-hour day—that makes 33,048, in one month 991,440, in one year nearly 12 million vehicles." A tally of individual people walking about Potsdamer Platz was "impossible. Each minute brings new masses of people, from the right, from the left. They come from all sides, forming each second a new image. The elegant world, laboring Berlin, the worker, the salesman, the intellectual—an extract of Berlin's entire population moves across Potsdamer Platz, a colorful jumble, a swarm as in an ant house."[32] "Potsdamer Platz," as another writer put it, "that is Berlin. The typical modern Berlin—this is what they can't replicate in the other cities. On Potsdamer Platz you can hear the heartbeat of the world."[33]

Berlin's dynamism was the envy of Paris and London, not to mention sleepy Vienna.[34] When Stefan Zweig described Vienna at the turn of the century, it was not in terms of movement, crowds, and nightlife, but rather of measured, controlled lives, cautiousness, and temperateness.[35] Paris admittedly had its grand boulevards and fashionable clothing and London its famous West End, but both lacked the frenetic newness of Berlin. It stood apart in the sense that its quintessential urban features—the crowds, the commotion, the sightseers, the nightlife, the crime, the prostitutes, the beggars—were exaggerated.[36] As Karl Baedeker put it in his 1912 guide to the German capital, Berlin may not "compete in antiquity or historical interest with the other great European capitals," but it is "the greatest purely modern city in Europe."[37]

BERLINERS WERE PROUD of this uniqueness and seem to have taken a special pleasure in imagining the way newcomers to the city felt as they stepped off the train. "The streets," one writer thought, must make quite an impression on them. "Here the city of three million shows its special flavor. The newcomer is surely bewildered by the gargantuan number of pedestrians (not even at his town's marksman's festival are so many people out on the street!), the row of streetcars stretching as far as the eye can see." Double-decker buses with men reading newspapers on their open-top roofs, countless taxis, automobiles racing by—these were the striking images of the big city, and Berliners took perverse joy in seeing newcomers confused, panic stricken, and lost as they tried to make sense of such a chaotic world. Indeed, when the visitor returns home to the provinces, the author concluded, he will have a hard time readjusting to normal life.[38] In the same way, the *Berliner Lokal-Anzeiger* proudly published letters written by a provincial woman visiting Berlin, who penned, "I freely admit it to you. I am overwhelmed by the big city."[39]

But it was not just newcomers and visiting provincials who were overwhelmed. Even for established Berliners, metropolitan life was not easy. To be sure, Berliners knew their way around the city, knew precisely where the Electric stopped (and laughed at those who misjudged it and had to run after the departing streetcar), and did not fall for the tricks of swindlers who waited at the city's train stations for clueless and unsuspecting victims. But life's more meaningful pursuits presented a challenge to even the city's seasoned veterans. Establishing oneself, making acquaintances, finding love—these were perhaps never easy, but something seemed to have changed.

That the conditions of urbanity might have something to do with this change was not lost on social observers at the time. Georg Simmel, the pioneering sociologist and native Berliner, became fascinated with the effects of Berlin's urban dynamics on its residents.[40] Simmel penned an article titled "The Metropolis and Mental Life" that considered how the rhythms and schema of modern urban existence worked on the mind of the individual. He described his interest in investigating "the adaptations made by the personality in its adjustment to the forces that lie outside of it."[41] The forces, in this case, were both the "swift and continuous shift of external and internal stimuli" occasioned by the city and the need to "organiz[e] and coordinat[e]" all of life's activities "in the most punctual way into a firmly fixed framework of time which transcends all subjective elements" as a way of coping.[42] Simmel was quick to recognize the differences between modern urban life and traditional rural life, noting that there is a "deep contrast with the slower, more habitual, more smoothly flowing rhythm of the sensory-mental phase of small town and rural existence." Whereas life in a small town "rests more on feelings and emotional relationships," the city is characterized by "the imponderability of personal relationships."[43] Simmel concluded that the individual ultimately assumed a "blasé outlook" on all matters of life as a way of "adjusting to the content and the form of metropolitan life by renouncing the response to them."[44]

More practically, what Simmel was arguing was that the effect of the big city on the individual was to discourage interpersonal relationships and instead promote a "mental attitude . . . of reserve" as a sort of coping mechanism. If, he pointed out, city people attempted to cultivate the same types of intimacies with the masses as they had in a small town, they would "fall into an unthinkable mental condition."[45]

Simmel may have overstated the divide between city and province, but historians have generally agreed with his rather pessimistic take on the city and its effects on interpersonal relationships.[46] Indeed, his diagnosis of urban life as fundamentally fragmented came to be applied to modernity, more generally. Historian Moritz Föllmer prefers to interpret urban fragmentation as individuality, but he also points out that a growing urban individuality quite often led to isolation and suicide.[47] Judith Walkowitz describes London as the "city of dreadful delight"—dangerous for isolated individuals, most notably women, given its "dark, powerful, and seductive labyrinth."[48] And Joachim Schlör, in *Nights in the Big City*, details the ways in which talk of nightlife in turn-of-the-century Paris, London, and Berlin was dominated by horror and danger, no doubt most famously in Alfred Döblin's 1929 novel, *Berlin Alexanderplatz*, in which a deafeningly modern Berlin figures literally as the main character's antagonist as he attempts to reintegrate into the world after a spell in prison.[49]

These studies all acknowledge that this notion of the city as a dangerous, alienating place was not so much a reality as a narrative that had uses for various groups, such as men wanting to control would-be independent women. And yet they have left us believing, as historian Anthony McElligott puts it, "that alienation is the overriding experience of urban modernity."[50] The dynamics of interaction in the city, of course, went beyond rape, murder, or seeing someone throw herself into the river. Berliners inevitably came into contact with one another as they walked down the city's busy boulevards, rode the streetcar, or did their shopping, but this was Simmel's point: these moments of closeness contrasted sharply with the isolation one normally experienced or even cultivated, and this was a jarring experience. Indeed, Simmel believed, as sociologist David Frisby put it, that various "neurotic forms of behavior . . . result largely from the oscillation between close confrontation with object and people," on the one hand, "and an excessive distance from them," on the other.[51]

Berliners themselves seem to have agreed with Simmel, as snippets from the daily newspapers attest. Men and women were alternatingly running into and seeking to avoid one another, and the entire experience was discomfiting, not to mention isolating. Sidewalk collisions, for one, were common in such a large and dynamic city; the *Berliner Lokal-Anzeiger* recounted as a daily occurrence—a "snapshot from the street"—the story of a flâneur strolling down the sidewalk with his signature cane and impeccable outfit. Behind him walks a young woman, and a scene erupts when she is hit by the cane he swings so gratuitously.[52] Berliners also complained constantly about bumping into people on the streetcar, having their toes stepped on, or having to put up with the cigar smoke of their fellow riders.[53] For that matter, the unwanted conversation of a fellow passenger could be supremely abrasive. The *Berliner Tageblatt* ran a story suggesting that Berliners were annoyed with anyone who wanted to converse on public transit and that most people considered a newspaper or looking out the window a way to avoid having to interact with others in the same car. "It's better to suppress the need to talk in the tram car," the newspaper counseled readers.[54]

The experience of being jostled and poked contrasted with isolation and loneliness.[55] One woman in her early thirties wrote to the *Berliner Lokal-Anzeiger* seeking advice from her fellow readers about how to escape the loneliness of big-city life. Signed "lonely girl," her letter detailed how terribly lonesome she was and suggested that, surely, many others shared her feelings. "Shouldn't it be possible in a big city like Berlin for women of equal rank to find social connections?" Bicycling—a new activity at the turn of the century—is nice but too boring to do alone, she wrote. Going out alone or joining a club of some sort does not work, either, since "not everyone is made for dancing," and one feels too old among the much younger people who are. "What should I do so I don't just read a little and then go to bed at 8:30?" she asked desperately.[56] The "public opinion" section of the *Berliner Lokal-Anzeiger* published other readers' responses to the "lonely girl," and, in one, another woman responded with words of comfort, writing that she, too, was lonely—but also a happy person who had found plenty to do. She first joined a "club for the lonely," which was full of nice women and even a few men, but even here it had been hard to make any close acquaintances. She coped with her loneliness, she wrote, by volunteering and, yes, bicycling alone. "Don't mope around," she counseled. "You'll find plenty in the big city if you just look."[57]

Journalists, authors, and artists were drawn to the theme of loneliness in the big city, and each city sketch, reportage, or short story strove, it seems, to emphasize the asymmetry between the giant metropolis and the tiny, isolated individual. A 1902 poem in the *Berliner Morgenpost*, for example, situated the city itself as the barrier to urban connection. It described a young man's efforts to meet Lotte, his beloved, for a rendezvous on Potsdamer Platz. He races after work to the busy square, and though he can see her red cap, his efforts to get to her are stymied by the streetcar, the omnibus, and the crowds of people. He can only watch as she walks away and leaves his life for good.[58] Ernst Ludwig Kirchner's famous Berlin street scenes likewise show crowds of men and women moving down Friedrichstrasse and across Potsdamer Platz, for example, but his subjects pass each other disconnectedly and anonymously.[59] The writer Johannes Trojan counted the short essay "Loneliness in and around Berlin" worthy of inclusion in his *One Hundred Snapshots* of Berliner life in 1903 and noted that one did not need to look far to see the pain of loneliness in a fellow Berliner.[60] And in a rather depressing Christmas Day piece, the writer Maria Janitschek described for readers the "Christmas walk of a lonely man"—a walk he takes at night, in the dark, wandering about various neighborhoods of Berlin. Nighttime strolls were by no means inherently lonely and were an aesthetic pleasure of the highest order for that modern, stylized figure, the flâneur. But for the man "who on this evening"—Christmas—"is free of any plans," strolling throughout the empty streets of the city is a sorry substitute for the scenes taking place in the glowing and merry apartments above. The man tries to enjoy vicariously the stories that play out for him in these rooms, but all he feels is a deep longing—"a longing that we all know."[61]

This admittedly stylized and heavily dramatized longing was Berliners' response to the city's curious mix of fleeting contact and oppressive isolation. Alternating experiences of being jostled by crowds and being painfully alone left Berliners wanting more meaningful contact with one another. But making contact was not so easy. There were rules and expectations governing making acquaintances, a script to be followed about how and where middle-class Berliners could meet potential spouses, and improvising came with certain risks, as a short story in the *Berliner Morgenpost* from 1913 conveyed. In the story, "Loneliness," the main character, Felicitas, has, like so many other women in the big city, failed to find a husband, so she bears "all of the joys and burdens of life" on her own. Contrary to her name, she is not particularly happy, and she tries to forget her loneliness by "wander[ing] among large crowds so as to seem less conspicuous."

One day while walking home from work a man approaches her and offers his umbrella so she can avoid the rain. She accepts, and he walks her home, telling along the way a little about his life, his work, and the restaurant on the corner he frequents. When they reach her door, he proposes that they meet again on Saturday. They do, and he arrives carrying a cake. He comes the following Saturday, too, and "imperceptibly these Saturday afternoons became her habit." Indeed, "She waited the entire week and looked forward to it as a child waits for a party." One day he comes in with wet feet, his shoes having been soaked by the rain. So she knits him slippers, and each time he comes they are hanging for him in front of the fire, already warm.[62]

And yet, as quickly as the relationship began, it ends abruptly when he announces one day that he is getting married. This of course shatters their hard-won domestic harmony, and Felicitas suddenly understands with bitter clarity the inherent limits of a relationship that began as haphazardly and randomly as theirs. "These two hours each week for two years had been ... merely the illusion of domestic bliss," she realizes, and now he wants to pin down the real thing, found the right way.[63]

When he leaves, Felicitas's isolation overwhelms her. "How lonely I am!" she murmurs to herself. She goes to the window and looks out into the rain and onto the street below. "How lonely I am!" she sighs again. "And without any effort, without any regret, almost without even wanting to, she bent over and let her head sink. Then she let out a weak sound—and fell."[64]

Felicitas's grim end is one many literary and real-life suicides that filled the pages of short stories and local news. The newspapers even ran stories about "the dangers of loneliness" and printed headlines like "I'm Alone and Forgotten."[65] But there is more to these stories about street encounters and oppressive loneliness than the annoyances of big-city life or the danger of depression and suicide. The remarkable thing about Felicitas's story is that she met the man seemingly by chance and not by the conventional, accepted methods. She met him, after all, on the street. But their relationship is practically doomed from the start because their meeting strayed too far from the traditional pattern, and even though the man, as he tells Felicitas, found the comfort of a marriage in their Saturday afternoons with his slippers hanging by the fire, it simply could not be permanent. It was fleeting because middle-class respectability was built as much on stability as it was on comfort. Stability came from meeting in society or through friends or family, not via unsupervised and unauthorized encounters on the street. But the stable approach had not worked for either of them (after all, they were both well past the average age of marriage and still single), the same way the matchmaking attempt by Frieda Kliem's friends failed. The failure of the traditional methods is, in fact, one of the most prominent themes regarding love in the turn-of-the-century metropolis. And yet where the modern metropolis had created a new path to romance—the street encounter—it was almost immediately crushed under the weight of "the real thing" and cast in the light of "an illusion."

FELICITAS'S STORY PLAYS on the tensions between traditional sensibilities and modern approaches created by the city. Felicitas and her companion find a degree of intimacy in their Saturday afternoons, but the way they find it and the restrictive proscriptions of middle-class society ultimately prevent them from making it official or permanent. Their union is, as Felicitas recognizes, a fantasy. For the man, it is a temporary substitute for the real thing. Middle-class people were supposed to meet in polite company and in the living rooms and ballrooms of their parents' or friends' homes. Most marriages were in fact still arranged by parents, who rarely looked very far outside of their immediate circle of acquaintances.

Yet men and women alike nevertheless continued be fascinated by other ways of meeting, and they seem to have placed a remarkable degree of hope in chance encounters like that of the fictitious Felicitas. In fact, fate was an aspect of city life that Berliners referenced again and again. Even more common than isolation or city collisions was the trope of the "missed connection." Alongside narratives of loneliness and of random encounters, alongside the longing this engendered, there was a hope that these brief, chance meetings might lead to something constructive or, better yet, romantic. Berlin was full of stories about fortuitous encounters—romantic meetings arranged or at least enabled by the big city with its masses and rhythms. There was a sense that, at any time, a woman might run into her soulmate or at least someone who might soften the pains of her isolation in the metropolis. These encounters were known as *Strassenbekanntschaften*, street acquaintances with whom one shared a brief—though often intense—connection. Walter Benjamin famously called this "love at last sight," though Charles Baudelaire deserves the credit for poeticizing this type of relationship in the 1860s in his poem "To a Passer-by" ("À une passante").[66] The gay poet Armand Ernesti wrote a similar poem about Berlin in 1903, a poem he called "Lost in the Maelstrom of the Capital":

> *He whom I will never see again, how my heart burned for you!*
> *You are the most beautiful man on earth, and so close to me, so like me.*
> *. . . O God, how closely we are connected. We were chosen for each other—*
> *And we once found ourselves but then missed each other eternally.*[67]

Newspapers picked up on Berliners' fascination with this way of meeting and began, around the turn of the century, running urban vignettes based on this unconventional romantic path. One story in the *Berliner Morgenpost* featured a man who accidentally grabs the wrong briefcase while leaving the streetcar on his way to work. In the briefcase is a picture of a beautiful girl, and he ultimately tracks her down and marries her.[68] In another, a young man meets his future wife because they both walk the same route to work each morning.[69] Chance encounters at the post office were another common plot of short stories, as were curious twists of fate such as the one whereby a working-class boy who was spurned by a middle-class girl finds success as a businessman and later happens to employ the same woman's son. Fate has brought them back together, and they get married.[70]

There were also real-life stories of fortuitous encounters, and newspapers were quick to publish accounts of them, too. In one case, a man who had recently sat for a portrait and given the photographer permission to display the photo in a display window heard from his friends that there was a picture of a beautiful woman next to his. Upon seeing the picture himself, he got her name from the photographer and ended up marrying her. The newspaper writer attributed this to the power of fate.[71] Stories like these, it seems, convinced city people that true love was out there and that fate might lead them to it. They also fanned the flame of interest in "what if" fantasies, and Berliners even took steps to try to foretell the work of fate. In 1907, the *Berliner Morgenpost* ran a news story about a man who had designed a vending machine that would show people a photo of their future mate. Wilhelm Strebel, the inventor of the machine, had acquired a pile of old portrait negatives at an auction and had used them to build his device, which he rented to various bars and restaurants throughout the city. The machine, which was apparently especially popular among young women, produced for a penny or two a reproduction of a randomly selected negative. Trouble arose, however, when a woman received a picture of someone she actually knew and who, upon hearing that his photo was being used thusly, sued Strebel.[72]

These dalliances with fortuitous encounters—both imaginary and real—nearly always combined the fantastical with the mundane. People were in these stories finding true love almost by accident, but they were finding it in the everyday locations of the train station, the streetcar, and the street. Whether it was the (fictional) pair that met at the post office when he thought she had left her umbrella at the mail window or the (real-life) couple who met when they both happened to be at the cemetery burying loved ones, these types of encounters seemed possible because they fit into the everyday rhythms of nearly all Berliners' lives.[73]

And yet, as easy as it is to get caught up in the romance of such stories, these examples of success were not representative or even particularly common. Far more often, the fortuitous encounter never took place or simply failed to work out, and this is precisely the point. In the case of the couple that met in a cemetery because both were burying their fiancés, the relationship ultimately failed when the woman started seeing someone else and the man turned violent. There was also a man who saw a woman each day on his way into work and began, gradually, to share with her longer and longer periods of eye contact as they passed until, one day, she was suddenly gone and never to be seen again. In these and countless other cases, fate rarely lived up to the hopes Berliners had placed in it.[74]

Although the newspapers might be expected to have either fallen hard for the idea of successful chance encounters or stuck unwaveringly to the narrative of the city's overwhelming power to divide and disappoint, they were instead ambivalent. Berliners and their press were clearly struggling to reconcile what they wanted and thought they needed with what middle-class orthodoxy deemed acceptable. One journalist, for example, penned an article about the intimate possibilities of a lingering glance between strangers on the street. But the strangers never connect: a day after their visual flirtation, he sees her walking with another man, and she does not so much as look his way.[75] Another story featured the fortuitous encounter of former lovers in Berlin's central park, the Tiergarten. Long ago, the man had broken off their engagement because his financial situation required that he delay marriage. Having established himself, he is ready to marry her, he says, and he has in fact been looking for her for years. "Fate ultimately helped me find you again," he tells her as he pleads for her to renew their engagement. But it is too late: she has already remarried.[76]

Perhaps most interesting is Lenelotte Winfeld's short story "Begegnung" ("Encounter"), which imagined the fortuitous encounter of a man and a woman who had long been carrying on a very intimate relationship via letters without having ever met. Here, again, the method of the fortuitous encounter seems to solve a problem created by the big city. But the norms of middle-class courting ultimately cause the potential mates to reconsider. In this case, a woman rides a train into Berlin but is sad because she has just ended things with her pen pal after she detected in his last letter an impatient desire to see her. She had feared that a meeting would ruin the beautiful relationship they had cultivated free from the pressures of real names and faces. "Would not every intentional, banal encounter throw disruptive shadows over the exchange of ideas that connected them so purely and deeply?" A man suddenly gets on the train, and she sees in his face something warm and welcoming that makes her forget her loneliness. This, she thinks to herself, is how she imagined her pen pal might look. The man is drawn to her, as well, and he promptly sits next to her and asks if he might share with her—the first person he has met in the big city—the reason for his trip into Berlin. "I'm looking for a woman I love but have never seen. I don't know her name; I have no picture of her. But I can picture her so clearly that I am sure I can pick her out, even among hundreds." "But you must have met the woman somehow," she reasons. "We're pen pals," he says simply. "One of my novels, 'Nirvana,' caused us to start a correspondence. But my partner broke things off when she detected my desire for us to meet." At this point, the woman of course recognizes her erstwhile pen pal in this stranger, but she does not let on and instead asks, "And so you think that you can find this woman in the metropolis without so much as a clue as to how she looks?" He replies, characteristically, "I trust benevolent fate that it will put her in my path," and then, suddenly, realizes that this has already happened. "Have I not already found her? I don't know what it is, but it seems to me that we've known each other for years." The woman still does not let on, saying only that her advice is to stop looking for her since the woman clearly does not want to continue the relationship. "Much the contrary," he replies, "I sense that she longs for me, too; only the banality of the rigmarole that comes with a rendezvous has scared her tender nature away. But how wonderful will our finding be," he continues, "when we, carried to each other by infallible intuition, stand in front of one another amid the throngs of people. 'It's you'—!—We'll know it intuitively at first sight." But the woman remains firm, saying coldly, "Stop looking for the author of the letters. You'll never find her." After realizing fully that the woman in the train and the woman behind the letters are one and the same and accepting that she does not wish to meet, he tries to salvage their correspondence. "Let us be good friends . . . continue our letters." "You know that's not possible," she says while walking into the crowds of Berlin's bustling train station. "We'd never find the old tone again. Our meeting has destroyed the magic that so held your fantasy."[77]

The remarkable thing about this short story is that the pen pals' meeting is entirely fortuitous, and both are no doubt excited and titillated by the prospect of a chance meeting. Indeed, they express a certain boredom with "banal," in-person meetups, having twice found success in the chance encounter (first through letters and again on the train). But their relationship, begun in this unconventional way, could never exist outside of the realm of fantasy, for it would clash with established patterns of middle-class intimacy. As soon as the man attempts to fuse fantasy and reality, the woman's adherence to the rules of middle-class life kicks in and ends things.

"Encounter" reads like a depressing version of the 1998 Tom Hanks and Meg Ryan romantic comedy, *You've Got Mail*, where the protagonists, who have only met in an internet chat room, meet fortuitously in real life without realizing they are already intimately acquainted. As in "Encounter," there are social pressures (their professional competition) that should prevent their union, but the movie has a happy ending because both are willing to overlook them. In one scene particularly reminiscent of the turn-of-the-century faith in fate, the protagonists go about their daily routines (walking to work, getting coffee, buying groceries) and pass right by each other, completely oblivious to their shared proximity. Indeed, the tagline of the movie reads, "Someone you pass on the street may already be the love of your life."[78] Both "Encounter" and *You've Got Mail* demonstrate a tremendous amount of interest and confidence in the power of fate, and yet the romantic strangers of each story, though led fortuitously together, struggle to recognize or accept when fate has, in a conveniently romantic and dramatic way, lived up to its billing.[79]

Physicians noticed that Berliners were mildly obsessed with fortuitous encounters or "love at last sight" at the time. In his 1907 book on the psychology of love, Dr. Georg Lomer suggested that while young people were especially predisposed to believing in love at first sight, neither age nor life experience could protect people from being struck by lightning, as he put it.[80] But Berliners hardly needed a doctor to tell them about their "psychosis," as it were; they had already diagnosed themselves and were debating the prudence, propriety, and safety of believing in the possibility of love at first sight and, more importantly, acting on this belief by approaching a stranger. On the one hand, meeting on the street was at once too quotidian (and thus far below the high poetry of love and respectability of a proper middle-class marriage) and too risky (for one did not know what one was getting and had no opportunity to vet the suitor properly). The street also connoted prostitution. On the other hand, the idea of fated meetings was enticing, and the newspapers offered plenty of evidence that they might just lead to something constructive.

The *Berliner Morgenpost* took up the topic of street acquaintances in an article in 1909, opening with the idea that city people were failing to make meaningful connections. Berliners, it suggested, struggled to find mates with whom they shared real "poetry," but not necessarily because poetic love was a fantasy. Much to the contrary, it reasoned, Berliners were simply looking in the wrong places. Each day, the article claimed, people meet each other in the street, in the theater, and in the café, and they may well be made for each other. Take, for example, the young woman walking home from work one day. She appears to be deep in thought, "perhaps she is even dreaming of the person she noticed on one of her recent Sunday outings . . . , perhaps somewhere on the tram, in the suburbs. . . . But she had not been able to approach him because there was no opportunity and because it would not look right" for a girl to approach a man she did not know. Perhaps if they had been in "society," in polite company, they would meet. "But on the street, in a train . . . that would never fly!"[81]

Now imagine, the article continued, there is a young man out walking, as well. This man is walking in the hopes of finding someone. This has, in fact, become a routine of sorts for him, but not because he is a "Don Juan." He is, rather, "one of the many who wake up each day with full hearts and look for their soulmates but return each evening with empty hands." He has "already a

FIGURE 1.4 A missed connection, perhaps? Otto Marcus, "Gross-Berlin," 1903
Source: Landesarchiv Berlin F Rep. 290, Nr. 121830.

hundred times looked around in his small milieu but cannot find a single soul
who could make his life poetic." Note, again, the failure of the usual methods
for finding connection and the resulting loneliness. "How happy he would
be," it continued, "if he could find his soulmate! How often has he found
instead the true curse of his suffering." But it is not his fault that he is alone.
It is, rather, "the big city with its colorful cluster of . . . people who appear as

if whirled together; the big city that keeps those who belong together from finding each other."

So this man has taken to the streets, as it were, to use the one advantage of the metropolis—its masses—in his favor. By now he recognizes that he will have to get her to stop. So he catches up to her and stammers out an attempt at an approach: "May the lady forgive me that I bother her . . . the urgent desire to get to know you . . . sudden encounter and unexpected feelings of warmth . . . I ask politely for the honor of accompanying you." The young woman "doesn't have a heart of stone—yes, she too felt something in the man's eyes; she would even like to accept his accompaniment, but . . . 'My father does not allow street acquaintances.'" So ends the brief contact between the man and the woman—"they who just found each other"—and since she is a respectable woman, she thanks him and heads on her own in the direction of home. "This is the poetry and tragedy of street acquaintances that do not come to fruition," the author concluded.[82]

A week later, a woman wrote into the "readers' letters" section of the *Berliner Morgenpost* saying she was glad someone had treated this subject in such a reasonable manner. "It is foolish," she wrote, "that we should still think about this in such a small town, provincial way." Provincial, of course, stood for outdated, old-fashioned, clueless. "I used to think . . . it was improper for a woman to react to the attempted approach of unknown men," she continued, but over time "I realized that I perhaps ruined my chance at happiness because of this." The woman went on to describe her own "missed connection." She had moved to Berlin from the provinces and, like so many others, had a hard time meeting anyone. One day while riding the streetcar she noticed that the man sitting across from her appeared to be interested in her and was, in fact, quite obviously trying to work up the nerve to start a conversation with her. The woman for her part ignored him and read deeper in the newspaper. She might well have chalked up this experience to the frequent annoyances of unwanted urban encounters, except that it happened again the next day. This time she got up and moved to the rear balcony of the streetcar, hoping he might take the hint. He did not. In fact, the man ratcheted up his efforts, and try as she might to avoid getting in the same streetcar as him, he seemed always to manage to make it into her streetcar, even if it meant literally ramming himself onto a nearly packed car.[83]

The man showed remarkable persistence, but she was unmoved. After three years, the woman was at a philharmonic concert and saw by chance an old work colleague. She had always known the woman to be single, like herself, but now she had a man with her—her husband, it turned out. She recognized the man from the streetcar. As it happened, they had met the same way—only in this case the woman had been undeterred by social conventions. The happy couple later invited her over to their apartment, and she saw firsthand how nice the gentleman was.[84]

The woman concluded by arguing that many young women—in particular those who came to Berlin from the provinces, as she had, and had no family connections in the big city—simply lacked any other means of meeting men and that Berliners should not look down on women who entertained the possibility of a street acquaintance. What had ultimately made the woman change her mind? Was it witnessing firsthand one such streetcar relationship find so much success? Was it perhaps the desperation after failing to find someone, made even worse by having let such a relationship pass her by? Or had the repeated theme in newspapers and novels of street acquaintances led her to see the norms of middle-classness as unrealistic, stultifying, and outdated?

A reader forum of the *Berliner Morgenpost* showed Berliners similarly willing to accept the premise that fortuitous street encounters were thinkable, even necessary in modern times. At the newspaper's prompting, men and women responded with a unanimous yes to the question of whether it was proper for a man to approach a woman on the street. In one response, a woman argued in poetic verse her point that "To profit you must risk / Without fear and without hesitation / I'd ridicule the world!" But the newspaper editors were less convinced and, in a rare intervention in the readers' forum, called on Berliners to consider the matter more carefully.[85] Not surprisingly, the paper was filled the following week with the responses of older, more conservative readers who still considered such a street acquaintance unacceptable. "We knew that people have not lost their moral compass," the editors concluded, satisfied somehow that Berliners were, in fact, still happy to remain inside the familiar walls of middle-class respectability.[86] The advice column of the more conservative *Berliner Lokal-Anzeiger* provided similarly traditional counsel to a mother asking if it was a good idea for her daughter to show up at a café for a rendezvous with a man she had met on the commuter train. "Even if a rendezvous in a café is not a capital crime, it does display a certain amount of trust—trust that is questionable after such a fleeting acquaintance," the columnist wrote sternly.[87]

The debate about the propriety of street-level intimacy is indicative of the way Berliners felt about love and dating in the big city more generally. Their initial response to the question of whether it was appropriate for young, single people to meet others in such an unsupervised, random way was enthusiastic. To be sure, some Berliners truly believed this (and acted accordingly). The sheer number of swindlers who seized upon gullible and starry-eyed single men and women on the street and in the streetcar stands as evidence of this fact.[88] Yet cooler heads ultimately prevailed and quickly centered the moral compass of the newspaper-reading public, just as Berliners generally continued to eschew the pursuit of romance that veered from the traditional, middle-class path.

Why did men and women find the idea of the fortuitous encounter so alluring? To be sure, it was partly because such stories of chance and unlikely romance were simply compelling and juicy, and Berliners fell in love with the idea of falling in love on the street and in the streetcar because it fit with and even enhanced their pride in Berlin as a modern metropolis that was disorientingly fluid. Just as they reported on the chaos of moving day, the crowds moving across Potsdamer Platz each hour, and the troubles of provincials as they got lost in the city, so too did they seize on the theme of chance meetings and the (im)possibility of finding love on the street because it fed the larger narrative of the chaotic metropolis. It was also in some ways a coping mechanism because the difficulty of finding a mate drove them to consider it as good a possibility as any. After all, the woman who rued having perhaps missed her "life's happiness" because she had not entertained the timid advances of a fellow streetcar passenger did so as a woman who wanted to get married but had failed. And she was but one of thousands who had failed to make connections in the city.

On a different level, Berliners' obsession with fate and the fortuitous encounter can be seen as a release valve for some of the tensions of the modern world. Many fantasized about actually making the fortuitous encounter a reality, which reveals some of the tensions of the middle-class sensibility in the modern city. A few people used the stories—real and imaginary—of random, fated connections as blueprints for their own lives, and these were men and women who had lost faith in the religion of middle-classness and were willing to risk losing the stability of a middle-class existence for a degree of love and intimacy. Many more, however, were like Felicitas's companion, for whom the fortuitous encounter, as comfortable as it was, could never provide the stability that was so central to middle-class identity. These are the stories that, on balance, outweigh the ones about ostensibly reckless and naive Berliners—real and fictitious—who subverted conventional mores. To be sure, men had greater freedom than women to take a chance on the fortuitous encounter without damage to their reputation. And working-class

Berliners no doubt faced less scrutiny with regard to street relationships than those in the middle class. But those, especially women, who were in between, who were either trying to adopt a lifestyle befitting a new arrival in the middle class or struggling to hang on to the pieces of a crumbling bourgeois identity, certainly had less freedom to indulge in fortuitous encounters.

BERLINERS' FASCINATION WITH fortuitous encounters fits with the city's larger narrative of failure when it came to finding love. For all of the articles and stories about Berliners failing to find marriage partners, one might conclude that love and marriage were becoming extinct in the modern metropolis. In reality, though, Berliners were actually getting married (with or without love) as much as or more than ever before. Newspapers simply did not report on this very much.[89] Indeed, while both contemporary urban rhetoric and later historical scholarship maintained that marriage rates were lowest in cities like Berlin and that it was easier to marry in the provinces, more nuanced analysis has concluded that Berliners actually married at a higher rate than the German national average due to the city's younger population.[90] In fact, marriage rates over the period of Berlin's rapid growth did not decline much, if at all.[91]

The fact that Berliners were marrying, of course, says nothing about whether they were finding love, and parsing out love marriages from the marriage statistics is impossible. Contemporary observers were interested in this distinction, though. One journalist announced in the *Berliner Morgenpost* that he had calculated a "statistic of love" by studying the city hall marriage registers, which apparently recorded whether marrying couples affirmed their desire to marry verbally ("yes") or merely signed the form in silence. His conclusion was that the verbal *Ja*'s were increasing and that the coming year would be a big one for love and marriage.[92] The *Berliner Lokal-Anzeiger* even published a front-page piece in 1905 declaring that the German economy was in good shape given the high number of love marriages. After all, couples could not afford to marry for love unless they had ample savings or earnings.[93]

Such estimates were probably misguided. After all, a large number of working-class men and women married as a means of surviving unemployment during labor off-seasons or to avoid signing another apartment lease with no foreseeable income. Marriages in just April and October—the renewal months for six-month leases—made up nearly half of all marriages in any given year, suggesting that Berliners either had good timing when it came to falling in love or, more probably, valued cheaper rent over emotional bonds.[94] Indeed, contemporary demographers were less sanguine about love's blossoming in Berlin. They argued that working-class Berliners married "carelessly," while middle-class men and women were postponing marriage out of economic necessity.[95] Recent scholarship has largely agreed on both counts, though it appears that only men were marrying later. Most women continued to marry in their early twenties, though the wait for a spouse was perhaps more uncomfortable than it had been in earlier generations.[96]

If marriage, with or without love, was not really so endangered, and if, at any given time, three-quarters of men and six in ten women of marriage age were married, why was scarcity and isolation such a compelling narrative?[97] For one, statistics like these make it easy to gloss over the fact that a quarter of a million men and nearly half a million women of marriage age were not married. Berliners around 1900 certainly did not look past these approximately 750,000 single city people. Indeed, for as much as newspapers celebrated the number of weddings in April or October, stories about the thousands of men and women who had been unsuccessful were much more common.[98] After all, this made for better copy.

Another explanation is that many Berliners felt that relationships had become harder to forge in the modern metropolis. Reader letters, novels, and diaries show single Berliners complaining that it was simply difficult to meet potential partners in the modern city. In nearly every case, Berliners laid the blame squarely at the feet of the city, which functioned as a sort of romantic antagonist. Hermann Schwabe, whose highly regarded 1870 "Observations of the People's Soul in Berlin" was published by Berlin's statistical office, painted a bleak picture of marriage in the metropolis, noting that big cities and the interactions they occasioned had turned dating and courting into a vexing "art," one that made it an "open secret" that Berliners, in fact, frequently left the city when they wanted to find a spouse.[99] An 1888 study by Dora Duncker described a man who "had as good as no acquaintances" in Berlin and for whom "his loneliness . . . grew to a nearly unbearable burden in the vivid, breathless ado of the big city."[100] In his case, singleness was made worse by the city's very vibrancy and commotion, which seemed almost to taunt the single person.

Matters were certainly worse for women, who were especially vulnerable to the metropolitan antagonist. Dorothee Goebeler, a journalist who penned countless insightful articles about the plight of women in the big city, wrote in 1912 that "women of times passed" had families to which they belonged; and while family ties do not necessarily mean friendship or a union of souls, "they give something to hold on to, and women of today, women of the big city, often don't even have that." A man has his pub buddies, she continued, but there is no analogous sphere of interaction for women. "Women thus stand alone when they enter the years in which they yearn for contact and connection."[101] Indeed, single women, widows, and newly arrived provincials had the hardest time, as Goebeler noted, and most newcomers were in fact both single and young (under thirty).[102] Thea Schmiets, a widow who had been married to a high-level civil servant until he succumbed to a terminal illness, complained in a letter that she had no real opportunity to meet any men.[103] In this, she was one of the thousands of women who, as Goebeler pointed out, found themselves isolated in the city. Another "lonely woman" wrote in a letter to the *Berliner Lokal-Anzeiger* that "a woman without a family stands completely alone with her heart, her thoughts, and her feelings."[104]

Frequent moves, too, presented an obstacle to urban connections. With so many provincials moving to the metropolis, as one letter to the *Berliner Lokal-Anzeiger* put it, "people have become increasingly estranged from one another. A person changes his apartment as he changes clothes, such that getting to know others in the neighborhood is not remotely possible."[105] Hermann Schwabe, for his part, had written already in 1870 that metropolitans had little or no shared experience and thus struggled to "harmonize" in any meaningful way.[106]

A lack of family in Berlin and the absence of a circle of friends were certainly two major obstacles to making intimate connections in the city.[107] Another hurdle frequently cited—especially by men—was the problem of time and opportunity.[108] One man complained in a letter that a man's career "leaves him only Sundays and a small amount of time and opportunity on the weekdays to figure out what his wishes and desires are, much less find entrance into the circles in which he might hope to find this object of his yearning."[109] The experience of "A. G.," a twenty-seven-year-old assistant manager in the government bureaucracy, exemplifies this. A. G. posed to the *Berliner Morgenpost* the ostensibly simply question, "How does one find a woman?" "I've lived in Berlin for several years now and know the city well enough," he began, "but while I have plenty of sophistication (*Bildung*) to be able to mix in good, middle-class circles, my wish to find a nice-looking, thrifty girl has failed thus far . . . even in giant Berlin." A. G. pointed out that he could not simply approach a woman on the street or "out of the blue" because she would be skeptical of his intentions. Berlin is much different from the provinces, he concluded, where everyone knows everyone else and you can just approach any woman. "My sense is that in Berlin, it's only possible through relatives and acquaintances."[110]

A. G.'s letter, while perhaps naive about the dating dynamics of rural towns, occasioned a flurry of responses in the following weeks.[111] Contrary to the editors' response—"Surely it cannot be so hard to find a fitting mate"—most of A. G.'s fellow readers agreed with him and shared stories of their own heartache.[112] "Mr. A. G. is absolutely right," a similarly exasperated postal assistant wrote. "For two years now I have looked for 'the right one,' but it has all been in vain."[113] Exemplifying Berliners' faith in fortuitous encounters, "H. S." from suburban Steglitz counseled A. G. by saying, "I would just wait until I happen upon a girl that pleases me *at first sight*, whether it's in the theater, at a concert, on the street, or any other place."[114]

The problems were also financial, for while disposable income meant that even working-class men and women could frequent dance halls and bars on Saturday night and Sunday afternoon, the reality of "the struggle for existence" was that one frequently had little left over after paying for rent.[115] Middle-class men also had to put money aside so as to be able to support a family in the future.[116] Those in between—women like Frieda Kliem who positioned themselves as lower middle class but earned very little and had no real dowry to offer suitors—had it harder still. Frieda's sewing work, for example, brought in a paltry DM 20–25 per month, and she received another DM 22–23 each month as interest on her inheritance. DM 31 of this went to rent each month, leaving her approximately DM 16 to spend on food, transportation, and clothing.[117] As Ottilie Baader, a fellow seamstress, wrote in her memoir, "My fate was the same as many single daughters who don't make their own happy life at the right time: they have to hold everything together, to be both mother and father at the same time, and support those family members who can't support themselves."[118] Leisure was thus mostly out of the question, and it is hardly surprising that women like Frieda complained often about their financial problems.

The economic plight of single women who were new to Berlin and trying to make ends meet could be quite grim. On August 9, 1905, the *Berliner Morgenpost* reported the suicide of Else Buchholz, a "twenty-two-year-old woman . . . [who] had only recently arrived in Berlin to work as a buffet lady, but after only finding employment as a waitress and then losing her job, her apartment, and finally her money, grew tired of life."[119] Stories like that of Else Buchholz were, sadly, so common that they became almost a fixture in the daily scenery of Berlin; indeed, in 1904 alone, there were 612 suicides—and 337 additional unsuccessful attempts.[120] Women without money—like Else Buchholz—had a hard time making connections with other Berliners because they simply could not afford the extravagance of a café or dance hall.[121] The

Berliner Morgenpost, which in 1898 ran a series titled "Women in the Struggle for Existence" that provided tips for women trying to make it on their own, argued in its introduction that advice for single Berliners was especially relevant because so many women (and men) lacked the job stability and wages to even think about getting married.[122] Indeed, one of the articles in the series suggested wryly that the best way to find a husband was to have "lots of money."[123]

Financial problems made it difficult to start a relationship, but even those Berliners who succeeded in making connections often found their intimacy cut short because of a lack of money.[124] One major obstacle was the dearth of opportunities to be alone for men and women who could not afford an apartment or even a room of their own. Keeping quiet and keeping secret were thus barriers well known to the Berliners living on tight budgets.[125] Financial worries also made it hard for relationships to blossom. The daily newspapers were filled with stories in which money was the root cause of a suicide, violence perpetrated against a lover, a broken engagement, or some combination of these. There was the case, for example, of a twenty-nine-year-old bookkeeper who had fallen in love with a salesclerk at a soap store and even bought soap each day so he could see her. They soon got engaged, but when the salesclerk realized that her betrothed earned very little and was wasteful with what he had, she broke off the engagement, only to find herself the victim of an attempted murder by the spurned lover.[126] The *Berliner Morgenpost* characterized as a common "street scene" a news story about former lovers who see one another on the street. The woman had moved on because it was clear that the man had no money, and in his despair he jumped into the river to commit suicide.[127] The stories did not always end in sadness. In 1909, for example, a seventy-two-year-old man finally took his eighty-two-year-old bride to the town hall to be married after waiting more than forty years to establish themselves financially—but exceptions like this only put the many tragic relationships into starker relief.[128]

Urban life was indeed especially hard for those Berliners teetering on the border between lower middle class and working class and who thus faced several of these problems at once. After all, Berlin was growing due primarily to the influx of provincials seeking work, and when they arrived in Berlin, they had neither reliable work nor support networks. Frieda's experience of bouncing around between jobs after landing in Berlin was in this sense typical. Most newcomers were able to state a profession of some sort when registering at city hall upon their arrival—only 19,400 (7 percent) of the 272,906 men and women who arrived in greater Berlin in 1904, for example, reported being without a profession, on the dole, or in training—but having a profession did not necessarily mean employment, much less a stable job.[129] By far the most common profession recorded by newcomers was simply "laborer" for men and "domestic worker" for women, followed by trade/sales, construction, food and drink, metal fabrication, and, for women, textiles—in other words, professions characterized by low pay and irregular employment.[130]

In terms of family connections, the vast majority of newcomers were both young and single. In 1904, 78 percent and 74 percent of newly arrived men and women, respectively, were between the ages of fifteen and thirty-five, and those in their twenties made up 52 percent and 43 percent (men and women) of all newcomers.[131] Men and women twenty to twenty-four years old were also almost all single (2 percent of men were married, compared to 9 percent of women), and by their late twenties, still only 19 percent of men and 27 percent of women were married. For that matter, even those in their thirties were mostly single: just 38 percent of men and 36 percent of women were married.[132]

No doubt some Berliners came to the city with at least some distant relations residing somewhere in the metropolis, just as Frieda Kliem had extended family in the city, even if she rarely interacted with them. But the limited data available suggest that Berliners—and European urban migrants, more generally—had little by way of meaningful family connections in the big city. Scholars have struggled to triangulate the existence of support networks for urban newcomers, but they generally agree on limited extended family structures for urban migrants in industrializing Europe.[133]

Berliners themselves confirm this conclusion. A lack of family connections in the big city was almost always near the top of the list of complaints made by newly arrived men and women looking for stability. The author of the *Berliner Lokal-Anzeiger*'s weekly column, the "Berliner Observer," called these newcomers "luck-seekers" and noted that they filled the Berlin metropolis by the thousand. They are "people who have lost everything back home or have won nothing at all and thus leave their quiet provincial nooks and flock to the gleaming, enticing imperial capital in the sure hope of finding here what they have searched for in vain." They come, he continued, to build better lives in Berlin. But all too quickly—when disappointment comes and their "castles on the cloud crumble"—they realize that it was a "deceptive luster" that led them here. They ultimately hit bottom "even faster and more helplessly, for here relationships were foreign to them; here they lived lonely and isolated in unknown surroundings, overcome by the foreignness to the point of diffident, timid vacillation and fear."[134] The "Berlin Observer" paints a grim picture of the fortunes of these thousands upon thousands of "luck-seekers," but the reality was, indeed, miserable, especially since Berlin neighborhoods did not break down by ethnic group, unlike Paris or Chicago at the time. Accordingly, provincials lacked even the basic comfort of a shared cultural background with the men and women who lived around them. When provincials landed in Berlin, they entered a city teeming with others like them but were, for the most part, completely alone.

Urban migrants naturally came from a variety of distances: some came from Berlin's suburbs, others from the surrounding Brandenburg countryside, and still others from further away in Germany or the continent. Demographic studies suggest that migrants with shorter journeys often did better, and this makes sense: they were more likely to have the assistance of family, if needed; they were more familiar with what city life was like; their language (or dialect) and regional/cultural sensibilities more nearly resembled those of the metropolis; and they probably had a larger support network than those who came from farther away.[135]

For that matter, studies of other European urban migratory patterns have suggested that most urban newcomers came from the "direct rural vicinity of the city," but migratory patterns were hardly a one-way street from rural to urban.[136] Indeed, men and women frequently moved back and forth between different communities as dictated by work, family, and other ties. Success and stability could be short-lived and fleeting, and those who seemed to have gained a stable foothold in the city often found their situations change quickly when a factory closed, a loved one died, or their fortunes plummeted.[137] Frieda Kliem is, in this sense, remarkably characteristic of the larger story of Berlin: born in Berlin's suburbs, she moved first out to rural Brandenburg and then back to Berlin, her finances and sense of stability vacillating and forcing her to adjust.

What worked against all single men and women in Berlin—whether working or middle class, newly arrived or lifelong Berliners—in addition to finances and a lack of family connections, was a set of long-standing mores and expectations for comportment that limited the ways in which they could interact in the city. Frieda Kliem is in many ways the perfect example. After all, she had her standards and refused the matchmaking attempt of her friends because she wanted to marry only a civil servant. This probably had as much to do with social standing as with income. Frieda's insistence on this point may seem curious if not downright foolish given her precarious situation, but it was hardly uncommon. One man wrote into the *Berliner*

Lokal-Anzeiger asking for advice because he feared he was doomed to become a lifelong bachelor. Despite having made some money of his own, he had come from a poor family and feared that any middle-class woman (or her family) would object to his humble beginnings. My sisters, he pointed out, were all domestic servants, "not even salesgirls."[138] The "Berlin Observer" tried to counsel single male readers like this gentleman to search for women in poorer areas, places where they did not normally look, places where women were not doing so well.[139] It would be a noble quest, perhaps, but also one fraught with the tensions of a society in which marriages across class lines were exceedingly rare.[140]

TERMS SUCH AS "the modern world," "nowadays," and "back then" were fixtures in the emerging lexicon of dissatisfaction and frustration metropolitan men and women felt about love in the big city. "Back when grandfather took grandmother" was how laments about a supposedly easier, and in any case bygone, time often began.[141] It was clear to Berliners from factory floors to Tiergarten penthouses that the modern world and the modern city had made things more difficult when it came to finding love.[142] Back then, as one writer remembered, "a young man, when he reached the marrying age, chose one of the waiting girls that pleased him, took her in if she said yes, and made her his wife in front of the pastor and then the city hall." It was similarly easy for women: "When a young girl reached marrying age, she went to a dance, where suitors appeared; she turned away the ones she didn't like and said yes if there was one she did want, and she soon afterward became his wife, had children, and lived happily and without any further desires until she died." By the turn of the century, these times had passed. "That beautiful time . . . is unfortunately irrecoverably lost. It's too bad, since it was a wonderful and happy time."[143] Whether it was the modern need to learn the current dance à la mode ("back then," one man complained, one learned a set of dances that lasted him his whole life), redecorate the connubial apartment with each changing mood ("in the good old days," another wrote, an apartment had a single decor that never changed), or the replacement of the "intimate sphere" of the coffeehouse or confectionary shop with the American-style bar that made life more expensive and less relaxed, Berliners invoked the beauty of yesteryear in the same breath in which they gushed about the metropolis's fluidity, tempo, and size.[144]

To be sure, much of this talk of "when grandfather took grandmother" was more perception than reality. City people were often confused about what life had been like in rural settings of ages past, in particular with regard to sexuality and marriage. Far from being an enclave of chaste young people, the old countryside had always been a place of casual sexuality, and marriage often came only after a pregnancy.[145] As a Frau Hoffmann describes rural life in her turn-of-the-century autobiography, "The bride and groom are already sleeping together regularly. How is the man supposed to be satisfied otherwise? I've got two illegitimate children myself—two boys. I never got any kind of support; in spite of that I raised them with dignity. 'That' doesn't really hurt you. There probably aren't any 'honest' couples."[146]

And yet there is evidence that things had, indeed, changed from the pre-industrial period that so often served as a vague contrast to modern times. Most evidence suggests that men and women had rarely looked beyond their preindustrial towns and villages in their search for marriage partners. But this changed around the 1860s; increasingly, one partner (usually the woman) had to be recruited from outside the village, even if the distance of recruitment was still quite small.[147] Rural communities, to be sure, had their own quirks and practices that made finding a partner more complicated than Berliners liked to remember. But turn-of-the-century impressions of the world offer compelling evidence that old and new were pitted against each other with astonishing force. The "modern women's journal"—a new offering by the *Berliner Morgenpost* in the 1910s—elucidates this antagonism, for here modern women could find practical tips for sewing, fashion, and homemaking, each section displaying first "the old method" and then "the new method."[148] But Berliners increasingly found "the old methods" inadequate in matters of the heart; when it came to meeting "the right one," as one woman claimed, "the old methods" were "broken."[149]

Most commonly, the problem with old methods in the new world was that they represented an outdated way of thinking about dating. Partly this was the problem of finding connections in a big city where anonymity and strangers cast a shadow upon meaningful intimacy. Many frustrated men frankly saw meeting on the street as their only real opportunity to come into contact with a mate due to the pressures of their jobs.[150] And yet, in most circles, a well-intentioned, intimate approach made on the street remained taboo. This was no doubt to some extent because of the prevalence of swindlers and prostitutes. They were, of course, not new with the birth of the big city, but, as period observers noted, the material pressures of metropolitan life—combined with the large pool of potential victims and clients—paved a road to perdition that proved too enticing for criminals and down-on-their-luck Berliners to resist. So any fortuitous encounter had to be taken with a healthy dose of skepticism.[151] But it was more than just the swindlers and prostitutes that had discredited street acquaintances. After all, street encounters between honest, well-intentioned people were disdained even after it was clear that neither was working a trick. It was also the optics, the unsupervised meeting of strangers, that did not accord with the values of middle-class life.

Those who avoided street acquaintances still faced the material pressures of the metropolis, and these were the very men and women who lacked the money and rank to mix in circles where the "older," time-tested methods were adequate. Dance lessons were well known for leading to a first love and often to a marriage, but they were extravagant luxuries that did not fit in the modern world of rising costs and meager incomes.[152] One had to think practically and weigh the likely romantic return on each little investment. Reflecting on these financial realities, one writer went so far as to suggest that the modern world had "made the goddess of love into the goddess of reason."[153] Berliners indeed seem to have agreed that the material realities of life could not be overlooked in modern dating.[154] "We live in strangely uncertain times," Dorothee Goebeler wrote in 1914. "Wealth shifts like sand; income is lost. What today appears to be sturdy lies tomorrow in pieces on the floor."[155] Whereas "the question of the heart [was] until recent decades nearly the only basis for marriage," the provocative columnist J. Lorm wrote in the *Berliner Lokal-Anzeiger*, "it is in our realistic time almost pure legend." Now, he continued, one only "speculate[s] . . . whether it is rational" to marry.[156] "Modern love is no longer the wild steed that jumps over gates," another wrote more poetically. "It is trained to step carefully and wears a bridle with reins."[157]

These writers emphasized without fail the struggle for existence, as well as increasingly expensive ways of life and increasingly complicated needs of urban people. Indeed, as Lorm wrote in another piece, "it has become so unmodern" to use words like "love," "happiness," and "peaceful home"—"as if one still looked for these phantoms in our time!" The old methods, as he saw it, were far away from the modern, urban world, where life was rushed and people had no time to devote to things that did not promise fame or money.[158] Modern life was, in this narrative, a struggle—a battle, even—between the sexes and required appropriate tactics.[159] "One no longer writes long letters [or] pours out his feelings in another's breast; one does not reveal himself," wrote social commentator Rudolf Lothar. "Much the contrary," he argued, "one closes himself off as well as he can."[160] "There is no doubt," he wrote in another article, "that we have been driven to skepticism by the struggle for existence."[161] Indeed, in 1902 the *Berliner Lokal-Anzeiger* ran a story that looked nostalgically (and a little bit humorously) at the guides to writing love letters that had been so popular in the nineteenth century but could now only be found in antique bookstores and flea markets.[162] Long, flowery declarations of love were apparently irrelevant in the modern world; so, too, was sentimentality in German novels.[163] Gallantry was out of fashion.[164] Even engagement rings—which were once made to order with great care and attention—were now mass-produced.[165] For that matter, the talk in 1913 was of a new law being proposed whereby men could recover and resell engagement rings if the wedding fell through.[166] And whereas wedding bells rang in small towns with an almost steady regularity, Berliners at the turn of the century would listen in vain for that singular announcement of a wedded pair. Wedding bells "are usually left out," the *Berliner Morgenpost* noted in 1907, "because in the turbulent, bustling metropolis one doesn't hear them anyway."[167]

Wedding bells, professions of love, florid love letters—these are, of course, but tiny parts of the intimate world of the turn-of-the-century metropolis. Taken together, though, they are indications of a new era. This self-conscious (if not altogether real) break with the past and the resulting new methods were Berliners' responses to their modern and urban surroundings. These two features were inextricably linked; they were both provenance and offspring of one another. Whereas the metropolis became the very symbol of the modern world, it was itself only possible because of the material transformation of Europe in the nineteenth century. Together, the metropolis and the modern world created a profoundly new experience for men and women at the turn of the century—an experience that was shaped by more difficult material conditions and a social world more antagonistic to intimacy because of the vast numbers of strangers and an equally static set of mores. This new reality affected Berliners in myriad ways, but they wrote with great similarity about the new intimate and interpersonal dynamics of the modern city. From first meeting to marriage, city people found that intimacy in the modern metropolis was difficult to find and just as hard to keep in their grasps. As they expressed their frustrations at being lonely, not having enough money to marry or to be a desirable mate, and lack of opportunities to meet other single people, they also displayed a fascination with fate and the fortuitous encounter—the idea that where logic, effort, or longing had failed, sheer luck or chance might succeed.[168]

And yet Berliners were, for the most part, careful not to try to coerce fate or aid Cupid, for to approach a stranger on the street or in the streetcar was to brush up against the boundaries of proper middle-class masculinity and femininity. For that matter, successful and lasting fortuitous encounters were mostly the topic of fiction. One newspaper story focused on a young man who met the eyes of a pretty girl late one evening while waiting for the streetcar. Shyness and propriety prevent him from addressing her, and this frustrates him as he climbs aboard. "But he comforts himself with the thought that he will see her again, that he will then . . . that, that—yes, that . . . he grows upset."[169] Working-class Berliners appear to have been more willing to entertain the idea of the city encounter, but would-be swindlers caught on to this and found in thrifty, hard-working, lonesome, working-class Berliners their most gullible—though not particularly profitable—victims. In fact, the fear of being swindled left only the most desperate willing to flout the old methods. Nevertheless, the high number of swindlers and victims suggests that many urban dwellers were, indeed, as desperate and lonely as the numerous short stories and reader letters suggest.

Moreover, while the swindlers got a lot of press, the dominant narrative about love and intimacy in Berlin was that of the fortuitous encounter or love at last sight.[170] For turn-of-the-century Berliners, this fantasy was not just the compelling story of strangers falling in love but an important imaginative space of adventure outside the bounds of traditional masculinity and femininity. Tracing Berliners' interest in fate mixed with the everyday adds another layer to the story of urbanization and modernity and gives city people a degree of imaginative agency not afforded them in studies of the city as dangerous or alienating.

While Berliners responded to the disorientation of the modern metropolis by embracing a narrative of fate and imaginary encounters, this was by no means their only reaction. Frieda Kliem turned down the matchmaking attempt of her friends and seemed poised to perhaps go under in the way so many single women who had come to Berlin from the provinces did. But she was also a modern woman, and, when the traditional methods failed, she responded by using the conditions of modern urban life to her advantage and succeeded in finding some measure of connection and love. This part of Frieda's story reveals a competing urban narrative, one of opportunity and adventure.

2

Urban Avenues to Love

IN THE LATE fall of 1900, Kaiser Wilhelm II made a rather curious comment—actually a command—to the group of young women selected to greet him at the dedication of a new monument to his great-grandmother, Queen Louise: "Do not ride bicycles!"[1] The kaiser's plea makes slightly more sense given that Queen Louise was frequently cited as a model of womanhood and that riding this new-fangled vehicle was considered most unladylike. In any case, Wilhelm II's command to women to abstain from bicycle riding came too late. Cycling had begun to take off in the 1890s, and women as well as men quickly became cycling enthusiasts. The phenomenon of cycling swept both Europe and the United States, with cities like Chicago boasting over five hundred bicycle clubs at the turn of the century.[2] In 1911, the *Berliner Lokal-Anzeiger* estimated that there were already over one hundred thousand bicycles in Berlin.[3] Berlin had so many riders that the *Berliner Morgenpost* started a regular feature called "Where Are We Bicycling to Tomorrow?" that suggested routes in and around the city.[4] Berliners soon donned special ready-made cycling apparel, and city planners even turned some walking paths in the beloved park, the Tiergarten, into bicycle paths.[5] Journalist Eduard Bertz wrote in 1900 that one could best appreciate Berliners' love for cycling by observing the "unending procession" of bicyclists along the road from Berlin to Werder (just west of nearby Potsdam) and that the bicyclists' little lanterns combined on the evening return to Berlin to look like an "endless procession of giant lightning bugs."[6]

Women were especially keen to take up bicycling, and manufacturers scrambled to accommodate this new market. Production of women's bicycles in fact overtook that of men's in 1896.[7] And yet its growing popularity among women notwithstanding, turn-of-the-century women who took to cycling were still largely regarded as daring, independent, and audacious, and not just

Grunewald Sphinxbrücke

FIGURE 2.1 Berlin bicyclists enjoying a ride through the Grunewald forest, 1905
Source: Landesarchiv Berlin, F Rep 290 (01), Nr. O317909.

because they flouted their kaiser's anticycling edict. This was partly because the bourgeoning women's movement had adopted bicycling as a symbol of independence.[8] As the generically old-fashioned aunt of a 1905 penny novel tells her niece, Marie, bicycling "looks like emancipation" and is "a corrupt idea."[9] Female riders were indeed often caricatured as *Mannweiber* (masculinized women) in the popular press.[10] But bicycling also struck older Europeans as unfeminine and unbecoming in a more general way. A recently widowed woman who wrote into the newspaper advice column asking if she could ride her bicycle during her mourning period received the stern counsel that bicycling anywhere other than to work was unflattering.[11] An article in the *Berliner Tageblatt* similarly suggested that a woman on a bicycle did not look right because she could not—as she had otherwise done "for centuries"—hide through clothing or artfulness the parts of her body that must be kept private.[12] Cycling costumes for women were indeed more form-fitting than normal clothes (some even included trousers), and riding a bicycle required as much or more exertion than other middle-class leisure activities for young people, such as tennis, golf, and ice-skating.

Women thus risked social censure when they mounted their bicycles. But the rewards were great. Bicycling was a unique thrill, a thoroughly modern take on horseback riding. A 1905 article in a popular women's magazine, for example, described the thrill of "fly[ing]" while riding a bicycle, noting that to ride is to "triumph over time and space."[13] Greater still was the bicycle's romantic utility: lovers could use its speed and easy maneuverability to find a moment alone together or perhaps even meet for the first time. A bicycle may at first seem a rather unsteady base for cultivating a love relationship—indeed, one writer commented that "skinned knees, flat tires, and bent handlebars are not really congenial to amorous feelings"—but there is evidence that it facilitated finding intimacy.[14] Berlin's daily newspapers, for example, warned about girls who had been "tempted away" on bicycles and about violent love triangles that had started on bicycling trips.[15] In the penny novel, Marie ultimately learns to ride in secret and risks her aunt's complete disavowal because she sees it as her only opportunity to meet a young man who has caught her eye. In this, the bicycle—and the distance it potentially placed between would-be couples and their chaperones—was more than just another leisure activity; for Marie, it was her ability to "have a say" in the person she would ultimately marry.[16] The *Berliner Morgenpost's* series on tips for single women in the modern metropolis likewise recommended bicycling outings as a good way to meet a man, especially if a woman made sure to teeter and crash in his direction so he could catch her. She should also make sure to "sprain" her ankle so that he might lead her to comfort under a tree, where "professions of love flourish the best."[17] Just as a young couple in the short story "Zu Rad" ("By Bicycle") race away from their older and less experienced bicyclist chaperone in order to be alone, so too does Marie ultimately escape with her bicycling beau and receive in due course his much-coveted profession of love.[18]

Frieda Kliem was one of Berlin's many passionate bicycle enthusiasts. Indeed, Frieda displayed an almost religious devotion to her bicycle rides. Any weekend with nice weather saw Frieda riding in the nearby Grunewald forest or in the Falkenhagen forest, which was only a short tram ride away. Frieda's weekend bicycle rides began alone, but, true to the advice columns and magazine features that suggested these outings as a way to meet people, she soon found others who shared her passion. In fact, Frieda's entire circle of friends was formed this way. She met not only her best friend, Antonie Köhler, on a bicycle ride, but also the Selkas—Anna and Hermann—to whom she grew so close that she took Anna in for a spell when she was considering a divorce from Hermann.[19] These friendships—Antonie's especially—were critical for Frieda to feel at home in the big city. In each case, the bicycle was the vehicle for the relationship.

Frieda's bicycle outings also occasioned several male acquaintances and marked her first real opportunities for lasting intimacy with men. In the summer of 1904, Frieda met a widower banker named Otto Buning, and the two bonded over their love of bicycling. It is not clear whether they met for the first time while on a bicycle ride, but Otto's first love letter to Frieda in July 1904 pointed to her love of cycling as a reason he had fallen for her. Frieda had also visited Otto at his home, and there she met his four children. They, too, were won over by Frieda and expressed their approval to Otto. This convinced him, as he wrote, to "give you my complete and utter trust" and tell Frieda, "I am falling in love with you."

Bicycling would also allow their relationship to continue to grow: "I'm especially happy that you also enjoy bicycling," he wrote, "and so I would like to allow myself a proposal: so that we can talk comfortably, let us take a little bicycle ride to Waidmannslust or Hermsdorf or wherever you would like." There is no record of how much time Frieda spent with Otto after this letter or even if she accepted his invitation for a second bicycle date. But Otto proposed marriage, and Frieda told him she needed to think about it. Otto's love letter went into a drawer with her other keepsakes, and Frieda pondered this coveted marriage proposal.[20]

As she was doing so, she fell in love with someone else. In 1906, when Frieda, Anna Selka, Antonie Köhler, and Robert Adam (a young stockbroker who joined the bicycle outings in 1905) were relaxing in a restaurant in the suburb of Halensee after a bicycle outing, Robert ran into a friend from the stock exchange, Emil Freier. Frieda and Emil soon fell into a deep conversation, and when she revealed that her store was not doing particularly well, he offered to help her find a new job. Frieda volunteered that she had once learned how to use a typewriter and could probably pick it up again quickly. This would work perfectly, Emil told her, because his position at the stock exchange afforded him ample opportunities to line up various piecework typing orders. This marked the beginning of a close friendship between Frieda and Emil, one that brought him to her apartment "nearly every day," as he remembered, to deliver new orders and help her complete the existing ones. When Frieda signed a lease on a new apartment, Emil helped her move. And when she later went on an extended vacation with her friend Antonie, Emil offered to store her furniture for her. Frieda eventually came to see in Emil her ideal husband and spoke openly to others about her desire to get married.[21]

Emil was indeed a great catch for Frieda: they shared similar interests, and she got on well with his siblings.[22] He also made good money: around DM 140 per month. But Emil did not share Frieda's feelings, and nothing romantic came of the relationship. "My sense," as he later told the police, "is that Kliem assumed I wanted to marry her. She even said as much to other people, notably to my family."[23] Emil's siblings attested to the purity of their

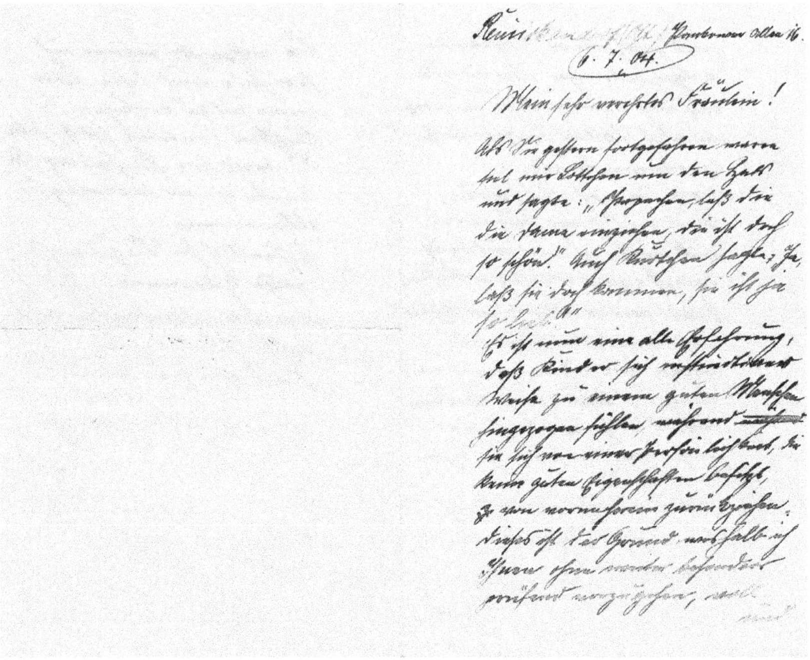

FIGURE 2.2 Otto Buning's love letter to Frieda Kliem, found among her papers in 1914, page 1

Source: Landesarchiv Berlin A Pr. Br. Rep. 030-03, Nr. 1232, Bl. 95.

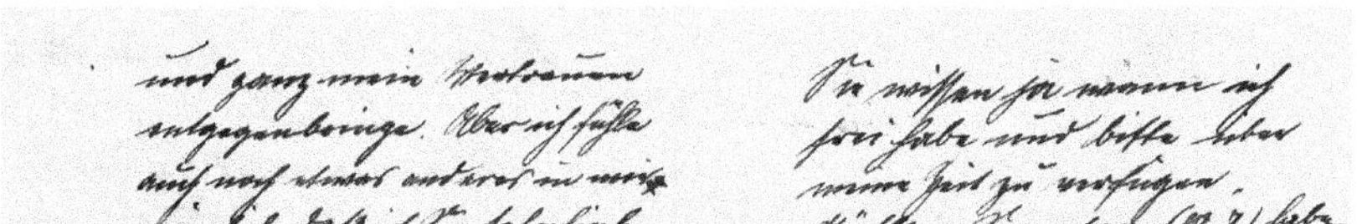

FIGURE 2.3 Otto Buning's love letter to Frieda Kliem, pages 2 and 3

relationship. "Her relationship with my brother," Emil's sister, Clara, confirmed, "was purely platonic."[24]

Frieda made yet another male acquaintance while bicycling, and this one was perhaps the most interesting. While the modern leisure activity of the bicycle outing had led to a marriage offer from Otto Buning and a desired pairing with Emil Freier, these relationships were more or less traditional in nature. This third one, though, was both fundamentally different and thoroughly modern. At some point between 1906 and 1910, Frieda met a man named Otto Mewes on a bicycle ride, and he became a fixture of every outing thereafter. Mewes was a three-times-divorced, eccentric, and finicky man of leisure who hailed from the nearby town of Brandenburg an der Havel and yet seemed to live everywhere and nowhere. Mewes is perhaps best described in the words of his friend, Paul Schambach: "He lives as a vegetarian and has a certain weakness for the fairer sex that has frankly cost him more than once. Even though he has been married and divorced three times, he apparently, in spite of his sixty-five years, is not completely healed." Mewes came from a comfortable bourgeois family and took a managerial job at a factory before he met two older French women and lived off of their largesse (in return for language and singing lessons). Mewes also became a Freemason, which seems to fit his freethinking, freewheeling persona.[25]

Whereas relationships with Otto Buning and Emil Freier appear to have been wholly respectable, Frieda's intimacy with Mewes is probably best understood as a sort of informal or casual dating relationship. She was careful to keep the details of their relationship secret—a fact that stood out to nearly every member of her circle of friends.[26] Frieda also repeatedly attempted to pass off Mewes to her friends, neighbors, and distant relatives as an "uncle," and since he came to visit every four to six weeks, she had ample occasion to rehearse this ruse.[27] But few seem to have believed this. After all, they observed how, during bicycle outings, Frieda made sure to ride near Mewes and how she grew visibly jealous whenever he was friendly to one of the other women or when another made the mistake of riding between them.[28] Frieda and Mewes eventually took to traveling together on their own and enjoyed a walking and bicycling trip along the Rhein River and to Monte Carlo in 1913. While Antonie Köhler came with them, Frieda and Mewes at some point broke off and traveled the rest of the way alone.[29] Time spent together by Mewes and his "Fritz," as he called her, abated only when Mewes decided to move for good to the south of France, where, as he put it, it was easier to live as a vegetarian and "get by on my own."[30] But Frieda still wrote him letters and signed them "with a kiss" up until the day before she was killed.[31]

Frieda Kliem, who initially struggled to get by and find connections in the metropolis, made several friendships with men and women as she settled into the big city. In taking up bicycling and showing herself open to the idea of relationships made in this way, Frieda formed a network of close friends and, at several points throughout that first decade of the twentieth century, male suitors with whom she enjoyed some degree of love and intimacy. But Frieda's found intimacy was more than just the result of patience or of being in the city long enough that fate finally got around to blessing her with a fortuitous encounter. The big city did create opportunities for single men and women at the turn of the century, but what lay behind those opportunities were fundamentally new avenues to and types of love and intimacy—each one with its own set of risks. As Berliners went about crafting their lives and selves in the modern metropolis, they were thus faced with the choice of diving into the choppy sea of modern, urban love or tethering themselves to the reliable but often frustrating shores of a more traditional approach to love and courting.

BICYCLING OPENED THE door to intimacy and love for Frieda Kliem and others, but it was not the only vehicle to love at the turn of the century. The explosion of the metropolis brought a whole host of new gathering spots, social offerings, leisure activities, and technologies that made it possible for men and women—especially those in their twenties—to make intimate connections, provided that they were willing to accept the attendant social risks. Those who did often found love or some more "modern" equivalent, but they talked about this modern love in a different, more practical way.

Take moving day, an extremely visible and sensationalized representation of Berlin's high apartment turnover rates. While apartment buildings with perpetually new neighbors were a reminder of the urban isolation about which Berliners so frequently complained, they could also serve as a matchmaker of sorts.[32] Berlin was filled with stories of people who met and fell in love because they lived on the same floor or in the same building. One woman described in her memoir how she met her husband precisely because, as lodgers at the same Charlottenburg boarding house, they ate lunch at the same table every day. They were married within a year or two of their first meeting.[33] The newspapers, too, reported on relationships that had germinated in apartment corridors and courtyards, such as that of a twenty-three-year-old book printer and his seventeen-year-old bride who happened to live in the same building and share the same path to work.[34] There was also the young man who lived with his mother and fell in love with the middle-aged divorced woman living next door.[35] For that matter, the city's many *Schlafburschen*—young, single men who rented rooms or even just beds from widows or larger families— were known to start relationships with the women they so frequently came into contact with, though these were often adulterous, short-lived, or both.[36]

One writer opined that apartments were a little slice of rural life in the big city: "Nearly everyone knows each other here. . . . It's like in a small town."[37] Indeed, another writer claimed that she shared a "window acquaintance" with her neighbors, whose windows she peered into every day.[38] Still another wrote that apartments offered one "a certain solidarity" with her neighbors—one that vanished once they passed from the apartment to the busy street.[39] In these ways, apartment buildings shrank the metropolis down to the size of the small towns where romance had allegedly been easier.

The apartment-based romance was popular enough that it featured in quite a few short stories.[40] Paul Bliß's 1913 short story, "Liebe macht erfinderisch" ("Love Will Find a Way"), for example, features a young woman who is locked out of the apartment she shares with her aunt one evening after coming home from work. Her aunt is out, though she had earlier informed the neighbor—a young, single man of her niece's age—of her whereabouts and asked him to come fetch her when the niece showed up. The man uses this to his advantage and tells the locked-out niece only that he will wait with her until her aunt returns. After he chivalrously produces some candles when the hall lights go out, he flirts with her and eventually professes his love for her, brushing off her avowals of middle-class respectability by telling her he will be patient. He then offers to take her to her aunt, confessing that he has known where she has been the entire time. "And you're just telling me this now!" she exclaims. "I needed to take advantage of this opportunity," he responds, as he kisses the hand of his smiling neighbor.[41]

Bliß's story showcases two characters who show themselves willing to adapt to the conditions of the modern city. The man resorts to this innocent trickery because, as he puts it, he had no other way; and the woman moves beyond her initial protestation that she does not spend time with men without a chaperone. Moreover, while the man does at one point mention the word "fortuity," his invocation of the much-beloved term is completely different than starry-eyed faith in chance encounters, for he takes an active role in arranging his own amorous destiny. Indeed, he makes clever use of a common residential space to jump-start his chance at finding love. Whereas a traditional, middle-class morality more often than not kept Berliners for whom the standard methods had not worked from doing anything other than waiting for their stars to align, a modern, enterprising sensibility potentially put young or uninhibited Berliners in intimate contact with one another.

Even more horizon-expanding was the workplace. For working- and lower-middle-class Berliners alike, the work milieu often provided a shortcut to making acquaintances in a vast, impersonal city of millions. Factory work was of course emblematic of the turn-of-the-century city, but men and women did not usually work side by side in factories and thus did not frequently find marriage partners or love interests among their work colleagues.[42] But factory work was by no means the only employment for Berliners around 1900, and a wide variety of service jobs—from waitresses to maidservants to taxi drivers to office clerks—did, in fact, occasion the romantic workplace mingling of men and women. For working-class Berliners, it was often the building and location, not the job itself, that served as the catalyst for connection.[43] Whether it was a young waitress who fell in love with a taxi driver working out of the same building,[44] a jeweler's apprentice who worked in the same building as a maidservant,[45] a beer distributor and a young woman recently hired as a servant to a family in the same building,[46] or new arrivals working in the same hotel, single Berliners found that the orbits of their work movements intersected with those of others who also longed for love.[47]

More interesting still were intimacies that developed between middle-class, white-collar colleagues, for these jobs were fundamentally new and modern, and they were the landing places for an entire generation of young women like Frieda Kliem seeking independence and professional identities as typists, salesgirls, secretaries, and even office clerks. In his famous study of white-collar workers, Siegfried Kracauer described these clerks, salespeople, and office workers as solitary types whose work compelled them to divorce themselves from the restrictive social expectations of the middle class and embrace a sort of individualistic hedonism.[48] Kracauer was writing in the late 1920s, when (lower-)middle-class morality was certainly different than at the turn of the century;[49] and it is no doubt true that many or most middle-class men and women considered a relationship with a work colleague a scandalous breach of morality around 1900. Indeed, one publicized court case from 1910 revolved around the question of whether a woman could quit her job as a salesgirl without notice because her boss had proposed marriage to her. The court ultimately ruled that the well-intentioned advances of her boss did not provide justification for a resignation without notice, but the legal delibera-tion speaks to the contention surrounding the issue.[50]

Still, as news reports, diaries, and short stories from the turn of the century demonstrate, men and women who were willing to move beyond the barriers of middle-class morality vis-à-vis "correct" forms of meeting and dating did, indeed, find some success when they considered their colleagues or business partners as potential mates. There was, for example, the case of the department store security guard who fell in love with a salesgirl who worked in the area he patrolled, not to mention the doctor and nurse who both worked at the Charité hospital and developed an intimate relationship.[51] One woman wrote to the *Berliner Lokal-Anzeiger* for advice on the proper next steps after she had fallen in love with a work colleague, and Aimée Gaber's 1911 short story "Seine Braut" ("His Bride"), plays on the theme of a woman's distrust of her fiancé, who works in an office full of attractive and aggressive women.[52] Short plays also featured office romances that went against the grain, as, for example, in Rudolf Schwarz's play *Liebesleute* (*Lovers*), where a factory manager falls for his secretary, as well as in well-known playwright Paul Lehnhard's comedy *Die Liebe im Kontor* (*Love in the Office*), which riffs on men's inability to re-frain from flirting with the female office workers.[53] Most of these anecdotes present the office marriage market in a wholly stylized, even farcical way; on the other hand, the fact of romance being found in the workplace is rarely the dramatic or comedic element in these stories and instead usually functions as a familiar, relatable backdrop, which speaks to its prevalence.

This narrative can be juxtaposed against somewhat more reliable autobi-ographical sources like the memoir of Helene Kuërs, whose path to marriage reveals the dissatisfaction with traditional dating, the careful adoption of a modern, more practical method, and the complexities of trying to fit these two sensibilities together. Helene, a Berliner whose childhood and adoles-cence was firmly middle class, had at least one suitor in her teenage years, but she reached her midtwenties without finding a man she wanted to marry. After finishing her schooling, she trained as a photographer's assistant and began earning money of her own. When she was forced to take a new job in 1901, she found work as a secretary in a large machine shop, which involved an-swering the telephone, doing the bookkeeping, and taking dictation from her boss. This last task had her moving frequently between her little office and the shop where Friedrich, her boss, spent most of his time. Helene remembered that they often spoke in the evenings when Friedrich came to sign the letters she had prepared and that, on one particular evening, he mentioned to her that he was interested in getting married but could not find a suitable wife.

"I told him he should go dancing, but he says he can't dance." "After a short pause," she continued, "he looks at me strangely and says, 'I would like to have you as my wife and thus ask you, will you marry me?'" Helene remembered that she was shocked he would ask her this so directly and was not sure how to respond. After a moment, she answered that she had to ask her parents. "So we agreed that if I did not come to work the next day that he could go to my parents and ask for permission. So I did not go to work the next day, and on Saturday my boss came with a bouquet of roses to ask for my and my father's approval."[54]

Helene's roundabout and clumsy solution to Friedrich's proposal suggests that a pairing with her boss—someone who was outside her family's social circle—was indeed unconventional and potentially disreputable. At the same time, Helene and Friedrich, like so many others, found in a fundamentally modern forum—a gender-mixed, middle-class workplace—the romantic success that had previously eluded them. In this, their story was actually quite typical. In fact, Helene could well have been the inspiration for the many short stories and works of fiction that played on the theme of office romance between boss and secretary. In the 1912 short story "Der Andere" ("The Other One"), for example, an older man named Georg proposes marriage to his secretary, Lore, in the same offhand and clumsy way. "You are no longer so young," he tells her one day, adding, "I think we are past tiptoeing around each other's feelings." Noting that he is a "creature of habit" and that he likes her so much as a secretary, he proposes that they get married as a practical arrangement so that he never loses her—as his secretary. Lore accepts, and only after they are married do they admit to each other that they love each other and feel their lives beginning anew.[55]

Georg and Lore's marriage, brokered under the guise of convenience, and Helene Kuërs's guarded response to her boss's proposal both underscore the point that flouting traditional mores vis-à-vis relationships born out of the workplace was not without its risks and had to be treated with caution. After all, aside from social censure, one could be fired for dating a colleague (or, worse, a competitor's colleague, as happened to a certain "Irma B." in 1907), though courts usually ruled that such a firing was unlawful and required restitution and back pay.[56] Still, it appears that, for those Berliners willing to be transgressive in matters of love and dating in the office, the reward was worth it. Indeed, some Berliners even argued that love found in these ways was actually more trustworthy than the traditional methods because they avoided the pressures and charades of family visits. Berliners were, as the writer Paul Kirstein noted somewhat hyperbolically in 1902, "in complete agreement that the relationships that develop in the hustle and bustle of one's work life are preferable to those constrained by domesticity and by the presence of family," where one puts on deceptively blissful airs.[57] A person, in other words, showed more of her true self at work. While most middle-class families no doubt would have preferred that their sons and daughters date and court the sons and daughters of family friends and business associates, Kirstein nevertheless gave voice here to the preferences of a younger, romantically frustrated generation.

Love found in apartment corridors, behind department store counters, and at bookkeepers' desks evinced an emerging romantic practicality, for here Berliners who had complained about a lack of time for dating and courting were adapting their search for love to fit the rhythms and movements of their daily and professional lives. They also adapted their leisure activities in the service of love, especially as modern sports occasioned new, casual interactions ripe for love's blossoming. Indeed, as women took increasingly to sports and active lifestyles at the turn of the century, the possibility of sports as dating became more thinkable (if still risky).[58] Bicycling was chief among these, probably because it was the most economically accessible, though golf, skating, and—for the slightly more affluent—tennis were popular middle-class sports as well.

As with apartment and workplace dating, sports were naturally not embraced specifically for their ability to facilitate romance. As writer Heinz Tovote maintained in 1909, "The sport itself is the main thing." But Tovote also admitted that the men and women who mixed while playing tennis, golf, or even hockey "happily accept all of the attendant perks thereof."[59] Sports were indeed increasingly being used as opportunities to socialize with potential love interests, not least because they allowed couples some unchaperoned time to themselves. Elisabeth Bäcker, a seventeen-year-old girl from the provinces who came to stay with her upper-middle-class relatives in Berlin and earn some money as a housekeeper, wrote in her diary that while the man she loved, Gero Kinzel, was engaged to another woman (but loved Elizabeth), they enjoyed their own bit of intimacy while playing tennis.[60] Quite a few plots of short stories relied similarly on sports to position a blossoming and independent protagonist close to her desired mate.[61] And the satirical magazine *Simplicissimus* put its own spin on this theme in a 1900 cartoon entitled "The Value of Sport," which features two women discussing the way "hearts find each other more easily" through tennis.[62] As with bicycling, a young woman's participation in sports was often shorthand for her emancipation from the restrictive femininity of her mother and grandmother, as Dorothee Goebeler noted in a 1907 piece on the growing chasm between mothers and

"modern" daughters.[63] Her readers saw it too, though they tried to suggest
that mothers were increasingly "allowing" their daughters to play tennis and
skate and study and were thus perhaps evolving, too.[64] Either way, it is clear
that sports were an emerging and nontraditional path to relationships for
young men and women.[65] For women, specifically, sports were a degree more
accessible and acceptable than work, particularly for middle-class women
whose families would have objected strenuously to their employment in a
shop or an office.[66]

Paths to love were also changing at the hands of various new technologies—
most notably, the telephone—that served to link urban strangers in intimate
ways. The most interesting such example here is the story of Frau B. and her
husband. Responding to a journalist's request for real stories of "how they
met," Frau B. overruled the objections of her husband and told readers how
she had met her husband because "it might possibly free many from a giant
prejudice." "I met my dear, good husband over the telephone," she wrote, cutting to the chase:

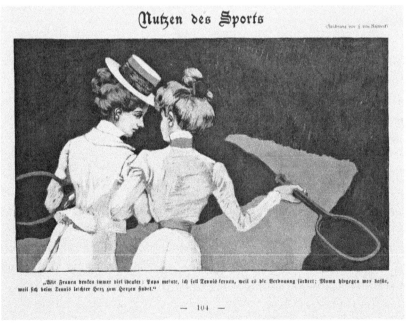

FIGURE 2.4 "The Value of Sport," 1900. The caption reads: "We women are always
much more idealistic: papa thought I should take up tennis because it helps with diges-
tion; mama was for it because she says hearts find each other more easily while playing
tennis."

"*Source*: Nutzen des Sports," *Simplicissimus* 13 (1900): 104.

I was employed as a telephone operator on Lützowstrasse. Among my numbers was a business on Kurfürstenstrasse from which, with extreme frequency, the same man always called. He was so polite and friendly that I—even though it was technically forbidden—usually gave him preference when he asked to be connected. He always thanked me and wished me good day and happy holidays, and one day he appeared at our office. I was, of course, stunned, but he claimed that the telephone in his office was broken and that he needed to make an urgent call—OK, I thought to myself, no harm in that. But that evening as I was leaving to walk home, he was standing there on the street. And he started talking to me! Of course very meekly and politely; he showed me every possible form of identification and was in every way a true gentleman. I finally allowed him to walk with me. And I was happy that he kept coming. . . . What should I say? We got engaged and married, and if you would like to see if this relationship made over the telephone is a good one, then come by and see our happiness for yourself. It couldn't have been better if a thousand mothers and fathers had arranged it.[67]

What is notable here is Frau B.'s hedging as she tells her story about breaking traditional taboos about dating. And while the end result was the same as (or better than, as she guarantees readers) marriages made through traditional means, it is clear that this was not always the case. Relationships made through or nurtured by the telephone do not seem to have been either more or less successful, but they were, as one columnist pointed out, potentially of a quite different nature because of the immediate and yet detached way modern technology brought people into contact. The telephone, as the author put it, was so revolutionary because it enabled the direct and real-time connection of two conversing parties—something extraordinarily useful for business correspondence, but also very helpful in intimate matters, where it allowed lovers to remain connected even if they were apart. "But the prompt settlement of matters, which, in business transactions, is so perfect, reveals itself over time—if not immediately—to be not without its risks in matters of love," the author warned. The expediency of the telephone, it seems, was making lovers less patient, less able to abide a lull or delay in communication, for "lovers with telephones don't write letters." If anything (for example, if the line is busy), they write postcards, which "replace a peek into one's soul with a view of a pretty landscape scene."[68]

This contrast between an effusive letter and a sort of placid, perfunctory postcard scene is powerful, and it underscores the point that modern avenues to and technologies of love were doing more than putting modern people in traditional relationships. They were actually changing the way people thought about love, more generally. Indeed, new and emerging technologies of love highlight a shift from finding one's true love to finding someone about whom one felt strongly at that moment.[69] As Nielandt, the protagonist in Erich Köhrer's 1909 novel, *Warenhaus Berlin* (*Berlin Department Store*), puts it,

> Love and happiness, wealth and peace, satisfaction, a delight in na-
> ture, art, culture: we no longer calmly select and enjoy these at our
> ease! Instead we rush into purchases, for carefully calculated chance
> has placed all the various possibilities, neatly presented, in our path!
> As people pass along the street, they acquire whatever suggests it-
> self, without lengthy deliberation, intoxicated by the sensation of the
> fleeting moment![70]

Similarly, Rudolf Lothar, the perceptive newspaper columnist, agreed with the assertion of a book he was reviewing that modern, urban love was not so much about finding one's soulmate but about the feeling itself of loving ("the feeling, not the object, is the main thing").[71]

It seems, then, that these more practical, inventive, and subversive approaches to finding love often positioned their happy discoverers differently vis-à-vis love. Approaching relationships more practically—countenancing the thought of finding love on the street or over the telephone, for example—had the unsurprising effect of making love easier to find. But Berliners who found love in these ways were, as Lothar acknowledged, also often less senti-mental, less emotional about love. "Only in the provinces" is the sentimental method at all common, he pointed out.[72] A front-page piece on the telephone put it similarly: "Longing is left to great-grandmothers. . . . Youth laughs in the face of [longing]. It laughs at tears and the pain of love." See for yourself, the author suggested: "In movie theaters, pretty young metropolitans laugh at the tears of the young sailor who sees his beloved torn from his arms." Indeed, "The youthful section of the theater always laughs coldly at the same tragic scene." For young people, the article concluded, love is "nothing more than a rendezvous arranged by telephone."[73]

It is, of course, reasonable to interpret such a melodramatic article as the cantankerous lament of an older Berliner disgusted with the flippancy and shortsightedness of turn-of-the-century youth. At the same time, the sheer number of articles and short stories that portrayed a novel and more practical approach to love and relationships in the modern metropolis can hardly be dismissed as all caricature. The sweet spot is probably somewhere in the middle. Any shift in turn-of-the-century approaches to love was, it seems, a very self-conscious and deliberate rejection of the idea of "when grandfather took grandmother."

THIS CONFLICT BETWEEN old and new becomes particularly apparent in the adaptation of the centuries-old tradition of the evening social and dance ball to "modern" purposes. Evening balls had long existed as an opportunity to see and be seen, to demarcate one's social position, and to pair off under the eyes of mothers eager to marry off their daughters, but enterprising Berliners were turning these into something new and more practical at the turn of the century. There had traditionally been two types of evening balls: so-called public balls, prominent events such as the exclusive *Presseball* ("Press Ball"), whose guest list included a heavy representation of royalty, dignitaries, and luminaries of the arts; and private "house balls," evening gatherings organized by middle-class families.[74] Young women from well-to-do families saw in private evening balls their best chance at marriage, and hovering mothers and austere fathers alike realized that these gatherings offered the best and most respectable matches. Time and again the story of a well-bred daughter meeting a fetching young officer at an evening ball played out in short stories and serial novels, even into the first decade of the twentieth century.[75] There was in fact a sort of idée fixe about evening balls as the tried-and-true path to intimacy and marriage.[76] Mothers obsessed over whether their daughters would be the ones "left sitting" without a partner to dance with and become "ball veterans," that is, soon-to-be spinsters.[77] Daughters scrutinized the words and behavior of their dance partners, as, for example, in the case of the woman who wrote to the *Berliner Lokal-Anzeiger*'s advice column asking if an especially long squeeze of the hand at an evening ball portended marriage.[78] And newspapers published full-page ads and articles about the latest ball fashions for the coming "season."[79]

For that matter, young women had been conditioned for evening balls from an early age.[80] Most upper- and upper-middle-class couples sent their children to dance lessons that mimicked the grown-up world of etiquette, dance cards, and white-gloved hands and prepared young Berliners for a successful debut when that first ball invitation arrived. Indeed, most teenagers' very first ball was actually the beloved dance class ball, which

was both the course's final exam and a junior-high-dance-like first exper-
iment with love, intimacy, and pairing off.[81] Teenagers and parents alike
took the dance class ball very seriously, not least because so many marriages
grew out of dance class ball pairings.[82] Accordingly, even those who, as
members of the petit bourgeoisie, could hardly afford the extravagance of
private dance classes for their children and who generally did not place
much importance on aping the customs and sensibilities of the upper class
nevertheless felt compelled to participate. They exchanged dance class ball
etiquette advice and tips for doing it on the cheap in the newspaper, so
important was this ritual of proper adolescence.[83] The dance class ball was,
indeed, "the end of a period of childhood," as one writer so eloquently put
it. "The young girl rapidly matures into the young lady, she soon views life
and society through different eyes, and no ball can bring back the magic of
that first one."[84]

By the turn of the century, though, there was a sense that evening balls
were becoming something fundamentally new. Andreas Schulz writes that
the "authority" of private social events such as these was "already somewhat fragile," and the playing out of a larger transition and tension can be
seen in the transformation of evening balls into something more practical
and individualistic.[85] One of the most easily recognized symptoms of this
transition was the increasingly widespread feeling—at least among younger
generations of Berliners—that evening balls were passé and old-fashioned.
Columnist A. von Wartenberg observed in 1907 that "modern" women no
longer trembled with nervous excitement when thinking about upcoming
evening balls or about a young cavalier coming to their table and asking
them to dance. Nowadays, he wrote, women who do so "belong to a dying
breed."[86] Wartenberg's claim here says perhaps more about men losing interest
in playing the part of the cavalier, but this is precisely the point: young or
modern men claimed to be growing tired of overbearing mothers and their
ball-crazy daughters and, in protest, apparently often refused to dance.[87]
Exasperated women—for example, "Annette," in a reader letter meant to pro-
voke a flood of responses—accused men of being too nonchalant at balls and
needled, "Are you too drunk from beer? Is dancing embarrassing? Are you
afraid to sweat? . . . Why do you leave us sitting?"[88] When pressed to explain
why they no longer found it fashionable to dance, men cited their frustration
with the fact that balls were so focused on marriage and courting and finding
a spouse under the eyes of eagle-eyed mothers and stern fathers. "[A dance at a
ball] doesn't have to be a dance that lasts one's entire life," Herbert G. declared
in a 1909 reader letter.[89]

These same changes were also affecting Berlin's famous masquerade balls, which proved especially adaptable to the changing tides of the modern world.[90] To be sure, they were less likely to go extinct than evening balls, and one apparently still frequently saw robber barons, holy men, noblewomen, and adult babies riding the subway and omnibus on the way to masquerade balls;[91] Berliners still wrote to the advice column asking for costume ideas;[92] and newcomers like Fritz Reinert still confided to their diaries that they had never had as much fun as at their first big city *Maskenball*.[93] However, the tastes and goals of younger participants, at least, were changing ever so slightly. Max Pollaczek observed in a 1908 article that "a masquerade ball is for the blasé society of our metropolis a rather antiquated amusement." Instead, "One nowadays would rather be amused than amuse himself and those around him."[94]

Pollaczek's dim estimation of balls points to a growing sense of individualism with regard to this old fixture of middle-class life. The same spirit that saw men unwilling to dance and modern women relatively indifferent to the cavaliers they might dance with was fueling a gradual rethinking of balls altogether. Berliners complained that evening balls were too expensive, and they polled each other for "better ideas."[95] All sorts of new types of balls sprang up around the city—working-class balls, widows' balls, and balls for the deaf.[96] There were gay balls and lesbian balls, too, some of which attracted over seven hundred people in a single evening.[97] There is evidence that some entrepreneurs used balls for the very practical and prurient purposes, respectively, of holding job fairs and attracting clients for prostitutes.[98] One enterprising Berliner went as far as to arrange a service that allowed ball goers to rent a "cavalier" for the evening, which probably speaks to the brittleness of this middle-class custom better than anything else.[99] And public ballrooms requiring no invitation or exclusive ticket and decorated in the style of the fine ballrooms of the upper crust sprang up around Berlin in great number (perhaps as many as nine hundred by the 1920s) and offered a sort of dance ball / nightclub fusion for all Berliners.[100] Even Franz Biberkopf, the down-on-his-luck, just-out-of-prison protagonist of Döblin's *Berlin Alexanderplatz*, heads to a ballroom for a night out.[101] Berliners, in other words, were both commodifying and communizing the ballroom experience.

This new approach extended to dance classes, as well. Berlin's newspapers noted that dance classes were now dominated not by the feeling of "our hearts mov[ing] for the first time like our feet" but instead by a very practical, businesslike approach aimed at mastering a dance, such as the ultramodern tango.[102] Columnist Else Krafft wrote in 1908 that there was a "fresh breeze" moving through modern-day dance classes, one that accommodated the styles and desires of the modern youth.[103] Young people, it turned out, wanted to dance. As influential writer, director, and artist Edmund Edel observed, "A dance madness, a dance epidemic has broken out in the city."[104] But "they don't dance to find suitors; they dance because it's fun."[105] Indeed, dancing had become like a sport, he continued, and the only thing that really mattered was "good dance music."[106]

Evening balls were thus becoming something more youthful, practical, and modern. Upper-class balls featuring dashing cavaliers and perfectly coiffed women gave way to alternative working- and middle-class balls more focused on instant gratification, blithe flirtation, and some measure of intimacy—enough, in fact, that by 1913, some of Berlin's more prudish ball-goers were complaining that there was far too much kissing going on and that they would boycott evening balls until something was changed.[107] Berliners who met at balls were, increasingly, more focused on having a good time than trying to discern their dance partners' intentions for marriage in the squeeze of a hand or the execution of a twirl. Women developed casually intimate relationships that existed only on the dance floor (so-called ball house boyfriends) and danced with reckless abandon, and the previously ubiquitous and vigilant "ball mothers" were apparently now a rare sight.[108] A sense of individualism, freedom, and frivolity had taken over all but the most austere balls, and the very purpose of evening entertainment was conforming to the more impulsive, fleeting fancies of a younger generation. This is not to say that one forgot about marriage altogether or that ball goers were uninterested in relationships extending beyond the walls of the ballroom. Indeed, old and new, traditional and modern still stood in tension with one another. But middle-class Berliners' populist repurposing of dance balls speaks to the currents of change running through the modern metropolis and marking an increasingly individualistic participation in dating, intimacy, and marriage.

In perhaps the most revealing anecdote about the gradual shift from old to new, Arthur Brehmer described guests at a very traditional and proper wedding ball who noticed that, as things were winding down, other guests started to arrive for an entirely different sort of ball. The wedding guests were intrigued by the colorful clientele this other ball attracted, and while they first merely observed their bawdy merriment, they soon lost their inhibitions and joined in to the can-caning and dancing and general felicity.[109] In the clash between old and new, in other words, Berliners increasingly found the modern and individualistic approach worth trying.

THIS SAME FRICTION between old and new can be seen more directly in the rise of casual urban dating. A 1912 novel by Leo Leipziger, for example, which the Berlin press reviewed as perhaps the best portrayal of the true nature of Berlin life, took the conflict between "back then" and "nowadays" as its pervasive and structuring theme.[110] The book's title, *Der Rettungsball* (*The Rescue Ball*), refers to the beach-ball-shaped life preserver one threw to Berliners who had fallen (or jumped) into the Spree River or the city canal, and in this case, the drowning Berliner is a young stockbroker, Max, who is the very symbol of modern, energetic, self-confident, and reckless twentieth-century Berlin. Max has speculated on American railroad stocks and lost big, and his only hope for a bailout is his wealthy spinster aunt, Ida Susemaus, who stands for stability, caution, and tradition—in a word, "old Berlin."[111] Ida lives on Fischerstrasse, which preceded the city's explosion, rather than in an upstart neighborhood or well-to-do suburb. Ida has never moved from her birth house ("the last remnant of old Berlin"), and she continues to run the family vegetable wholesaling business from this old home filled with classic Biedermeier furniture and various other remnants of the past.[112]

Max, by contrast, goes from "flower to flower"—job to job, woman to woman, apartment to apartment—and this is the complicating factor for his rescue. Indeed, Ida's single stipulation about helping Max is that he give up his casual relationship, his so-called *Verhältnis*, with his girlfriend, Meta, and marry a respectable girl of Ida's choosing.[113] The plot progresses rather predictably, with Max first ditching Meta and then ultimately benefiting from the labors of his friend, Moritz, who smooths things over with Ida and procures her blessing for Max to marry Meta, who does her own part by proving to Ida that she is a respectable, independent, hard-working businesswoman.

Max's *Verhältnis*, his casual girlfriend, Meta, serves as the book's catalyst. Indeed, the term *Verhältnis*—which includes a spectrum of relationships ranging from casual dating within one's class to an incongruent, mostly sexual relationship between a middle-class man and a petit bourgeois or lower-class woman that functioned as a sort of placeholder between a boy's adolescence and his social and economic establishment as a man—crystalized modern, practical, and individualistic ways of thinking about love and relationships at the turn of the century. Casual dating (a shorthand translation for *Verhältnis*) was not really new in 1900 and did not necessarily start in Berlin. Indeed, loosely defined, physically intimate, on-again, off-again relationships with little prospect or likelihood of marriage have undoubtedly always existed in some form or another. But as debates about relationships, dating, and marriage crescendoed at the turn of the century, the notion of the *Verhältnis* became especially controversial. In part, this was because—as so many critics claimed—nearly every man had a *Verhältnis*. By some accounts, most women had them, too.[114] Dorothee Goebeler even quipped that "nowadays, even schoolgirls have a *Verhältnis*."[115] Frieda Kliem had one, though it is perhaps more accurate to think of Frieda as the *Verhältnis* to Otto Mewes, since he seemed to dominate the relationship and came and went as he pleased. Either way, it is clear that a person's feelings about the propriety of a casual dating relationship with no immediate intentions for marriage broke down along the old/new, traditional/modern divide.

A young, working-class woman who did not believe that an upstanding girl could tolerate such a relationship wrote that her friends derided her as "unmodern," just as a bachelor recalled how, when he refused to marry a girl of (in his eyes) questionable morals, she called him old-fashioned. "Everyone can have one *Verhältnis*—as long as it's just one—without anyone thinking anything of it," she said. "Am I just outdated?" the man asked his fellow Berliners.[116] Conversely, those who embraced casual dating nearly always described themselves as modern or referred to the reality of the world "nowadays."[117] A 1907 book called *Die Frau von Heute* (*The Woman of Today*), for example, suggested that the *Verhältnis* was simply the modern, refined, freer form of the coquetry society had known for so long.[118] Dorothee Goebeler put it succinctly when she referred to the growing chasm between "mothers of yesterday and daughters of today"—mothers who would not dream of dating casually and daughters who did.[119]

Casual dating for young men and women of both the working and middle classes often started as a result of fortuitous encounters on the street, interactions with neighbors in apartment buildings, affection for work colleagues, and sports. But the most common path to casual dating was, without a doubt, the dance floor. Saturday nights and Sunday afternoons spent dancing the polka at a dance hall were without question the weekly highlight for working- and middle-class Berliners alike. "This dance frenzy is at its craziest on Saturday night," writer Edmund Edel reflected, when "the dance halls are so crowded that one can hardly breathe."[120] There was also the popular saying, "Can't wait for Sunday; no dancing, no fun."[121]

The energetic atmosphere of the dance hall can be experienced by following "Sylvester," a reporter for the *Berliner Morgenpost*, into a dance hall late one Saturday night in 1899:

Down the hall to the coat check. From somewhere the muffled sound of a waltz. The coat check attendant stumbles up to us and hangs our overcoats with the rest of them. Judging by the abundance of coats, it must be very full inside. Someone kindly pulls back the portière hanging over the door. A sea of light hits us, a hot, stimulating air. White and gold everywhere; on the walls and ceilings are paintings; the motif of eternal femininity appears again and again in stark nude hues. A gypsy band strums a Strauss waltz with titillating verve. On the parquet there is dancing. . . . Watching them, one almost understands how certain puritanical sects in America could consider the waltz immoral. It is this pressing together of bodies, the swaying of elastic bodies, the sly tricks.[122]

Whether it was the intimacy of the waltz, the tantalizing melodies of the band, or Berliners' desire to let loose after a long week of work, Saturday nights and Sunday afternoons at dance halls found couples pairing off by the thousands throughout the city. For those who were up for it, this kind of "dance floor love," as it was called, often led to real intimacy and connection.[123] Indeed, "typical" was how a news story about a 1908 murder trial referred to the fact that the murderer had met her lovers at dance halls.[124] Sometimes the connection was merely sexual, as was the case when an undercover policeman caught two individuals at Luna Park dance hall doing an "American dance" that, in characteristically chaste police language, involved "coital movements."[125] Historian Carola Lipp has also shown that dance floor couples often slept together afterward and frequently did so outside in the bushes after the dance was over.[126] Older Berliners even complained about the way dance floor couples brought their intimacy onto the train on the way home from the dance.[127]

In some cases, intimacy found on the dance floor even led to marriage, which—the changing nature of balls notwithstanding—was no doubt still the ideal outcome for many Berliners.[128] In some ways, dancing was the perfect way to find a marriage partner, especially if one bought the theory presented in the *Berliner Morgenpost* that dancing was essentially a sort of human mating call.[129] Indeed, men who were looking to get married were often told simply to go dancing, where they would surely find someone. This, after all, had been Helene Kuërs's first suggestion to her boss when he told her he wished to get married.[130] Many women were still eager to find a spouse on the dance floor, and swindlers soon became wise to this fact.[131] There were times, too, when the incongruence of a dance floor couple's intentions led to awkwardness, as was the case for a distraught twenty-six-year-old Berlin man who kissed his dance partner and then found himself being introduced to her parents as her fiancé.[132]

But the most common outcome of dance floor love was somewhere between sex in the bushes and a promise of marriage; it was, in a word, the *Verhältnis*, the unchaperoned, unadvertised, normally undefined dating relationship that, for the most part, Berliners saw as the practical and harmless means to an intimate and less lonely end. These relationships were often fairly fleeting, perhaps most absurdly so when a young worker started a *Verhältnis* with a girl he met on the dance floor and then promptly fell in love with the girl's sister (and then her mother);[133] or when a drunken police officer overzealously broke up the intimate embrace of a couple who had left the dance hall and were sitting quietly in the Tiergarten.[134] Newspapers seemed to enjoy publishing these sorts of tragicomic endings to "dance floor love," and many relationships started on the dance floor no doubt fizzled out or were so heavily discouraged by disapproving parents or friends that they were not worth continuing.[135]

Fleeting or not, these relationships nevertheless provided warmth and connection, and Berliners seemed to have valued them enough that they often did risk nurturing them. Here the anonymity of the big city was naturally of great advantage, since such a casual but intimate relationship was usually kept under wraps, but there were additional tricks to keeping a *Verhältnis* going. Love letters left at the "messages" counter of the post office were one option— one that was apparently so common that a *Berliner Morgenpost* article in 1906 suggested that the postal service paint a large cupid on the wall of its building since it served so many Berliners as a sort of love-courier service. The article, whose author perched himself among the lovesick crowds, also gives a taste for the excitement of dating:

> It is interesting to examine their facial expressions, for they so clearly reveal the emotions of their love lives as they read the written correspondence of their beloveds. Does she (or he) smile while writing the lines with such joy—"Are you happy, Schnucki? I am too"—; does she bite her lip nervously—"I am starting to wonder about the meaning of your silence"—; does she longingly close her eyes halfway—"Oh, if only I were already at your place."[136]

Often these notes set up a rendezvous at one of many Berlin hotels that were well known for the fact that their guests almost never had any luggage and checked out at midnight. "It's funny how many *Herr Meyers* there are," a piece in the *Berliner Morgenpost* quipped of the pseudonyms Berliners used to register for hotel rendezvouses with their dates.[137] Other times the rendezvous spot of choice was something easily recognizable like the public clock on Potsdamer Platz or Friedrichstrasse.[138] Most common, though, was one of the many parks—Humboldthain or the Tiergarten, for instance—which offered seclusion from prying eyes.[139] Julius Knopf, in a poetic ode to the Tiergarten published in 1905, could not keep his eyes off the many lovers in Berlin's beautiful central park:

> *On a bench, hidden from the eagle eye of the policeman*
> *Sits a couple, hand in hand . . .*
> *And in front of me, walking, deep in an embrace*
> *She sways with him in ecstasy.*[140]

The Tiergarten also served as the favorite meeting spot of gay Berliners.[141] Hans Ostwald, the writer, journalist, and amateur sociologist, wrote about the men who sat, alone or in groups, near the Tiergarten's Goethe monument and waited for their boyfriends.[142] There were in fact so many that Berlin's chief of police felt compelled to write a memo in 1911 to a city magistrate suggesting that lights be installed in various points of the park. This, he claimed, would deter the large number of gay men who were not breaking any laws but were using the Tiergarten to find dates.[143]

Of course, for gay Berliners, casual dating was the only possibility for connection. Germany's infamous §175 criminalizing gay sex and effectively driving gays underground made finding love even harder than for straight Berliners.[144] Indeed, one of Berlin's most famous (but anonymous) gay men described in his diary how, when he made his first gay friend, he "realized how terribly isolated I was in this city of millions."[145] Another gay writer lamented the fact that his era's "closet morality" prevented Berliners from finding each other.[146] Gay Berliners had, in many ways, to rely upon fortuitous encounters but risked penal threat by approaching someone on the street.[147] One gay Berliner described the beginnings of a relationship with a medical student who had moved to Berlin from the provinces because he wanted to take in the maelstrom of the city. But the medical student turned out to be straight, and the author detailed his pain at lending him money for a prostitute:

> On our way home, he asked me for [three marks]. I gave them to him but became suddenly silent even though I had just so happily conversed with him; and a feeling of indescribable melancholy shot through my heart. We reached the street corner where we normally parted ways. He stepped off the sidewalk and I turned around. I looked back once

at him with deep sadness and wild inner turmoil, but still feelings for
him, whom I loved dearly despite everything. . . . A heterosexual can
only understand the feelings I had in doing so if he imagines that he is
deeply and madly in love with a woman whom he must lay in the arms
of a roué while he, having paid the man a sum of money and essentially
sold her off, must stand by with a feeling of failure.[148]

A poet described a similar feeling when his lover turned his attention to
women: "It's all over now. . . . A woman sits atop the throne of his heart."[149]
While some people thought that gay Berliners had some mysterious talent for
finding other gays on the street, others pointed out that gays had to rely on
the same uncertainty, the same tentative, hopeful glance as straight Berliners
when attempting to make a street acquaintance.[150] Even the dark and typically anonymous space of the bordello was unsafe, for if a man fell in love not
with one of the girls but with a fellow guest, as the writer Josef Kitir imagined
in 1899, that encounter could be discovered and exposed.[151]

Casual same-sex dating was also generally more fluid than heterosexual
dating, and this made it less likely that any found intimacy would last.
Literature, especially, gave particularly frequent voice to the short, fleeting
nature of gay encounters, as, for example, in Adolf Brand's short poem about a
brief encounter at the Friedrichstrasse train station.[152] In another short story,
two men meet on the street amid the hustle and bustle of the city and enjoy
a period of intimacy and connection before they have to part. The author
does not specify why, though perhaps the unspoken, unspecified force pulling
them apart is more powerful than a mundane need to return home. "It is said
there are people who only love once," the narrator begins, "only once in a
long life. Oh to love just once—and then—? Then, if this love did not last a
lifetime—if it was but an ecstasy of hours and days, then—what then—?"[153]

If casual same-sex dating was often fleeting, it was heterosexual marriage
that most often brought it to an end (or prevented it from ever starting).[154]
A wide variety of sources refer to the fact that many gay and lesbian Berliners
did end up getting married, whether because of family and social pressure or
simply the need to fit in and conform to middle-class sexual norms that were,
not surprisingly, staunchly heterosexual. A letter published in the literary
journal *Der Eigene* portrays the distraught confession of a young gay Berliner
to his mother that, despite her wishes that he marry a respectable girl, he loves
Oskar.[155] In another short story, a man commits suicide because of the pressure from his mother to marry a woman. "My mother is pushing me to marriage," he writes in his suicide note. "I cannot admit to her that, while I can

admire and honor the best of women, find them beautiful, even, I cannot love them. . . . I would have to hate myself."[156] In 1903, a sexual science journal published a letter from a "Frau M. F." describing how she had conformed to her parents' expectations by marrying at seventeen and having children but, at the same time, fell in love with a woman and started an extramarital relationship with her. But this woman then suddenly got married as well, and the author felt a giant blow to her happiness.[157] Reinhold Gerling, in one of his many guides for young men about sexuality and marriage, warned that lesbians normally marry straight men. He may well have been referring, among other cases, to the 1905 news story about a couple whose marriage was "ruined" by the wife's lesbian *Verhältnis*.[158] And Magnus Hirschfeld, founder of Berlin's first sexual science institute and himself a closeted gay man, published a selection from his patient notes in a 1901 article asking whether gays were suited to married life. Among other case studies, Hirschfeld presented the account of a young gay man who had resisted heterosexual marriage for a long time before ultimately giving in.

> I wanted to put an end to this sorry situation. Everyone my age was already married; my family and a few friends suggested I do the same. But I could not tell anyone the reason I did not want to get married. This is one of the sad parts of our fate, namely this secret, which is so deeply ingrained in us and must not be told to anyone, not even our closest relatives. I saw others happy and satisfied and wanted to be happy, too. While I had no desire for a marital union [with a woman], I did hope to find inner peace and satisfaction in it.[159]

Hirschfeld also noted that it was "more common than one might think" for gays and lesbians to simply marry each other as a way of fulfilling social expectations and having a sympathetic partner in the difficult world of gay relationships.[160]

There were examples of casual same-sex dating leading to lasting intimacy, though. One of Hirschfeld's most interesting cases is the autobiography sent to him by a man who dressed as a woman and fell in love with a woman dressed as a man. This arrangement, as he describes it, allowed them to experience long-term connection and intimacy.[161] In another case, a woman met another's eyes on the street and found them so enthralling that she followed her for a spell. It happened that they kept running into each other, and the one woman finally approached the other and said simply that she loved her and that she hoped she would not hate her for it. The two appear to have become a couple afterward.[162] The most illustrative example comes from the autobiography of E. Krause, published in Hirschfeld's sexual science journal in 1901. It is the account of a seemingly well-off, university-educated lesbian who resists the pressure to marry and ultimately meets her lifelong partner at a party on one of Berlin's suburban lakes. Her lighthearted retelling of the many suitors she has while growing up—and her steadfast rejection of them—suggests that she had not come particularly close to marrying simply for the sake of middle-class respectability; any wavering was quashed for good when, as she writes, she read Richard von Krafft-Ebing's famous 1886 study (and detailed list) of nonnormative sexualities, *Psychopathia Sexualis*. "It was now clear to me that I could never marry a man," she wrote.[163]

The most interesting thing about Krause's account of her relationship is the fact that she intentionally refers to her girlfriend as her *Verhältnis*. In fact, she characterizes the relationship as both a *Verhältnis* and a "marriage," noting that, once they expressed their love for one another, they "lived together as a married couple." She even understands the relationship in terms of a heterosexual marriage: "My dear, homey little wife is a true German housewife and has complete control in our cozy home, and I work and make a living for us both as the go-getting, fun-loving husband."[164] Krause's choice of words here is remarkable because it suggests a blurring between casual dating and marriage and a tweaking or modernization of the meaning of marriage. At the same time, it reveals the extent to which marriage itself was so utterly crucial to the stability of middle-class life that even Krause casts her same-sex union as a marriage. While legalized marriage was impossible for gay couples, many indeed used casual dating as both a path to intimacy and connection and, sometimes, a replacement for a state-sanctioned union.

It is impossible to gauge the extent to which gay Berliners used the *Verhältnis* simply as a brief, sexual connection or as something like Krause's longer-lasting union, but the *Verhältnis*, or casual dating, was clearly not just about sex. It certainly had little in common with prostitution, though there were gay prostitutes and this was how authorities usually characterized it. Gay dating, as the medical student Edwin Bab told a Berlin crowd in a 1903 lecture, was, indeed, often conflated with prostitution, probably because of the "occasional happenings" in bars and other places of ill repute. "But as little as one would claim to see love . . . in the bar with the red lantern" (that is, in a brothel), he continued, "so little can one condemn gay love because of prostitutes and pimps."[165]

While heterosexual dating was nowhere near as transgressive as gay dating, Bab's rhetoric can be extended to casual dating for straight and gay Berliners alike. There were no doubt some dating relationships that had little to them other than sex and some that were one-sided in terms of a sense of connection and intimacy; but many more were the wellspring of marriages, lifelong partnerships, or, at the very least, belonging and closeness that lasted long enough to counteract the alienating and isolating forces of urban life.

There is, indeed, evidence that some Berliners—especially working-class and petit bourgeois women—saw in the *Verhältnis* an opportunity to marry up, to use emotional and physical intimacy to propel themselves into a middle-class existence. Some were successful: Mary Jo Maynes and Alfred Kelley both present autobiographies of several working-class women who parlayed *Verhältnis*-like relationships into marriage and upward social mobility.[166] Andreas Schulz, too, cites a pairing between a middle-class girl and her petit bourgeois boyfriend that is all but quashed by her parents before she demonstrates his sterling and business-savvy qualities and, in the end, prevails (not unlike Max and Meta in *The Rescue Ball*).[167] On the other hand, *Verhältnis* relationships started as a desire for "traditional marriage" usually ended in bitter disappointment.[168] This was the case for the coworker of the anonymous author of the 1908 autobiography *Im Kampf ums Dasein* (*In the Struggle for Existence*) who is "in the family way" thanks to "one of the higher functionaries of the factory. [But] he didn't intend to marry her, and she was very unhappy about this." Worse yet,

> Since the man in question had to stop bothering her, he was looking for another victim for his lust; his eyes fell on me, but he didn't have much luck because I bluntly brushed him off. The result of this was that after two weeks I was back out on the street again, which was unpleasant for me mostly because the work had been easy and the pay relatively good.[169]

Moreover, casual dating relationships (and all or most intimate relationships, for that matter) were usually intertwined with the complicating dynamics of pregnancy. After all, the prospect of a child on the way added an entirely different element and calculation to casual dating and potentially made any fleeting or frivolous relationship a good degree more serious—certainly for women. The abandonment and isolation of the pregnant woman was probably the most common outcome, though violence, shaming, extortion, marriage, and occasionally even love were all surely possible fates of casual dating relationships where sex led to pregnancy. Abortion was also a common element of these stories, increasingly so during the Wilhelmine era as a result of medical and pharmacological advances, expansions in insurance coverage and fertility education, an explosion in the marketing and sale of abortifacients and other birth control products, the professionalization of abortion practices and providers, and the gradual and generational shift in women's approaches to abortion, birth control, and family planning.[170]

In fact, the shift in approaches to birth control dovetails with the changing ways in which Berliners thought about love, dating, and intimate relationships. What was primarily at stake vis-à-vis birth control, abortion, and family planning was, in essence, upward mobility of the sort petit bourgeois women like Frieda Kliem strove for time and again. Advertisers of contraceptives and patent medicines certainly recognized this, luring customers with a chance to "move up in life."[171] Social Democratic groups and libraries, not to mention social reformers like Helene Stöcker and even sexologists like Magnus Hirschfeld and Paul Näcke, sought to spread information about the proper use of contraceptives in the hopes of "raising up" working-class women.[172] And proletariat-oriented health insurers (the so-called Health Insurance Program, started in the 1890s) sought to reduce the costs of contraceptives and prophylactics like the popular, newly invented diaphragm, intrauterine devices (IUDs), and condoms—again, in the service of helping working-class women in their quests for upward mobility.[173] For that matter, domestic servants often learned about contraception from their middle- and upper-class employers, whose status they longed to attain for themselves.[174]

All of this added up to a veritable explosion in birth control (from about 1880 to 1900) and abortion (from about 1900 to 1920) in Berlin and elsewhere. Statistical studies and crime demographics show that it was especially those women on the cusp of middle-classness, like Frieda Kliem, who embraced these forms of intentional family planning. Indeed, sales clerks, office workers, and secretaries made up the bulk of those who sought abortions (usually illegally, though there were exceptions and semilegal methods). Although testimonial justifications or explanations are exceedingly rare in the historical record, young single women for whom unexpected children would have rendered unattainable the next rung of that ladder upward to respectability and stability were the most common seekers of abortions.[175]

This, then, was part of a more individualistic approach to love, intimacy, and relationships that privileged practicality and self over tradition—in the interest not just of enjoyment and pleasure but also of connection and stability.[176] Though the story of birth control, abortion, and family planning has a great many other dimensions to it than the *Verhältnis* and the pursuit of love and intimacy in the modern metropolis, the shared ground of these two themes of turn-of-the-century urban life is nevertheless instructive and illustrative of a broader generational shift.[177]

The *Verhältnis* was thus a mix of connection and pain, success and failure, repression and individualism; it was, in most cases, ultimately merely a means to a practical, individualistic, and less lonely end. As a letter to the *Berliner Lokal-Anzeiger* noted, "Every even halfway independent girl goes for walks with an upstanding man, not out of interest in him, but rather for her own enjoyment. . . . It has nothing to do with love."[178] Much as Frieda escaped her loneliness and connected with others through bicycling, and as countless others considered apartment and workplace relationships, so, too, was the increasing acceptance of casual dating a gradual reworking of gender norms to accommodate the changing times and environment. This process might be called the urbanization of sexuality, though there was much more at stake than sex and intimacy.[179]

Casual dating—dating that was not merely courtship for marriage but rather itself a means of connection—was emblematic of the new Berlin, where endeavoring young men and women found themselves actively "browsing," "searching for the happiness that lies on the street."[180] And yet this new Berlin, which would become so emblematic of the 1920s, was only still emerging at the turn of the century. The columnist Dorothee Goebeler closed her discussion of modern daughters and old-fashioned mothers by concluding that "we live in a period of transition. New ideas, new ideals rise up everywhere and battle with the old ones."[181] In this transition period, Max and his Meta, Frieda and her Otto, and many other men and women were, increasingly, turning to casual dating because it offered a means to intimacy, closeness, and connection.

But casual dating was risky. Its prevalence notwithstanding, those men and women who dated with no marriage in sight operated outside the bounds of hegemonic masculinity and (especially) femininity, where marriage remained the be-all and end-all of middle-class life. For men, the risks were not great. Men were indeed chided for "sowing their oats," but this was done more with a wink and a nod than any intention of changing their behavior. And while young men were occasionally warned about the financial and health costs of casual dating, it left no indelible social mark on them.[182] When, in 1905, for example, a young woman asked the advice column of the *Berliner Lokal-Anzeiger* whether she should accept the marriage offer of a man who had already had several girlfriends before meeting her, the advice was simply that she could either accept him or get used to living alone. "You cannot hold a man responsible for what he did before meeting you," the columnist reasoned. "You won't find angels on earth, not even among the most noble men."[183]

The stakes were much higher for women, who risked being labeled disreputable when they dated casually. It did not matter whether a woman was the one dating casually or the casual date herself; critics—from mothers and grandmothers to social observers and pastors—were quick to connect casual dating with prostitution. These voices against women and the *Verhältnis* formed a chorus in newspapers and newsletters, and some women—in particular, a Frau Manko, who admitted to having had ten to fifteen *Verhältnisse*—were openly upbraided by the news editors as "Bluebeards" and nymphomaniacs.[184]

It is thus not hard to see why Frieda Kliem shrouded her relationship with Otto Mewes in secrecy and tried, unsuccessfully, to pass him off as her uncle. Frieda longed to be seen as a respectable, middle-class woman, and she walked a thin line between maintaining a certain propriety and becoming, in the parlance of the day, one of the "fallen." In truth, Frieda only wanted the connection, intimacy, and stability of a mate, and she was as entrepreneurial and practical about her love life as she was about her business ventures. Having opened her own business and seen it fail, she moved almost seamlessly to a new, different career. Her movements—on her bicycle, with Otto Buning and Emil Freier, and with Mewes—were similarly enterprising: the path to each offered a reward but was marked with substantial risk, and she acted shrewdly. In both her business and intimate pursuits, Frieda was in this way thus emblematic of the emerging new Berlin.

3

Reimagining Marriage

IN 1899, DR. HERMANN Müller-Sagan, a member of parliament and father of six, announced to the Reichstag that there were over fifty-four thousand "old maids" living in Berlin. Whether this was the result of a new study or his own tabulation based on Berlin's statistical almanacs is unclear, but Müller-Sagan was careful to point out to his fellow representatives that this figure should give one pause. After all, these were not merely aged, gray-haired ladies "with chewing tobacco tins and the obligatory dog on their laps," but rather all women over the age of thirty-five who had never "landed safely in the harbor of marriage."[1] Müller-Sagan, it seems, was concerned about the number of unmarried women in Berlin, women who could not or would not fulfill what was widely understood as their most essential and natural function.[2] And while there is no further record of any specific parliamentary action on this announcement by Müller-Sagan, it is perhaps fitting that his own eleven-year-old daughter, Ilse, seems to have herself ultimately joined the fifty-four thousand who never married.[3]

Like Ilse, Frieda Kliem was under thirty-five when Müller-Sagen announced the number of "old maids" in Berlin in 1899, and perhaps like Ilse she might have thought she would never come face to face with spinsterhood. And yet, like the many women who could not escape the problems of the big city or for whom the modern methods of dating were distasteful, too risky, or otherwise insufficient, Frieda found herself still unmarried as she entered her thirties. To be sure, there were certainly women who liked it better that way, not to mention women for whom marriage was a legal impossibility. For Frieda, though, her lack of a husband eventually became a burden, an instability, and an embarrassment. So she decided to wear a wedding ring (actually, two for good measure) so that others might simply assume she was either married or a widow.[4] This was clever and enterprising, for in addition to connoting respectability and middle-class cachet, Frieda's fake wedding rings also served a strategic purpose. As her friend Antonie Köhler pointed out, "Men are more interested in widows than old maids."[5] Therefore she went by Frau Kliem, as opposed to Fräulein Kliem.[6] Her landlady reported that Frieda had even signed her apartment lease as a widow and only admitted the truth much later.[7]

Frieda's behavior is a little surprising given the success she found through bicycling and her embrace of a modern sensibility about love and dating. She had enjoyed three relationships that could have led to marriage. For that matter, she had an actual offer of marriage from Otto Buning, the widower father of four who worked at a branch of the Dresdner Bank. Otto was in many ways Frieda's ideal match, not least because he loved Frieda, he loved bicycling, and he made good money as a banker. Indeed, Frieda had told her friends that she would only marry a civil servant, and here was one of a roughly equivalent ilk proposing marriage. The issue seems to have been the four children. Frieda, who was remarkably independent, was not eager to become a mother to four young children, as she told her friends and neighbors.[8] But Otto's offer was nevertheless a compelling one, and Frieda treasured it. While she spent years trying to make up her mind, Otto proved a patient man, and his offer was apparently still good as late as the summer of 1914. In all likelihood, Frieda spent so long contemplating Otto's proposal because she thought she might find something better but did not want to give up his offer in case she did not.[9]

There was also Frieda's intimate relationship with Emil Freier, the stockbroker who arranged her work as a typist and came often to her apartment. On these visits, Emil often stayed for coffee; other times they went to Aschinger's Café, where he treated her to a drink and a bite to eat. Frieda was keen on marrying Emil—a fact she told his siblings and parents—and was careful to take off her fake wedding rings whenever she was around him. "I don't remember ever seeing them," Emil later told the police. In any case, Emil, in his own words, "told her that [marriage] was out of the question. I didn't have any special feelings for her to make her my wife. I [only liked] her as a friend with whom I could converse." Frieda apparently felt compelled to tell her friends that Emil had a lung condition that hindered him from marrying anyone, and he may have told her this so as not to hurt her feelings. But when, in 1907, Emil suddenly got engaged to a woman named Clara Maerker, Frieda was crushed and more or less broke off their intimate friendship. They occasionally took bicycle rides together, but Emil only saw her two or three times over the last few years of her life.[10] Her interactions with Emil's siblings were also tense after Emil's engagement (which he later broke off), and Emil's sister, Clara, remembered that the last time she saw Frieda, in June 1914, she had seemed uncomfortable and mostly looked at the floor.[11]

Frieda's third potential marriage was to Otto Mewes, the eccentric older gentleman she was dating casually. Frieda and Mewes were quite close, and Antonie Köhler, their mutual friend, remembered that Mewes had actually thought about marrying Frieda at some point. This would have been a good match, for the two loved bicycling and traveling, and Mewes, as punctilious as he was about his finances, seemed to have plenty of money. But despite Frieda's concern about money, her thrift, and her entrepreneurial nature, it was, ironically, Mewes who gave up his idea of marrying Frieda because he did not think she would make much of a housewife. "She had little interest in constant work," Antonie Köhler told police when explaining why Mewes had decided against marrying her. "She started all sorts of things but never made anything lasting from it."[12]

It is not clear whether Frieda would actually have wanted to marry Mewes, but his rather traditional stance on the desired attributes of a suitable wife clearly did not prevent him from engaging in a modern dating relationship with Frieda. This was probably as close as Frieda ever came to a real marriage of the kind she had so often spoken of to friends and family. Indeed, her relationship with Mewes was, in time, no longer a so-called *Verhältnis* but closer to what turn-of-the-century Berliners referred to simply as "free love" (*freie Liebe*) or "wild marriage" (*wilde Ehe*). When he came to visit, Mewes stayed with Frieda in her apartment and even had his own set of things there, including his bicycle and a host of other items. Mewes always paid when they went to cafés and restaurants, and they even opened a joint bank account together. Frieda in fact set up her will such that Mewes would receive everything she owned.[13] Perhaps most telling of all was the portrait of Mewes placed lovingly on Frieda's piano.[14] In the end, though, Mewes moved away permanently, and Frieda found herself approaching her fortieth birthday wearing fake wedding rings and worrying about becoming an old maid.

For all of the relatively intimate acquaintances Frieda found because of her modern approach to love and dating, she had remarkably little success turning any one of these relationships into marriage. Frieda quite obviously wanted to get married, and while she found both fast friends and some degree of connection with potential mates, marriage remained for her an elusive goal. But Frieda was only one of many women facing similarly bleak outlooks.

Novels, short stories, newspaper articles, guidebooks, and diaries all register the problem of marriage in turn-of-the-century Berlin. The problem—a crisis, to many observers—revolved around the same old/new, traditional/ modern conflict as street relationships and casual dating, though, in this case, practical sensibilities about love called into question the very institu- tion of marriage, which had an almost sacrosanct quality in middle-class life. In the face of marriage's perceived incompatibility with the modern world, emerging masculinities and femininities offered alternative visions of inti- macy in the turn-of-the-century metropolis. As they debated and tried on these alternatives, Berliners were engaging with questions of tradition, re- spectability, and individualism on the most personal level. The conflicted na- ture of this engagement, and the ultimately limited proliferation of marriage alternatives, however, reveals just how resilient middle-class respectability and marriage were to the revisionist impulses of "modern" Berliners.

IN THE FALL of 1906, readers of the *Berliner Morgenpost* were engaged in a hot debate. This itself was nothing new, but ever since the start of the new century, Berliners seem to have relished more than ever their weekly opportu- nity to trade blows with each other in the reader letters section. Topics ranged from whether women's hats were too large and obstructed people's views in the theater and omnibus to whether men should be allowed to smoke in the streetcar, and in most cases, battle lines were drawn according to gender. Up for debate in September 1906 was the question of whether unmarried women should be addressed as *Fräulein*, which was the diminutive of *Frau* com- monly used for young women, or if one might extend the more generic *Frau* (simply the counterpart to *Herr*) to women who were quite clearly no longer teenagers but deserved to be respected as adult women regardless of their marital status. Opinions differed among the respondents, one pointing out that no "upstanding woman without a child wants . . . to be called *Frau,*" an- other asserting that one should take a cue from the Russians, who use simply the first and last name, and still a different woman reasoning that while it would take a federal law to change Berliners' habits, *Fräulein* was demeaning because it suggested that women who had not married by the normal age were somehow lesser women. The editors of the *Berliner Morgenpost*, for their part, weighed in by agreeing that *Fräulein* was clumsy but that there was little reason to change to something different.[15]

The discussion about *Frau* or *Fräulein* is emblematic of the many impas- sioned exchanges between Berliners at the turn of the century. What most often got their tempers flaring were the modern, emancipated femininities emerging in the city.[16] The "modern woman" in fact became a mélange of polemic rhetoric and real dilemmas rooted in everyday life, and it seems that everyone had an opinion.[17] Indeed, far from mere parlor banter limited to intellectual elites or prominent leaders of the women's movement, this was a debate across all segments of metropolitan society. It crossed dinner tables, enlivened living rooms, echoed through office corridors, buzzed through streetcars and omnibuses, and filled the pages of the daily newspapers. Hardly a week went by without a provocative column or lively reader letters section about gender norms.[18]

The "modern woman" was, for the purpose of these debates, almost always single, and her singleness was so provocative because it was elective, part of a new lifestyle based not on hearth and home but on a career, leisure, and independence.[19] "Modern life has, as we all know, freed the young woman from all boundaries and chains," Dorothee Goebeler summarized in 1914, and "relationships between girls and men are different than they always were."[20] What had changed, she believed, was that "the girl of today no longer waits for 'the man,' at least not in the way that our mothers and grandmothers did." Nowadays, Goebeler continued, a woman has her career. "If a 'prince' comes to deliver her [from having to work], all the better; if he doesn't come—one comes to accept that, as well."[21] Goebeler, whose columns appeared almost weekly on the front page of the *Berliner Lokal-Anzeiger*, defended this shift, pointing out that work "brings [modern women] into contact with the most distant circles" of people and "protects against the embittered calcification of the spinsterhood of earlier days." After all, this modern "comradeship," as Goebeler described it, between middle-class working women and their male colleagues, resulted in a new "tone" that "no longer weighed each word on a scale and asked of each glance: what did he mean by that?"[22]

Passive, pining women were said to be a dying breed and were being replaced by modern women who had career prospects and who embraced casual dating.[23] Modern women were indeed real, but casual dating only actually replaced marriage completely for a select few women. The perceived prominence of independent women nevertheless compelled observers to muse about whether women really could be friends with men without having to think of marriage; or, more generally, if there might in fact be more to a woman's life than marriage.[24] "The thought of a husband and marriage is no longer the central focus of all of life's emotions," Heinz Tovote wrote in 1909. "There is so much more, so much that is equally interesting." Indeed, "nowadays" a woman can talk openly about her love life and her happiness "without thinking of herself as wanton" or unfeminine. "Women," he concluded, "are moving into everything, and they stand expectantly before all of life's closed doors, seeking entry."[25] Young women were now supposed to have more time to luxuriate in their independence and even delay marriage indefinitely. And whereas one used to laugh at "older girls"—also referred to, somewhat euphemistically, as "aunts"—when they expressed a desire to do anything remotely feminine or flirtatious such as dancing or ice-skating, "the mature woman . . . nowadays dances, does gymnastics, swims, rides a bicycle, and no one bats an eye."[26]

It was a great time to be a modern woman, according to this line of discourse—even better to be in love or to look for love. Berlin observers noted that "modern women" were increasingly active in pursuing men and starting, managing, and even ending relationships.[27] Newspapers reported on the new (limited) marriage and divorce rights created with the passage of a new civil code in 1900. And they published reports about women speaking up and asserting their rights if they were not happy.[28] Indeed, newspaper advice columns were filled with women asking for practical advice on how to divorce their husbands.[29] To hear newspapers tell it, a "modern" girl could go to bars on her own;[30] she could smoke cigarettes;[31] and she could cultivate her intellect, whether through attendance at lectures and presentations in the evenings or simply reading, which was recast as intellectual stimulation, not idleness or daydreaming. Being smart was, as Goebeler put it, becoming socially desirable, something fashionable.[32]

The result was that singleness (also referred to as "female bachelorhood") was now said to last two or three times as long as it had in grandmother's time, and statisticians struggled to calculate the number of old maids, given that Berliners were marrying later and often more than once.[33] "At what age does an unmarried woman actually give up her hopes for marriage?" asked one frustrated statistician.[34]

Taken together, these traits rounded out the emerging image of the modern woman who took seriously her own life and happiness and for whom all "attractions of life" were pursuable. As Hans Ostwald wrote, "All of these various opportunities for enjoyment call to her: 'Come—enjoy your youth! One only lives for a short time!' "[35]

The thousands of pages of print this discussion of new women constituted sparked approval and disapproval among Berliners of all stripes. Rhetoric and love are different, however, and all women, "modern" or not, had to chart a course between what they said they wanted and their actual relationships and lifestyles. More specifically, urban women found themselves confronting what was increasingly referred to as "the problem of marriage" and reconciling the

FIGURE 3.1 One of the first cigarette ads featuring a woman, 1914
Source: Berliner Morgenpost, July 25, 1914, Nr. 201.

desire for a respectable union with someone they loved, on one hand, with maintaining the independence (or the allure thereof) they were just beginning to enjoy, on the other. Indeed, the improvements of the new civil code notwithstanding, most women recognized that while marriage remained in many ways the supreme marker of middle-class respectability, it also often meant an end to the independence they were enjoying as they went to bars, smoked Manoli cigarettes, and attended lectures.[36] They thus had to decide for themselves whether breaking with tradition, not to mention family expectations, was worth the risk and potential freedom.

Fashioning one's life as single and independent became increasingly think-able when compelling examples appeared in the pages of the ubiquitous daily newspapers. One fiction writer even admitted that he and his colleagues had been forced to adjust one of their oft-used "types" or set characters—the young woman from Berlin's famously swanky west side whose unwavering path to an early marriage to a respectable suitor was never in doubt—to reflect the inde-pendent yearnings of modern readers.[37] Popular literature was indeed rife with images of happily independent modern women, and this no doubt tempted some women to marry later. Well-known, famously independent women like Henrik Ibsen's Nora and Karin Michaelis's Elsie Lindner served as hallowed inspiration for putting off marriage for a while or even for good, but writers of far lesser fame were, for their parts, weaving similarly maverick, independent women into their Berlin-based stories, and these perhaps struck more of a chord with regular readers. In a skit by A. von Wartenberg, for example, the experience of the recently married Helene is juxtaposed against that of her friend, Bertha, who, having delayed marriage, still has her independence and time for amusements. "No, she would never marry, never, ever," Bertha thinks to herself after witnessing the marital discord and resulting bitter dis-appointment of Helene firsthand.[38] In Julie Jolowicz's 1907 short story "Zwei Briefe" ("Two Letters"), a modern woman tells her suitor, Paul, whom she has made wait for two years while she traveled the world and tested his love and commitment, that she has become a different woman and that she loves her newfound freedom and will not be returning.[39] Gertrud Steinbach's short story "Liebe" ("Love") similarly portrays a young couple sitting together on the shore of one of Berlin's lakes. The female protagonist cannot shake her longing for independence and, breaking her lover's embrace, runs toward the setting sun and the expansive, freely flowing water.[40]

To be sure, delaying marriage out of a reluctance to give up independence and freedom in real life clearly required some measure of money and was thus mostly limited to middle- and upper-class women.[41] And while there were quite a few members of the women's movement who articulated the point that marriage was a patriarchal institution designed to subjugate women, the valence of this discourse was relatively small for women like Frieda Kliem.[42] Instead, the motivations of working-class and petit bourgeois women to post-pone marriage were, like those of their male counterparts, often more prac-tical than anything else and based on the need to continue to earn enough money before even thinking about marrying.[43] In this way, the "struggle for existence" was as much of a cause for women marrying later as were the amusements and freedoms of independent life. Columnist upon columnist noted rising costs in the modern city, especially for food, and observed that "the question of money" had become the pivot point in the lives of all but the very wealthy.[44] Since only a minority of women gave up the idea of marriage altogether and most were still focused on the idea of eventually marrying, the money issue had the effect of pushing back marriage and forcing women to consider establishing themselves financially before taking vows. After all, as simple as marrying for money and stability may have sounded, doing so was actually quite difficult.

On some level, the security of at least a small amount of savings left modern women in a better position to look for a real amorous match and not simply accept "the first best," as the well-worn phrase went.[45] On a different level, the "struggle for existence" left Berliners, especially women, more skeptical about the true aims of potential husbands—so much so that newspaper columnist Rudolf Lothar considered a straightforward, traditional love story no more than a "fairy tale."[46] Indeed, Lothar and others noted elsewhere that the time of a woman "los[ing] her head is long past," "turned on its head by our modern time," and that it would be impossible to go back to the "romance of old."[47] Whether it was the increasingly accessible jobs and career opportunities open to women or a dearth of opportunities for marriage and the sheer necessity of looking out for oneself and earning what money one could (for "just in case"), singleness held a multifaceted appeal for a great many Berlin women.

It seems, then, that images of single women in books, skits, and newspapers likely hewed quite closely to many women's real experiences. Still, not all turn-of-the-century women were so convinced that the "romance of old"—and the idea of marriage at an early age—was all that bad or that changes were necessary. "Modern" women were often scorned for their newfangled ideas about love and marriage, and even established newspaper columnists took potshots at such women by suggesting that emancipated women gave off a "masculine allure" with their "short hair," reform dresses, and beliefs about free love and political equality.[48] Others confirmed that most men interpreted modern women and their beliefs about independence, work, and marriage as meanness or, at best, indifference to their male suitors.[49] For that matter, the very adjective "emancipated" was meant to deride and was largely applied as an epithet.[50]

Whether because of the power of hegemonic femininity or because, as Dorothee Goebeler observed, many women simply were not happy trading family, hearth, and home for hard, long hours as office workers and secretaries, many women actually joined the chorus of male voices against "the emancipated" and embraced early marriage as they had long done.[51] Coverage

and thematization of such "traditional" women often took on vaguely deter-
ministic and clearly conservative terms, for example, suggesting that women
would rather have a husband than work. The intent here was clearly to
compel women to embrace traditional femininity.[52] But a variety of sources
nevertheless indicate that quite a few women actively eschewed the women's
movement or found the femininity it trumpeted to be tiresome and unful-
filling.[53] Alfred Holzbock, in a 1906 newspaper piece, attested that not all
women were "hypermodern."[54] A. von Wartenberg perhaps put it best when
he commented that the modern woman was, at the turn of the century, still
more "inkling than reality."[55] These are conservative, male takes, no doubt;
and certainly one tactic of the male, antiemancipation establishment was to
denigrate the women's movement by calling it disjointed, aimless, and nas-
cent. But the many voices speaking to the appeal of marriage and, occasionally,
their indifference to the women's movement suggest that these observations
perhaps had some merit.

Marriage statistics largely bear this out. In 1904, for example, a full
42.7 percent of women married between the ages of twenty and twenty-five.
Another 29.9 percent of women married between twenty-five and thirty.
As 7.4 percent married very early (before twenty), almost 80 percent—four
out of five Berlin women—had married by the age of thirty.[56] In fact, when
compared with the statistics from a generation earlier, the marriage age for
women actually seemed to be dropping.[57]

The turn-of-the-century calculus about marrying early, delaying marriage,
or remaining single is thus best interpreted as complex and multivariable.
Frieda Kliem embodied the ambiguities and complexities of emancipation: she was in many ways a model of emancipation—owning, as she did,
her own business, refusing to marry the "first best," and embracing bicycling,
among other things—but she also quite clearly wanted to get married and
leave at least some of this independence behind. A popular women's magazine held an essay contest in 1905 that highlighted these tensions, asking
readers to submit their best responses to the question: "How do I marry
off my daughter?" The responses chosen for prizes were neither wholesale
rejections of marriage nor paeans to the propriety of early marriage. Rather,
all attempted a sort of balance between work, dating, and marriage, the conservative approach of the question notwithstanding. They argued that "the
choice of a career should not be an obstacle to marriage" and admitted that
women with salaries and work skills held an advantage over other girls when
it came to being chosen by a man for marriage.[58] The *Berliner Lokal-Anzeiger*
lauded the prize committee's selections, praising their decision to give prizes

to the entrants who wrote about raising their daughters for usefulness and happiness, even if this precluded marriage.[59]

A serial novel by Arthur Zapp that ran in the *Berliner Lokal-Anzeiger* from December 1903 to January 1904 offers a similar portrait of the ways "modern girls" sometimes struggled to match their heads and hearts in the midst of fast-paced Berlin life. "Moderne Mädchen" ("Modern Girls") features three young women in their early twenties—Klara, Eva, and Fritze— who share a Berlin apartment. Each has her own opinion about what being a "modern girl" should mean. Fritze, the youngest, is perhaps the most easily classifiable, as she is pursuing a university education and spends her days and evenings studying for her entrance examination on a scholarship from the Berlin women's club. She is the most pessimistic about marriage, men, and love, telling the other two, "Rubbish! Love is for teenagers, I have more serious things to do than fall in love. Such a thing is totally out of the question for me. You know my plans."[60]

Eva, who came to Berlin from the provinces and works as a secretary and bookkeeper for a publicist, reveals her more moderate position vis-à-vis love in responding, "That's true in theory. But in practice things are always much different."[61] "You are right," she continues, "we modern girls shouldn't give ourselves to a man who will require our subservience and treat us like a pet who is just there for his comfort; and we shouldn't just get married to be taken care of financially. That is shameful for a girl of today. We should all become independent and be free to pursue a career so as to avoid such an ignoble fate and make decisions independent of the material question." But, she concludes, "The best is marriage—our natural and best occupation is to be wife and mother."[62]

Klara heartily approves. Despite having worked her way up from a streetcar ticket taker to a civil servant for the transit authority, she makes no secret of the fact that she longs for a husband, for children, and for love. Klara, the author tells us, has always dreamed of this "female happiness," and while she takes great pride in her job and enjoys the independence her rather sizable salary (well over DM 1,000 per year) brings, she hopes more than ever that "Cupid would come to her aid and rescue her from the dry office tasks that are not fulfilling to a woman."[63] Klara's financial independence is more useful to her in allowing her to leave behind a rather bitter family situation than in prolonging her single status.

These three modern women all end up falling in love and dropping their reservations about men, love, and marriage. This plot of a story about "modern girls" thus seems on its face to fit with the relatively conservative position taken by many men, some women, and a variety of social observers in deriding "the emancipated" and lauding those who married.[64] But Zapp's story is more nuanced than this. It ends with Klara's wedding ceremony, where Fritze's new husband raises a glass to modern women everywhere:

> My toast is to modern girls, the eager-to-work, energetic, independent, modern girls. I may not be any friend of the efforts of those women's rights activists who work to open all careers without exception to women and who want to make women equal to men in every respect. But I recognize and laud one positive effect of the modern women's movement, to wit, that it has created the opportunity for modern girls to be able to earn an adequate wage in honorable . . . careers. . . . The independent young woman who takes care of herself does not need to sell herself to a man she doesn't love out of fear of scarcity. She can wait until her heart speaks. . . . So I raise my glass and declare: to the modern girls!"[65]

One can assume that neither Fritze, Eva, nor Klara felt compelled to stitch a speech so qualified and guarded in its acceptance of the women's movement onto a pillow to cherish forevermore. But amid an atmosphere of acrimony and public squabbles between women pushing for independence and a majority of men who aimed to stop them, the limited concessions of Fritze's husband sound somewhat less misogynistic and indeed speak to the complicated interplay between urban women, emancipation, and marriage at the turn of the century.

A WEDDING TOAST like that of Fritze's husband might even be read as relatively progressive alongside an emerging trend of men's widespread and general aversion to marriage, or *Ehescheu*, as it became known in Berlin at the turn of the century. A few anecdotes from the daily newspaper will give a flavor of what *Ehescheu* looked like in a city that featured, as one newspaper article claimed, an entire "marriage-averse generation."[66] In one case, a man who tried to drown himself was pulled kicking and screaming out of the water and later admitted that he was about to get married and had attempted suicide "out of a fear of marriage."[67] In another, a man vanished on the day of his appointment at city hall and then, after a new date was set and he actually was married to the daughter of a businessman, fled both the wedding reception and the country.[68] The headline writers called it "the same old story" when a young man had to move to six different apartments in order to escape his former girlfriend, who was hell-bent on marriage.[69] Still another example involves the reporter who, for the sake of a good story, divorced his wife so that he could marry her again, take a honeymoon trip to Paris in an automobile, and document the whole episode, day by day, for the readers of the *Berliner Morgenpost*. On the day of his remarriage, the reporter was gripped with fear at town hall and had to summon his courage: "The devil knows why, my heart started pounding. As we started up the stairs it was still going. And I had to think very intentionally on the old phrase: 'To marry, one has to know what he's getting into but keep courage.' And I wanted to have courage."[70] A final example is of a young groom who somehow escaped the coach that was carrying him to his wedding ceremony in April 1901. When he could not be found, the *Berliner Lokal-Anzeiger* announced an essay contest for readers to come up with their best guesses about where he could have gone. The response was overwhelming, and Berliners were so taken with the story that they apparently even submitted hefty novels imagining and embellishing the disappearing groom's entire life story.[71]

Of course, not every case of cold feet was so sensational as to occasion a citywide essay contest, but the topic of *Ehescheu*—and the trend of men preferring bachelorhood to marriage—had everyone talking in Berlin, especially toward the end of the first decade of the twentieth century. On some level, this was just good copy that bolstered the standard narrative of the city as the world upside-down. At the same time, this talk of *Ehescheu* was not mere fluff. There were points of resonance throughout Berlin society: stories about "famous bachelors" in history, jokes about how bachelors were terrible cooks and had to rely on their landladies for anything resembling sustenance, and warnings to men that it was easy to get tricked into an engagement on Christmas Eve.[72] There were also books that discussed strategies for avoiding marriage and tips for making a wedding seem like an utter impossibility when the chiming of church bells was imminent.[73] Men sought advice from their fellow newspaper readers about whether or not to break off an intended marriage for a lack of compatibility and received helpful responses with practical tips for how to do it gently.[74] And the mothers writing in to the essay contest about raising (and marrying off) daughters felt compelled to address *Ehescheu* in their prize-winning entries. Each gave suggestions for how women could overcome this problem.[75]

Even the writer and sociologist Hans Ostwald could not resist commenting on the way men often felt trapped, caught in marriage, and forced into it to avoid unpleasant situations. In the case of Ostwald's "Liebe im Rausch" ("The Rush of Love"), Heinrich sits in a bar with other

members of a club he belongs to, and it is the first time he has been amid such
sociability in a long time. Even though "he [becomes] utterly intoxicated
by the life . . . that surround[s] him," he is careful not to drink too much
because he does not want to get sick, and the others turn to making fun
of him as an awkward outsider. Falling in a sort of spell while gazing at
the dark brown hair belonging to the girl sitting next to him, Heinrich
offers to buy her a drink. "Without even realizing it," Heinrich gets closer
and closer to the girl, their feet touch, and their heads move closer and
closer together. Suddenly, Heinrich is so warm that he has to go outside for
some fresh air. She follows him, and while "at first Heinrich [feels] himself
refreshed, this freshness merely increase[s] the rush, the lust, the intoxication that [fills] him." In a haze, Friedrich puts his arms around the girl
and they start kissing. "They [cannot] tear themselves apart," but then her
brother appears and is about to pull out a knife to attack Heinrich. The girl
is quick, though: "We're getting married—leave him be—he's my husband
now, after all." Heinrich "repeat[s] mechanically: 'We're getting married!'
But that was cold, deflated, sober. That was not stammered or screamed in
the frenzy of love. That was the devastating realization of a hard, bitter fate
that has suddenly appeared. He was trapped."[76]

Ostwald cleverly juxtaposes intoxication and sobriety, the "rush of love"
and the cold realization of an unwanted fate, and the glut of books and articles about men wanting to prolong their bachelorhood and delay marriage
would lead one to believe that, for most Berliners, marriage was a bitter sentence.[77] A closer look, however, suggests that Berliners were not simply re-
belling against the idea of commitment, monogamy, or family as such but
were instead responding to a particular set of developments in the turn-of-
the-century metropolis.

According to some, casual dating was replacing marriage. Plenty of
critics suggested that men had simply been spoiled by increasingly popular casual dating and that they saw no need to get married when they
could have connection and intimacy without any of the financial and legal
commitments.[78] These were largely the same people pushing for a so-called
bachelor tax (*Junggesellensteuer*) proposed sometime around 1907, which
would require some sort of yearly sum from men who were of marrying age
and had not yet married.[79] One poem sent into the *Berliner Morgenpost*
argued that casual dating would become an expensive pleasure if such a tax
were actually enacted, implying that it was because of a man's *Verhältnis*
that he had little desire to marry.[80] Writers, too, imagined plots that featured men plagued by earlier, and casual relationships, suggesting that

casual dating was a real impediment to marriage even for those who actually wanted to marry at some point.[81]

For the most part, though, Berliners seemed to agree that casual dating was not at the root of the emerging problem of marriage. Indeed, as one reader wrote into the *Berliner Lokal-Anzeiger*, "One must not confuse cause with effect. [A bachelor] dates casually because he is not married; rarely does he refuse marriage because he is dating."[82] Others pointed out that since there were hardly any "old bachelors" in Berlin, most men must end up marrying after all, even if they were waiting longer and longer to do so.[83]

When challenged, Berliners themselves gave a variety of responses about putting the brakes on marriage. Some cited the desire to pursue a career without distractions;[84] others complained, hypocritically, about the fact that so many women had already had lovers or even been married.[85] But the most commonly cited reason was money. Daily living was expensive and wages were low in the turn-of-the-century metropolis, and men were as concerned about their finances as single women. Many men, as the Sunday columnist for the *Berliner Lokal-Anzeiger* observed, did not feel financially ready for marriage. Realizing how much it costs to support two (and eventually more) people, they saw their current situation as bachelors as much easier.[86] The columnist was on to something: the men who defended their aversion to marriage nearly always cited the fact that they were fully aware of the increase in their expenditures for food, clothing, and insurance if they got married. And this was not even counting the costs of amusement, luxury items, or the wedding itself.[87] A 1913 *Berliner Morgenpost* piece homed in on the bridal carriage as the bane of a newly married man's existence. In this case, the protagonist, Gustav Blümke, tells his bride-to-be that, given the rising cost of food and the expensive new apartment, they will have to do without a fancy bridal carriage and instead take a taxi to the church, thereby saving the thirty marks for their household budget. But Kläre responds "categorically" that a bridal carriage, as well as a top hat and patent-leather boots for him, are all "just part of the way things are done. No bridal carriage, no wedding." Frustrated, Gustav tells Kläre to just get the bridal carriage, and she ends up picking a very extravagant one. The wedding continues as planned, but Gustav is so angry that he cannot enjoy it and instead considers it a "source of bitterness" that he carries into the marriage.[88]

Small sketches like that of Gustav Blümke did little to ease the economic trepidation many Berlin men felt about getting married. The result, as the "Berlin Observer" noted in his weekly column, was that men increasingly looked for a woman who already had money so that the impact of their wives'

expensive tastes would be easier to absorb.[89] The idea was simple: by com-
bining the savings of a bachelor and a "wealthy daughter," as such brides were
often called, bride and groom, once married, would not have to adjust their
prior standard of living.[90] They would be able to "afford everything," as one
woman put it.[91] Of course, a sizable dowry also helped, and while men were
frequently criticized for still caring about the dowry "in this day and age,"
they defended it as entirely reasonable given the costs of modern life.[92] More
often than not, though, dowries were refused or simply nonexistent.[93] After
all, many young Berlin women had come from the provinces seeking work
and thus had few if any family connections, and so men were left to weigh the
emotional pros and financial cons of marriage without dowry.[94] They had, as
J. Lorm wrote, to reach the point of satiation where "the effects of a 'temper-
ately enjoyed youth' make peace, quiet, and a lovingly prepared meal appear
desirable."[95] They also had to examine their budgets and decide whether they
had saved enough for marriage, as Dorothee Goebeler attempted to do for
them in a 1913 feature piece called "What One Needs to Marry."[96]

Getting to the point where one was ready to marry, then, was for many
Berliners neither easy nor something to be taken lightly. A peek into diary
of Ernst Schwarz makes this clear. Ernst was a very thoughtful, often melan-
cholic Berliner who, at twenty-four, met and fell in love with Meta Brückner
but found himself tormented by the imagined financial ramifications of marrying her. Ernst was neither poor (he became a rather successful businessman)
nor miserly (he generously covered the copious costs of his sister's wedding
celebration), but he was extremely cautious and plagued by chronic rheuma-
toid arthritis. Ernst hardly had time for women as he was working his way into
stable employment and a reasonable income, and though he and his friend
met two young women at a lake in the spring of 1911, his diary entry from that
evening evinces an offhand aversion to early marriage: "Nice, well-to-do girls,
early twenties, would actually be a good match for marriage if we were already
thinking about such things."[97] They were not, though, and when that winter
one of the girls, Käte, started "getting her hopes up for something serious that
I cannot fulfill," Ernst broke things off. "It's really too bad," he confided to his
dairy that December. "Perhaps I met Käte a year too soon. I always have the
same misfortune—or is it good fortune?"[98]

Ernst would be tested again just two months later when he met twenty-
year-old Meta at an evening ball for bankers. The two hit it off, and Ernst was
at Meta's home in suburban Köpenick by the next afternoon. They developed
what Ernst called a "very close friendship"—"here . . . I have learned what passion means"—and Meta was soon intent on getting married. She introduced

Ernst to her parents and relatives, who in turn waited expectantly for Ernst to propose. Here Ernst was again cautious, though in this case his misgivings about marriage carried the extra weight of not wanting to leave behind his independence as a bachelor: "I am not yet mature enough for marriage, though the fact that I have it so good at home [on my own] and want for nothing certainly has something to do with it." "Meta doesn't have a penny," he reasoned with his diary, "so, given my financial situation, it would be foolish to even think seriously about marriage." So Ernst "let Meta go," which was not easy, but "apparently reason speaks louder than my heart at this point."[99]

Ernst tried to distract himself with his work, but he admitted to his diary that his thoughts were still on Meta, and when she asked to talk four weeks later, he agreed.[100] They resumed their relationship, and while Ernst at first maintained that he still could not "wrap my head around the idea of marrying Meta," he found himself ultimately won over by the love and affection of his "friend and comforter," Meta. "In spite of my miserable financial situation and unstable prospects for the future (career, health, money)," he wrote, "I gradually warmed up to the idea of marrying Meta."[101] It had not been an easy decision, for "I could not come to terms with the thought of a life full of anxiety about having a decent living and lasting health," but Meta's "courage and . . . love" had, in the end, convinced him to "lay down my weapons" and surrender. They were engaged on Easter Sunday 1913.[102]

But things did not get immediately easier for Ernst. A promised dowry of furniture fell through, there were more health and business problems, and a bout of depression left Ernst wondering if he was "one of those for whom the devil chooses to make life on earth difficult and test how much a person can take. I don't know; I only know that I am soon finished if happiness does not return soon."[103] Happiness and good fortune did indeed return, though Ernst thought seriously about calling off their engagement in those tormented months of uncertainty. But by the end of the year, his income had finally increased to a satisfactory level of DM 420 a month—"that should be enough for the beginning of a new marriage; why shouldn't I finally be happy?"—and he decided the time was right to get married. Ernst and Meta were married on April 26, 1914, and appear to have enjoyed a long and happy life together.[104]

Ernst was in many ways a typical Berliner, and though he rarely referred to the modern world as such or used language like "nowadays," his steady aversion to marriage, financial concerns, and hesitance to give up his comfortable life as a bachelor follow the contours of the larger trend of *Ehescheu* at the turn of the century. His diary entries also suggest something of the genuine nature of *Ehescheu* for ordinary Berliners. As with the aforementioned newspaper

writer who remarried his wife for the sake of some good copy, it is tempting
to view all of the hullabaloo about *Ehescheu* as a sort of hypermasculine
posturing. So, too, is there a temptation to read the constant handwringing
about money as a masculine facade for the timidity and insecurity about
relationships, dating, and love that many men surely felt. Both readings are
compelling and perhaps accurate for a great many of the Berliners under study
here. On the other hand, the specific quality of Ernst's diary entries—their
brutally honest self-assessments and his steady and seemingly honest steps
of progress toward marriage—suggests something genuine, indeed, something unvarnished in his pecuniary concerns about love and marriage. Ernst's
hesitation and economic caution were clearly self-destructive, and it seems
clear that he was not sowing his wild oats and enjoying a libertine bachelorhood while debating his readiness for marriage. He seemed genuinely to desire marriage and connubial connection, and his financial anxieties appear as
authentic—if a touch neurotic—concerns about entering into marriage in a
world where financial security seemed as important as ever.

On the other hand, if both men and women were so concerned about
money and refrained from joining in Berlin's many leisure and nightlife
offerings, how can the dance craze, the masquerade balls, and the many
other evening entertainments be explained? How can Ernst's shrugging off
his myriad concerns about career, health, and money and meeting Meta at
the bankers' ball be understood? The answer, as one Berliner remarked in
a debate about marriage with other *Berliner Morgenpost* readers, had to do
with class. "Only princes and proletarians can marry young. The middle-class
person has to wait until he has a stable existence."[105] This, of course, was the
tricky thing about middle-class marriage, for while marriage was one of the
middle-class bedrocks for stability, Berliners like Ernst Schwarz realized that
they needed to have accumulated a great deal of money to be able to make
marriage possible.

Indeed, Ernst's concerns about marriage reveal the complex interplay between class and love at the turn of the century. For the most part, *Ehescheu* was
a middle-class trend, not because middle-class men like Ernst were actually
poor, had an especially high number of casual girlfriends, or lived particularly
spectacular lives as bachelors; rather, it was a middle-class problem because
class belonging carried a heavy set of expectations and assumptions.[106] These
in turn were the driving force behind Berliners' desire to delay or avoid marriage. Ernst, for example, refers to the need to secure a "decent" or "respectable" living, which naturally meant a salary large enough to support all of the
fixtures of proper middle-class life. The nuptial apartment Ernst ultimately

rented was a three-room apartment that was "very nicely appointed" and in a brand-new building in the suburb of Tempelhof. Ernst wrote that all of this would allow them to live there "perfectly."[107]

Middle-class marriage was about this perfection, and perfection meant not just a posh apartment but, more importantly, a domestic lifestyle with all of the trimmings. As one frustrated newspaper reader wrote to her *Berliner Lokal-Anzeiger* interlocutors, "How often have I heard," she wrote, "a man from 'better' [i.e., middle class] circles say, 'Well, as long as she does not start working!' What is that supposed to mean?"[108] It meant, of course, that providing a wholly sufficient income for the family was an important part of hegemonic middle-class masculinity and that to permit one's wife to work was to fall short. These men "constantly forget," she continued, "that they also come from simple families, that their mothers scrimped and saved so that their sons could study."[109] They forgot, in other words, that their respectability emanated not from genteel breeding or profound wealth but from tuition money gathered by industrious and thrifty mothers; in sales clerk positions attained by luck; or in career promotions earned thanks to the timely retirement or death of a senior salesman. Middle-class life was tenuous, and *Ehescheu*, fear of or aversion to marriage, was an attempt to hold on to it.

ALL OF THIS talk of *Ehescheu*, modern women, and old maids added up to a growing conviction that marriage itself was at a sort of crisis moment. There were the rising number of divorces, the widely publicized cases of marital violence, the women who complained that marriage was no longer a stable economic base, the men who tried to avoid it, and the growing opposition to marriage by women's rights advocates.[110] Conventional marriage did, indeed, seem to be under frequent attack. In 1907, the activist Hedwig Dohm levied her critique in the form of "marriage aphorisms," each offering an explanation for why marriages were so frequently unhappy. "The compulsion to marry is pernicious," went one of them. "We have stopped using straitjackets on the insane. When will we get rid of them for the reasonable?" Another aphorism was equally colorful: "Marriages are indeed made in heaven, but Lucifer is still there, too."[111] Rudolf Lothar put it differently but spoke to the same malignant qualities of modern marriage: "Those who marry are happy; those who don't are happier. Those on the outside want in; those inside want out. Men are afraid of marriage but marry anyway; women all want to get married and are unhappy and unsatisfied when they do."[112] While some complained that young Berliners entered marriage too starry-eyed and naive, that they needed

to be more practical, or that modern-day individualism was ruining everything, others saw in these developments the potentially devastating possibility that the institution of marriage was simply incompatible with modern,
metropolitan life.[113]

Berliners filled lecture halls to discuss this apocalyptic rhetoric. Staff at the
Ethnological Museum of Berlin had to close the doors on long lines of people
waiting to hear a talk by Ferdinand Freiherr von Reitzenstein in 1910. Those
"lucky" to get a seat, as the newspaper reported the next day, heard a presenta-
tion on "the big, if not biggest question of today": marriage, which is "a matter
of opinion—or to put a finer point on it—fashion." Reitzenstein, author of
numerous studies of love—*The Ancient History of Love* (1908), *Evolutionary
History of Love* (1908), *Cultural History of Marriage* (1908), *Love and
Marriage in European Antiquity* (1910)—gave listeners his take on the history
of marriage "from the time when there was no such thing as marriage to now,
when there is already a movement to do away with marriage in its current
form."[114] Large crowds gathered again to hear Grete Meisel-Heß discuss the
pros and cons of marriage in the modern world at the Berlin *Singakademie*
in 1911, though the *Berliner Lokal-Anzeiger* reporter sent to cover the lecture
was more taken by the speaker's good looks than her proposal that marriage
be made easier for young people by giving them a sort of marriage bonus that
they could later pay back in taxes.[115]

Reform of marriage was, indeed, a hot topic in turn-of-the-century Berlin.
J. Lorm wrote that one could not open a newspaper, read a brochure, or go
to the theater without seeing discussion of marriage and proposals to adapt
it to the modern world.[116] Even the wedding industry publicized "reformed"
bridal fashions as a way of staying au courant and profitable.[117] And newspaper readers in turn took their debates to the readers' letters sections of the
newspapers, arguing over the idea of giving each marriage a set expiration date
(term marriages, in other words) and, more basically, about whether or not
marriage was designed to preserve gender inequality.[118]

In the end, most of the debate centered around one basic question and what
most saw as its three possible answers: given the realities of the modern metropolis, which form of marriage makes the most sense—city hall formalities,
traditional church ceremonies, or "free love" unions whose longevity (or lack
thereof) would be of no legal or moral importance? In some ways, this was
actually two questions, the first hinging on the nature and jurisdiction of
marriage—state or church—and the second on the viability of doing away
with marriage altogether. Many Berliners felt no connection to the church
and saw little point in expensive church ceremonies once the introduction

of civil marriage in 1875 made them legally superfluous.[119] Siegbert Salter put it best in 1906 when he quipped, "It's a long way from city hall to the altar."[120] City hall marriages were indeed seen by many as the more modern, practical approach, a proper advance over the tradition-laden church service custom. Friedrich Bohn, whose 1907 lecture on modern approaches to marriage was heavily praised by the newspapers, told listeners that "those who are just married at city hall but have love and loyalty in their marriage are ethically superior to those who marry in a church with all sorts of pomp but have no idea of the true nature of marriage."[121]

On the other hand, quite a few Berliners still believed in having the sacrament of marriage administered at a church. For some, it was a sentimental attachment to tradition, as, for example, in Alexander Elster's short story "Erikas Hochzeit" ("Erika's Wedding"), where, after the marriage nearly falls apart before it begins, the couple finds a friend—who happens to be a town hall clerk—to marry them and then scrambles to the church "since the bride in her overflowing happiness did not want to miss out on the church blessing."[122] Indeed, many couples who skipped a church ceremony found themselves regretting it, as the advice column of the *Berliner Lokal-Anzeiger* warned a reader who wrote in asking to have the difference between city hall marriages and church ceremonies explained.[123]

In some ways, the dilemma of whether to have a church ceremony paled in comparison to the larger debate about whether marriage should continue to exist.[124] Many argued that marriage was simply incompatible with modern times and that free love was the only sensible solution. Traditional marriage was based, they said, on a fundamentally hypocritical morality that allowed men to stray and satisfy their "polygamous instincts" while denying women the same opportunity.[125] Indeed, women complained that men were constantly trying to convince women that they should embrace free love even though, when choosing a marriage partner, they would never consider a woman who had already experienced intimacy.[126] This was the experience of Olga Th., who had divorced her husband and then likely felt the sting of social reproach as a divorcée looking for love. Even before the divorce had been finalized, Olga "felt very isolated," so when she met a businessman who proposed that they forgo "the awkward formalities at city hall" and live "the good life" in free love, Olga agreed.[127]

But free love, as a number of writers suggested in short stories and novels, was motivated by more than convenience or laziness. In the case of Konrad, the main character of S. Sborowitz's 1907 play, *Freie Liebe* (*Free Love*), marriage with Martha, the woman he loves, is simply out of the question given their vastly different social backgrounds. Indeed, when Konrad's father finds out about their free-love union, he disowns Konrad, after which Konrad falls ill and ultimately dies despite Martha's best efforts to revive him.[128] Hermann Heisermans's short story "Liebschaft" ("Amour") portrays free-love relationships in a similarly tragic light, though in this case the drama comes from the awkward interaction of a recently deceased young man's parents and his lover, who is bereft at the loss of her free-love husband but embarrassed by the scorn of his mother. Only the father, who recognizes that they lived "as man and wife," shows any compassion toward the young lady.[129]

Free-love advocates recognized that it was young women who suffered the greatest stigma from such unofficial though often quite stable relationships, so they proposed that women be granted the moral freedom to enjoy "free love" as they matured from teenagers to women.[130] The Association for Maternity Rights, for example, announced a resolution in 1907 calling for the legal recognition of free marriages, their protection from interference by state authorities, and the legal equality of children born out of free-love unions.[131] Even Reinhold Gerling, a popular and prolific author of advice manuals for young people, argued that free love might actually lead to a strengthening of traditional marriage. For Gerling, free love was not so much the dissolution of state- or church-sponsored marriage as it was the complete overhaul of marriage law, marriage practices, and marriage education. "We realize," he wrote in his 1907 advice book, *Freie Liebe oder bürgerliche Ehe* (*Free Love or Civil Marriage*), "that things cannot continue in the same old tracks. The new age, with its violent economic unrest, demands a restructuring of individual life."[132] As it is, civil marriage "inhibits the development of the individual" when it should ideally be about "developing two complementary people into one being without destroying their individuality."[133] Proclaiming that "love . . . must be free," Gerling thus proposed that marriage laws recognize that "true marriage is made manifest in the instant that two loving souls plunge into one another, that they either silently or jubilantly give themselves to each other."[134] State and religious rules governing marriage must be abolished, Gerling concluded, for they "killed" love by constraining it, codifying it, and pushing it into an unnatural mold.[135]

Gerling's ideas were obviously radical for his time, calling as he did for the dissolution of all obstacles to divorce ("to give a promise for life, to sign a contract of indefinite length, is, given the current [social and economic norms], positively absurd!"), the end of a double morality regarding virginity before marriage, the delay of dowry payments until after the first year of marriage, and the entrance of women into all careers.[136] As it turns out, they were too extreme and challenged the core of traditional, middle-class mores too directly to be considered seriously at the turn of the century. Traditional marriage indeed remained the bedrock of middle-class life, and most Berliners—like Frieda Kliem—felt a strong compulsion to try to land in its safe harbor, as it were.

Although Gerling, like other advocates for free love and marriage reform, was responding to what so many saw as a failure of the church and the state to fit marriage to the pace and desires of modern life, it seems that the problem of marriage was above all about tensions between the patterns of traditional, middle-class life and an emerging, more individualistic sensibility spawned and encouraged by the modern metropolis.[137] Gerling, after all, had pointed to the need for marriage to accommodate the full individuality of both spouses, and he insisted on the importance of raising boys and girls equally and according to their individual preferences and predilections.[138] Other insightful commentators, too, situated the entire marriage debate in terms of the conflict between individuality and individual freedoms, on one hand, and the stability of middle-class life, on the other.[139] Rudolf Lothar, for his part, argued that reform—whether in the abolishment of church ceremonies or the establishment of free love as a legal reality—would not work so long as individualism was a reality. Until something changed, he concluded, one simply had to "make do with marriage as it is for now" and "suffer through marriage" with humor. This was easier for a columnist to write than for those frustrated with unhappy marriages, restrictive social stigmas, and oppressive loneliness to endure, but it seems that most nevertheless tried.[140] After all, few of these reforms ever took hold.

But marriage indeed seemed more and more at odds with a modern, metropolitan sensibility at the turn of the century. The sheer amount of debate makes this unmistakable. The way "grandfather took grandmother" had become outdated and irretrievable, as commentators had proclaimed, but not because it was simply passé or had fallen out of fashion; it became unthinkable and impossible because it seemed utterly incompatible with modern city and the way modern Berliners were positioning themselves in it. The things that had Berliners talking at the turn of the century—the propriety of women who preferred work to marriage and broke with the feminine models of their mothers and grandmothers; the prominence of bachelors in the city and the potential threat men refusing to marry posed to the health of the German state; the costs and benefits of allowing free-love unions, trial marriages, and hassle-free divorce; or even what it meant that Berlin had over fifty thousand old maids—were the sounds of Berliners young and old attempting, with varying degrees of success, to come to terms with a wave of individualism that challenged the core values of middle-class life.

4

Emerging Technologies of Love

ON OCTOBER 15, 1914, a young woman walked into a bank in the Berlin suburb of Weißensee and told the teller she wanted to make a withdrawal. She slid a small booklet across the counter and waited expectantly for her money while the teller read the account number, 4244, off the booklet's first page and searched for the corresponding file in the bank's ledgers. "One moment, Fräulein Kliem," he said, and disappeared into the back of the bank. As she was waiting, her mind flashed back to earlier that day when her sister told her a man had come by looking for her. He reappeared in the afternoon, and this time she had been there to meet him. It was Paul, who had sauntered up next to her on Alexanderplatz more than a year earlier and asked if he could walk with her for a bit. The man was much older and, better yet, had said he was single and wanted to start a relationship. It had almost seemed too good to be true. Indeed, it was, for he soon disappeared, and she lost all contact with him—until the day before, when, at the same place on Alexanderplatz, Paul had approached her again. This time he had a wild and desperate look in his eyes, and he asked her if she was still living in the same place. He had been there already twice that day looking for her. Her thoughts wandered to the possibility of a relationship with him, but she suddenly became aware of the teller walking back to the counter. When she saw that he was carrying a small envelope, she exhaled with relief. So it had worked after all, she thought. The teller did not seem suspicious about handing her all of Fräulein Kliem's money. Paul had said there would be no problem; he would withdraw the money himself, he said, except he could not risk being seen. "Just say you're Frieda Kliem if they ask," he had told her.[1] She did not know who Frieda Kliem was, but she, Anna Piegors, was taking her money. There were DM 144.24 in the account, but to take all of them might have looked a little suspect.[2] So she had filled out the withdrawal form for DM 125. After all, times were tight, budgets were stretched, and single women were dipping into what little savings they had all the time. She knew because she was single herself, and only nineteen years old.[3]

But the teller did not give her the envelope. A man suddenly grabbed her and told her she was under arrest for theft. This was part of an ongoing criminal investigation, she was told. She protested that she was withdrawing the money for a man around the corner. They told her to wait while they decided on their next move. She was to take the envelope with her, leave the bank calmly, and wave the envelope at Paul. The police would handle things from there. Anna was nervous, but she had no choice. So she left the bank and walked a few feet to the corner of Landhanstraße and Goethestrasse. There was Paul at the rendezvous point, and she waved the envelope at him.[4] She could see from his face, which bore pince-nez eyeglasses and a graying goatee, that he was agitated, and he hurried over to her to take the envelope. At that moment, the police rushed in and placed him under arrest as a suspect in the murder of thirty-nine-year-old seamstress Frieda Kliem, whose killer had remained at large for over three months and whose meager savings and bankbook he now held in his hands. Despite his agitation and attempts at resistance, the police whisked Paul away and took Anna Piegors to the precinct headquarters for questioning. Paul eventually cooperated and gave police his full name, Paul Kuhnt; his age, forty-nine; his occupation, retired pharmacist; his marital status, married with five children; and his address, Handjerystraße 15, Berlin-Friedenau. He admitted to having a criminal record. He went with the police as they searched his house and feigned ignorance when the police found a variety of objects hidden inside a cabinet: six gold-plated coffee spoons; three silver soup spoons; two small spoons with decoration; and several pieces of tableware with black handles. These precise items had been reported missing from Frieda's apartment by friends and neighbors. Kuhnt, though, denied any knowledge of Frieda Kliem and claimed that he found the silverware abandoned under the seat of a commuter train.[5]

The search through Paul Kuhnt's apartment continued and eventually turned up a bundle of envelopes with letters inside. Only the letters were not addressed to Paul Kuhnt; they were addressed to the dispatch departments of several newspapers, including the *Berliner Lokal-Anzeiger* and the *Berliner Tageblatt*, and were unmistakably responses to a classified ad. There were thirty-eight envelopes in all, each one bearing different handwriting. They dated mostly from late September 1914, just a few weeks earlier. These too were of great interest to the police, who were searching for some connection between a murdered seamstress and a forty-nine-year-old retired pharmacist

who was married with five children.[6] And classified ads were a great lead.
Indeed, ever since classified advertising took off at the turn of the century,
swindlers and others criminals had used ads—personal ads, especially—as a
way to ensnare unsuspecting women with clever or too-good-to-be-true ads
so as to rob, murder, or slowly swindle them. Berlin was still reeling from a
well-publicized and unsolved murder case just a year earlier involving a forty-
year-old seamstress named Emma Schäfer, who was found dead in the Tegeler
forest outside Berlin, having been beaten to death with a hammer. The man—
her would-be groom—made off with her keys and money and was believed
to have broken into her apartment shortly thereafter in hopes of finding a
stash of money. Neighbors apparently heard noises in the apartment, and
there were stains from where he had tried to wash the blood off of his hands.
But the murderer, Max Kirschstein, who had initiated contact with Emma
Schäfer under a false name—Karl Schmidt—using a personal ad, somehow
escaped and had not been found.[7]

The police opened the letters, one by one, and saw that these were well-
intentioned responses to Kuhnt's personal ad from lonely women—some
single, some widows—who were looking for love in Berlin. The ad, which the
police easily tracked down using the corresponding number, 679, at the dispatch center of the *Berliner Tageblatt*, was, indeed, impressive:

Senior teacher, Dr., widower, no children, 51 yrs., looking for spouse.
Responses to Schbg. P. 679, Exp. of the Berliner Tageblatt, Schöneberg,
Hauptstr. 23/4.[8]

It was the perfect hook. It was simple, striking but not pretentious, and un-
assuming. What slightly older woman looking for love in the personal ads
would be able to resist? The women responding ranged from thirty to forty-
eight years old, old maids to widows, and poor to quite wealthy. None of the
women was ready to send along a photo quite yet, but each of them was excited about the prospect of meeting the widower-teacher who was seeking
companionship.[9]

All of the women gave Kuhnt their names and addresses in the hopes
that he might contact them for a rendezvous or, at the very least, start a correspondence. The police wasted no time interrogating them, hoping that
they might be able to provide more details about Kuhnt. Fortunately for his
correspondents, Kuhnt appeared to be lying low as he waited for the right
time to drain Frieda's account, and, as each woman told the police in a sworn
statement, he had not yet contacted them to meet. Kuhnt's silence was no

FIGURE 4.1 One of the thirty-eight letters seized from Paul Kuhnt's house

Source: Letter from Erna Gärtner to Adolf Mertens, Landesarchiv Berlin A Rep. Pr. Br. 030-03, Nr. 1232, Bl. 26.

FIGURE 4.2 Kuhnt's ad ("Oberlehrer..."), placed rather inconspicuously in the *Berliner Tageblatt*

Source: Berliner Tageblatt, June 29, 1914, Nr. 323.

doubt disappointing to these women, who had selected his ad, picked out special stationery, and carefully chosen their words in the hopes of striking gold and finding love. But, given the fact that Kuhnt was neither a retired teacher nor a widow but a dangerous killer, this was clearly the much better result.[10]

In spite of the great interest his personal ad had sparked, the police concluded that Paul Kuhnt must have focused his attentions on Frieda Kliem, though the lack of a letter from her was perhaps confusing at first. Kuhnt's denials of ever having met Frieda rang hollow in light of the fact that he had tried to clean out Frieda's account and had her valuables in his apartment. Moreover, any uncertainty the police might still have had vanished when Kuhnt, while being hauled into the police station, attempted to make a run for it and, having failed at that, tried to get at a hidden package of morphine in an apparent attempt at suicide.[11]

With Kuhnt in custody, the police were faced with the matter of finding evidence that specifically linked Kuhnt to Frieda's death. There was also the question of how Kuhnt had met Frieda in the first place, not to mention why he had selected her among other potential victims. Kuhnt's flimsy explanation for how he had come across Frieda's valuables was hardly convincing, but the police needed at least a working theory for how Kuhnt had been able to gain access to her valuables and bank account. The most obvious answer was that Frieda, like the other women, had responded to Kuhnt's ad and arranged a rendezvous, but where was her letter to him? Had Kuhnt responded to an ad by Frieda?

This theory fit with what the police had found in their initial investigation of her murder. They had discovered a personal ad registered in Frieda's name in the June 7, 1914 edition of *Berliner Lokal-Anzeiger*, and interviews with her friends confirmed that she had been posting ads. Frieda had become slightly desperate in her search for a husband, they said. They had seen various suspicious men lingering around her door, coming by and asking about her, and, so Frieda had claimed, renting rooms from her.[12] Antonie Köhler told police that Frieda had "tried all sorts of ways to make relationships with men that would lead to marriage" after her previous attempts to find a husband had failed and after realizing that "she wouldn't be able to live on the little she earned and on her savings."[13] Köhler was certain that Frieda had "responded to personal ads and even wrote her own ads," all with the aim of finding someone—though not just anyone. "Even then it would only be men . . . who were from better circles," as Köhler told police—to support her and love her.[14]

So Frieda had posted a personal ad in the newspaper. It was straightforward and to the point:

> **Single** widow, 35, wishes to make the acquaintance of a respectable gentleman for the purpose of marriage. Poste restante 236, post office 14.[15]

Actually, it was not entirely straightforward, for Frieda was neither a widow, nor thirty-five (she was thirty-nine). But, as she had for years worn a false wedding ring and lied to others about being a widow, she had few scruples about bending the truth if doing so served her search for love and intimacy in Berlin. It was also characteristic of her commitment to middle-class respectability, noting that she was only interested in a "respectable gentleman."

It is not clear how long Frieda had been posting ads or how many different ads she posted, but she did receive at least a few responses. Not long into their investigation, the police discovered several papers and letters among Frieda's things, and two paper notes in particular caught their attention. The first was two-sided, and on the front were roughly nine lines of nearly inscrutable jottings that appear to be Frieda's notes about planned meetings with men.

On the other side was a response to her ad. The writer expressed his heartfelt wish to meet Frieda and start a relationship, and he proposed a meeting for the following Tuesday, June 9 (two days after the ad ran in the Sunday paper), at 3:30 in the afternoon at Aschinger's Café on Moritzplatz. Frieda was to carry the letter in her hand as a means of recognition, and the man requested that she be on time. It is not entirely clear whether Frieda did, indeed, go to Aschinger's Café on Tuesday at 3:30, but this rendezvous appears to have been one of over a dozen she had planned.[16]

The second letter was dated just a few days later and bore messy, almost childlike handwriting. The writer apologized that he would be unable to make their rendezvous and that they should meet Friday at noon at "the same place," where he would be holding an old book. Interestingly, the man this time included a name—Adolf Mertens—and a photograph, and Frieda was apparently so enthused about him that she doodled "I want Adolf Mertens to marry me" on the back of the letter and "Adolf Mertens you will soon marry me" on a piece of scrap paper. Next to both pieces of paper was a business card—Julius Foth, Royal Prussian Chamber Musician, Harpist—that suggested Frieda was perhaps already thinking ahead and planning a wedding.

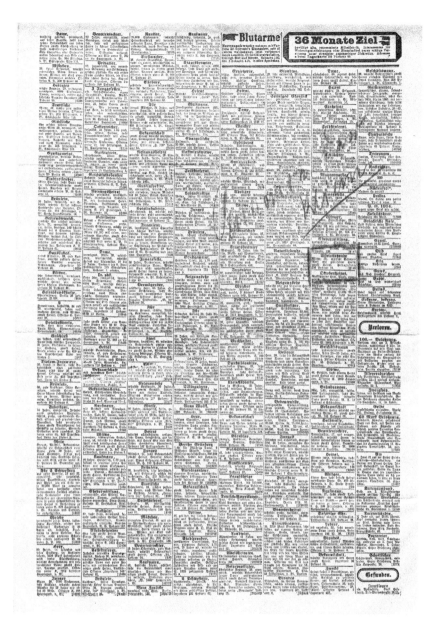

FIGURE 4.3 Frieda's personal ad, located and circled by the police in their characteristic red crayon. The handwritten text, scrawled on the ad by the police in the heat of the investigation, reads "Kliem's personal ad"

Source: Landesarchiv Berlin A Pr. Br. Rep. 030-03, Nr. 1232, Bl. 40.

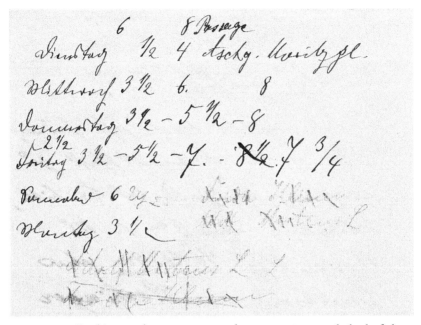

FIGURE 4.4 Frieda's notes about upcoming rendezvouses, written on the back of a letter found in her apartment

Source: Landesarchiv Berlin A Pr. Br. Rep. 030-03, Nr. 1232, Bl. 40.

She had also started writing out "Frieda Kliem" and "Adolf Mertens" next to one another, visualizing their future union.[17]

Adolf Mertens was, from the beginning of the investigation, thus a person of extreme interest to the police, but tracking down the real Adolf Mertens had proven frustrating. There were, in fact, a number of Adolf Mertenses in Berlin, and the police sent telegrams to all of Berlin's various city halls hoping to narrow down the list of candidates. The responses they received each provided a date of birth, marital status, and the profession of the Adolf Mertens in question, but the police soon concluded that these Adolf Mertenses were either too old or were longtime family men who could not possibly have corresponded with a single seamstress looking for love. This, of course, was a flawed assumption, for personal ads attracted both single and married Berliners alike, honorable individuals as well as swindlers. There was one Adolf Mertens who was of some interest to the police based solely on the fact that he lived rather close to the post office where the letters had been mailed, but he was seventy-four years old and retired, and the police concluded that he "can hardly be the man in question." So the police marked his file—like

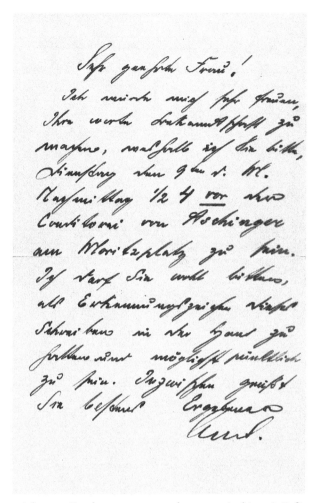

FIGURE 4.5 A letter to Frieda proposing a rendezvous at Aschinger's Café
Source: Landesarchiv Berlin A Pr. Br. Rep. 030-03, Nr. 1232, Bl. 40.

all of the others—with the words "No further action," and noted in an internal memo dated July 9, 1914, that "the persons in the phone book named Adolf Mertens are, according to reliable sources, of good repute, all married, and family men. Each also goes about his work with consistency."[18] As far as Berlin's chief of police was concerned, these were the cornerstones of middle-class respectability and, as such, wholly incompatible with an act of personal ad treachery.

Adolf Mertens had thus turned out to be a dead end, and this was where the initial investigation into the murder of Frieda Kliem had stalled. It was not

FIGURE 4.6 Adolf Mertens's letter to Frieda proposing a rendezvous

Source: Landesarchiv Berlin A Pr. Br. Rep. 030-03, Nr. 1232, Bl. 40.

FIGURE 4.7 Adolf Mertens's photographs, as found in Frieda Kliem's apartment by the police

Source: Landesarchiv Berlin A Pr. Br. Rep. 030-03, Nr. 1232, Bl. 40.

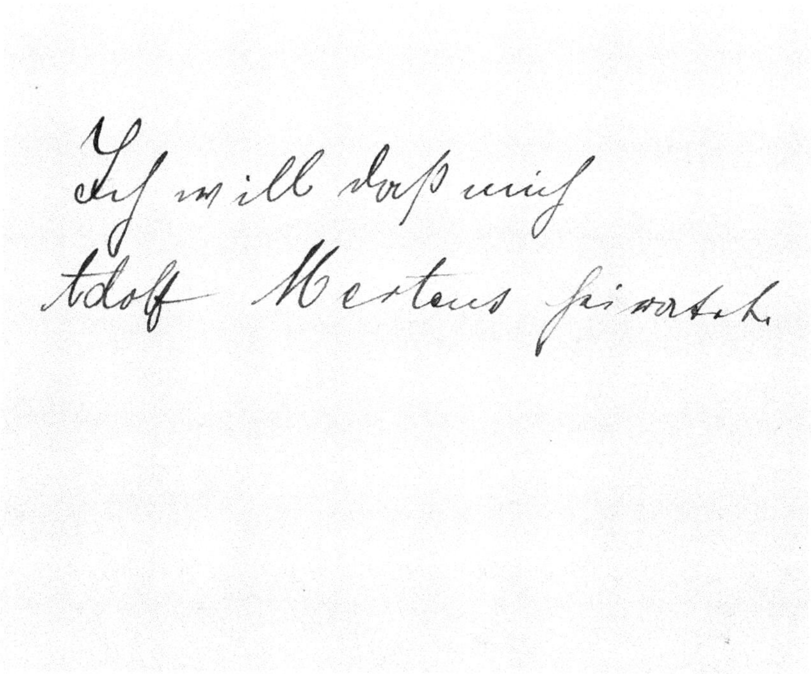

FIGURE 4.8 Frieda's hopeful doodles about a marriage with Adolf Mertens
Source: Landesarchiv Berlin A Pr. Br. Rep. 030-03, Nr. 1232, Bl. 40.

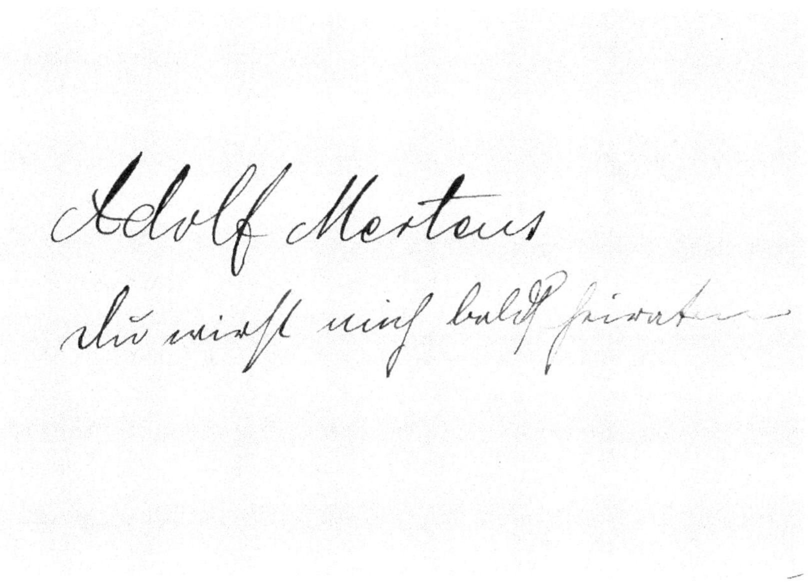

FIGURE 4.9 More of Frieda's doodles about marriage with Adolf Mertens
Source: Landesarchiv Berlin A Pr. Br. Rep. 030-03, Nr. 1232, Bl. 40.

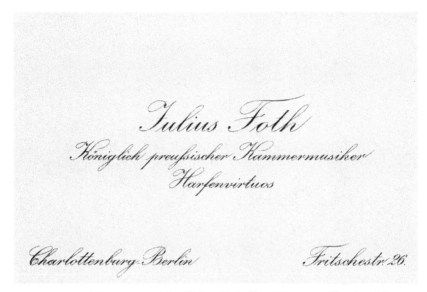

FIGURE 4.10 A business card for "Julius Foth, Royal Prussian Chamber Musician, Harpist"

Source: Landesarchiv Berlin A Pr. Br. Rep. 030-03, Nr. 1232, Bl. 40.

until Paul Kuhnt emerged—while trying to withdraw Frieda's money from the account authorities had frozen and were monitoring—that the police realized that "Adolf Mertens" was merely an alias used by Kuhnt to cover his tracks. Now all of the pieces fell into place: Kuhnt held in his possession the various items that had gone missing from Frieda's apartment; he matched the photo of "Adolf Mertens" found among Frieda's papers; and he had the exact same messy, childlike handwriting as "Adolf Mertens." These facts, combined with Kuhnt's efforts to flee from police and apparent suicide attempt on the way to jail, pointed to Paul Kuhnt as the obvious murderer of Frieda Kliem, and the investigation was closed.[19]

The police's work was not quite done, however. There was still the matter of explaining the cause of Frieda's death in the Falkenhagen forest near Finkenkrug, not to mention the specific part Paul Kuhnt (alias Adolf Mertens) had played in her murder. Here the sworn statements of Frieda's friends, family, and neighbors proved helpful, for it seems she was so excited about her future with Adolf Mertens that she had let down her usual mask of secrecy and told them about what she had planned.[20] Whether or not Frieda met with Kuhnt/Mertens on that Friday at "the same place," the two in any case decided to meet in a suburban forest on Wednesday, June 17, 1914. She wrote as much to Otto Mewes—her former *Verhältnis* and still one of her closest friends—in a letter dated June 16. In the letter, which Mewes later handed over to the police as evidence, Frieda wrote, "Early tomorrow I'm going to Finkenkrug, as long as the weather is nice; I was invited and am looking forward to the *Partie* (no bicycle)." Frieda's use of the word "Partie" is interesting, for it was a double entendre that meant both an outing and a marriage match. It is also curious that Frieda was not bringing her bicycle along, especially given the fact that she loved bicycling and had perhaps even suggested that they ride out to Finkenkrug.[21] But Kuhnt, her would-be husband and future assailant, had never learned to ride a bicycle, as he admitted to police, and had offered to pay her train fare instead.[22]

In her letter, Frieda sounded excited about the planned trip to Finkenkrug, though her characteristic loneliness and pessimism about the future pervade parts of this last correspondence with Mewes. "Too bad I have to ride alone," she wrote. "It would be much nicer in good company." "Business is bad," she continued farther down the page; "the latest fashion is that men don't wear hats, women are complaining about their hats, and a man from Kiel who's visiting friends says it's the same there, even with the fanciest men. How will fashion change next and destroy people's means of existence?" Other parts of the letter evince a striking and seemingly newfound contentment. "We've had summer weather for the last eight days," she wrote. "Sunday I was in Gorinsee and went swimming, then I went into the forest and lay in the hammock until I went home. It was a wonderful trip: in the morning [there] was at first a rather strong headwind but then a Linden breeze in Buchholz and a stretch to Schönerlinde with the scent of flowering acacias, which I love." Frieda had always drawn a degree of happiness from time spent in nature, but she conveys here a serenity that was perhaps the result of her belief that her time had finally come.[23]

There were other signs, too, such as the conversations Frieda had with her next-door neighbor, Marie Schönemann, in the days before her death. Marie told police that she had mentioned to Frieda her happiness at having found work. Frieda responded, "You're lucky; I on the other hand am not so lucky. But I have something planned in the next few days, and I'll tell you about it when it's all set up." Marie noted that she "didn't give much thought to what she meant; I can't say whether she was referring to a new job or an engagement," but when, two days later, she saw Frieda again, it became clear that Frieda was anticipating an imminent engagement with Adolf Mertens. Marie accepted a letter for Frieda from the mailman on Monday morning, since Frieda had said something important was coming, and when Marie handed her the letter ("postmarked in Berlin, written in a nice hand"), Frieda looked

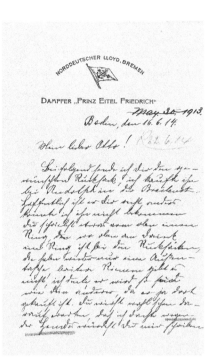

FIGURE 4.11 Frieda's letter to Otto Mewes, page 1, written on reused stationary (note the crossed-out date) the day before she was killed. The police, naturally, studied the letter and marked it up with red crayon.

Source: Landesarchiv Berlin A Pr. Br. Rep. 030-03, Nr. 1425, Bl. 95.

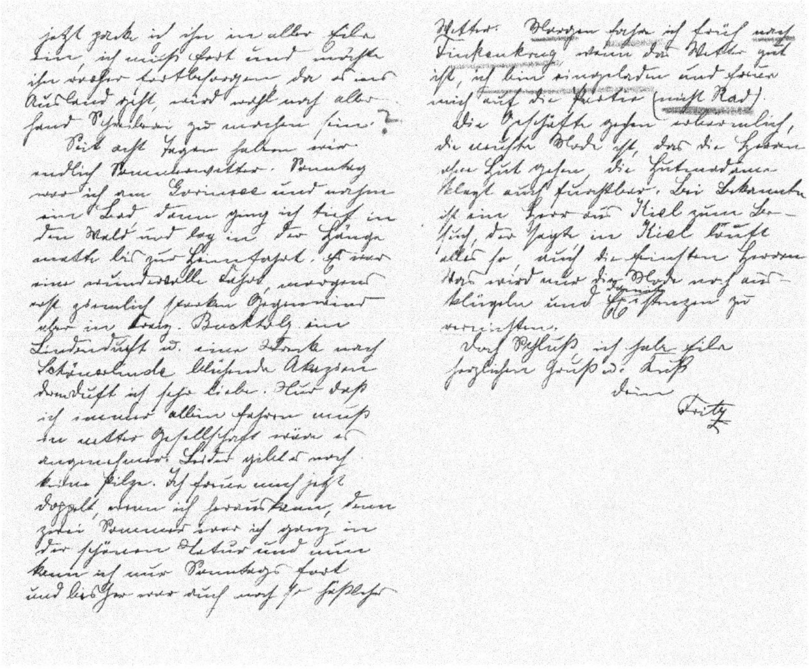

FIGURE 4.12 Frieda's letter to Otto Mewes, pages 2 and 3

relieved: "This is it, actually."[24] It is not clear who the sender of that letter was, but all signs point either to Kuhnt/Mertens, confirming their outing on the seventeenth, or, more likely (since no such letter was ever found and the handwriting was remarkably "nice"), a response from Otto Buning, the banker with four children who had proposed to Frieda back in 1904. Frieda hinted as much to another neighbor, Hulda Sello, who told police that though Frieda "had wanted to get engaged with a banker, a widower with four kids, . . . she gave up this desire because of the large number of children. He was supposed to come back from vacation on June 15, and she wanted to give him her decision—no—then. She told me about all of this on June 5; I know this for a fact because I was doing laundry that day."[25] The letter, in all likelihood from Buning, was his acceptance of her decision to turn down his proposal once and for all. It brought closure, the end of a long search and the beginning of a new life of stability.

Frieda, in the days leading up to her planned outing with Kuhnt/Mertens, was thus so hopeful, so confident that it would lead to marriage that she did not renew her personal ad and, more significantly, turned down the marriage proposal she had been mulling over for a decade. The fact, moreover, that she took such care to give Otto Buning her official and final decision before heading to Finkenkrug provides yet another fascinating glimpse into the world of middle-class respectability. Frieda, a middle-class woman in mindset and lifestyle if not in income or savings, was very careful to maintain at least a show of propriety by having only one serious love interest at a given time, even if she had found some measure of intimacy with other men during the time since Buning's initial offer of marriage. Frieda was not simply running away from her previous life. Indeed, she told the mailman to hold her mail and even mentioned to her grocer that she would be back shortly.[26] Her use of personal ads was not an escape from her heretofore difficult life; it was the promise of a better life.

Before heading out to Finkenkrug for her long-anticipated rendezvous with Adolf Mertens, Frieda put on a blue suit with white collar and black buttons, a white crepe blouse over a white knit camisole and a light gray corset, black "reform" slacks over purple hose with green hoops, and black lace-up shoes. She wore a black straw hat with a silk band and a small bunch of roses affixed to it, and she carried a green silk umbrella. She took the time to clean, trim, and polish her fingernails, and she gave the same attention to her feet. She also put in a false braid, thinking, perhaps, that it made her look younger than did her normal short, dark-blonde hair. Frieda was dressed to impress, and, having arranged for everything to be in order when she returned, she left for Finkenkrug that Thursday morning to meet the man she wanted so badly to marry.[27]

There is no record of Frieda's trip via train out to Finkenkrug, no transcript of the words she first spoke when seeing Kuhnt/Mertens, no map of the route they walked together in the forest. The police did find a depression in the grass not far from where Frieda's body was discovered, presumably, they concluded, created by the couple reclining together.[28]

It is, of course, possible that Kuhnt's intentions were more or less harmless, if extramarital, and that he had no intention of killing Frieda on that day. Perhaps he wanted intimacy. Perhaps he was consumed by the thrill of meeting a stranger through the personal ads. Frieda's closest friend, Antonie Köhler, thought as much; she was in Monte Carlo at the time of the murder, but she theorized to Mewes that the man "got pushy" and that Frieda would not have stood for that.[29] It is far more likely, though, that Kuhnt knew all along that he was going to kill Frieda. He clearly liked what he saw the day they rendezvoused: perhaps it was the gold watch, pearl ring, and gold brooch she wore.[30] Or maybe he liked what he heard: as cautious as Frieda had been, it seems likely that, in her excitement about her new love, she tipped her hand regarding her inheritance, the family land in Wilsnack, or the fine silverware that had been passed down to her from her family. Kuhnt in all likelihood saw the possibility of some money, and it is doubtful that his intentions were pure; after all, he was in debt, owing a total of over a DM 1,000 to various people. As a retired father of five, he might have seen crime as the only way of repaying his debts. Kuhnt knew the Falkenhagen forest well from his summer vacations, and he likely lured Frieda to a particular spot in the woods where he figured no one would bother them or find her body.[31]

However things progressed that day in the forest, the result was the same: eight days later, a forester ventured off the beaten path and found Frieda's corpse—face down, her body mostly decayed or rotted already—and called the police. When the police arrived at the scene, they examined what remained of her body and sent samples to a forensic chemist for analysis. There was, sadly, little to analyze, since her head was completely skeletonized and her organs unrecognizable. Frieda's jaw was separated from the rest of her skull and broken in three places. This "could only have been caused by violence," investigators concluded. "It is not impossible, however," they later admitted, "that this could have happened from a fall." They were therefore unable to determine a cause of death, especially since no other parts of her body showed the effects of trauma, poison, or foul play. The depression in the grass suggested that the assault was potentially sexual in nature, but the decomposition of her body made this almost impossible to determine. Indeed, there were neither signs of a struggle in the immediate vicinity of the body nor marks in the dirt from her body being dragged. In fact, the only things truly out of place in the whole murder scene were Frieda's keys, which were oddly absent (especially since her wallet—with a mere three marks inside—was still there). The missing keys fit with what the police discovered over the course of their investigation, for Frieda's killer had in all likelihood gone straight to her apartment, purloined her valuables, and then waited for things to quiet down before draining her bank account. Neighbors claimed that they had heard footsteps in Frieda's apartment that Friday, the day after Frieda was killed. The Friday newspaper was also inside the apartment, so someone must have brought it in.[32] Paul Kuhnt thus fit into the most plausible theory of the case, and the state soon jailed and charged him with the murder of Frieda Kliem, the thirty-nine-year-old, unmarried seamstress from Berlin.[33]

When she heard about Frieda's death, Antonie Köhler penned a letter Otto Mewes, who was in Locarno, Switzerland, at the time. "Never before in my entire life have I been so shaken," she wrote. "I feel horrible; I always told her she should be careful." She then moved on to the practical matters of dealing with the death of a close friend (contacting Frieda's aunt—"which will be a complete mess since she's so difficult"—and settling Frieda's debts).[34] Should Frieda have been more careful? Was her use of personal ads reckless, wanton, unladylike? Or were personal ads a modern-day necessity, something one did because they were effective or because one had run out of other options?

Frieda's death raised these questions for everyone who knew her. Frieda's friends, her neighbors, and her relatives had no doubt followed the case of Emma Schäfer and her violent death at the hands of a personal ad lurker, but they were now forced to consider the use of personal ads in a startlingly real and personal way. Despite the many similarities between the murders of Emma Schäfer and Frieda Kliem, murders like this were actually quite rare in Berlin, which had a low incidence of violent crime relative to other European metropolises like Paris or London.[35] On the other hand, murder rates in Berlin had been rising sharply since the turn of the century and were, by 1914, at their highest level in many years.[36] Indeed, twelve women were victims of murder or manslaughter in 1900; in 1914 the number was thirty-two.[37] These are small numbers given the massive size of the city, yet this increase was nevertheless enough to put the fear of murder in the hearts of single women and their

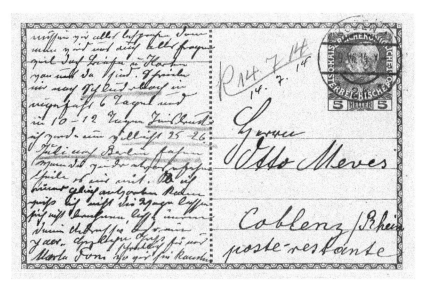

FIGURE 4.13 Antonie Köhler's postcard to Otto Mewes, dated July 14, 1914, address side
Source: Landesarchiv Berlin A Pr. Br. Rep. 030-03, Nr. 1425, Bl. 95.

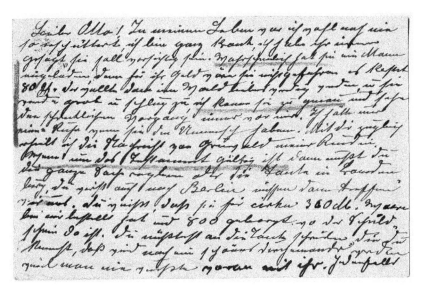

FIGURE 4.14 Antonie Köhler's postcard to Otto Mewes, reverse side
Source: Landesarchiv Berlin A Pr. Br. Rep. 030-03, Nr. 1425, Bl. 95.

families all over Berlin. The inherent riskiness of an unknown rendezvous, not to mention the newspaper ads that often occasioned such encounters, thus colored this path to intimacy in a menacing hue.

The growing popularity of personal ads, moreover, meant that nearly every Berliner knew someone who had used or was using the newspaper to find love or marriage. Accordingly, questions about their use, purpose, and riskiness played out all over Berlin and across all levels of society. At its core, the debate was about emerging and dramatically new technologies of love that aimed at a complete reimagining of the entire system of dating and intimacy. Some aspects of these new innovations no doubt sought to capitalize financially on the problems of isolation, dating, and marriage that pervaded both people's lives; others, though, represented the emergence of a new system of urban encounters that was so practical, so brazenly modern, that it registered more poignantly than ever before the clash between middle-class propriety and the ferocious advance of the modern world.

ON APRIL 8, 1863, Berlin police received a lengthy letter from S. Backhaus, a teacher and bookkeeper who had a rather curious request. With the help of his wife, he wanted to open Berlin's first and only official "Matchmaking Bureau" out of their home in central Berlin.[38] Backhaus knew what he was up against in obtaining permission to open such a business, and he was quick to differentiate his proposed venture from the "so-called marriage bureaus [that] have always been accompanied by at least the appearance of question-able uprightness." Berlin authorities had no interest in permitting these types of "businesses" and were quick to shut down any that attempted to operate in secret, but Backhaus promised that his would be different. For one, the "Matchmaking Bureau" would never serve as a meeting or rendezvous place for men and women and, thus, had nothing in common with brothels or other sites of prostitution. The "Matchmaking Bureau" was also sure to have a great deal of success "particularly in Berlin," Backhaus wrote, because finding a mate was getting harder and harder. "Pure chance does not often enough lead to suitable acquaintances," he continued, and it was as important as ever to find a "path to marriage" that was as "irreproachable" as marriage itself, that "godly and most moral institute." Berlin's elites, especially, lacked other worthy options, according to Backhaus, and the "Matchmaking Bureau" would fill this void with its honorable and straightforward business model. "My wife and I are completely respectable, and I therefore allow myself to hope that I am granted the permission requested." Backhaus included a de-tailed and rather impressive prospectus outlining a file he would keep of men

and women who were looking to get married and then match them according
to their desires and attributes. Nevertheless, the police promptly denied the
request, citing the need to protect "morality" in Berlin. A letter of rebuttal
from Backhaus was similarly unsuccessful, and the lack of any further correspondence about the matter means that Mr. and Mrs. Backhaus either ran
their "Matchmaking Bureau" in secret and without police approval or simply
gave up the idea altogether. In any case, Berlin's first official matchmaking
service never got off the ground.[39]

Still, as Backhaus's request reveals, the police were so bent on preventing
prostitution from gaining a foothold in Berlin that official matchmaking services did not have much of a chance. In fact, this is what makes the Backhaus
request for an official "Matchmaking Bureau" so interesting: it was an attempt to mesh an underground and, in the eyes of the police, subversive practice with middle-class respectability. Mr. and Mrs. Backhaus pointed to their
carefully designed system and numerous safeguards against matchmaking becoming something less reputable, not to mention their own respectability and
clean criminal records, but none of this mattered.

Neither did the fact that matchmaking was supposedly seditious make
a difference to Berliners starting matchmaking services, legal or otherwise,
for these would-be cupids saw a ripe market and a way to make money from
one of the growing metropolis's largest problems. By the turn of the century,
matchmakers had become so numerous that the journalist Paul Kirstein referred to them as an "army." Since established businesses dedicated to matchmaking were basically out of the question, most matchmakers did this work,
he wrote in a 1902 newspaper column, as side careers. So it was that furniture movers and factory workers, insurance agents and tailors earned money
on the side by matching up people (often their own customers) and skim-
ming off a percentage of any applicable dowry.[40] Other writers, too, noted the
prevalence of marriage "middle men" in Berlin, and columnists and writers
alike often chose to make these hobbyist matchmakers the subjects of their
sketches of Berlin life.[41] In most cases, matchmakers come off as itinerant,
somewhat weaselly types, men and mostly women who perhaps sat on park
benches in the Tiergarten or at empty tables in cafés and looked around for
their next prey. The so-called Berlin Observer, the weekly columnist in the
Berliner Lokal-Anzeiger, for example, claimed to have done some covert field
reporting as a way of understanding the methods of Berlin's matchmakers.
A July 1902 column describes his observation of a rather portly woman sitting down innocently next to men on park benches, starting conversations,
and then gradually and stealthily steering the topic to choosing the perfect

mate and her skills, in particular, at doing so for others.[42] Similarly, in Oscar Pitschil's play *Die Heiratsfälle* (*Marriage Cases*), the matchmakers Panse and Lerchenfeld come off as greasy salesmen who care only about closing deals as quickly as possible and increasing their business revenue accordingly. As one man reminds the other, paying off their debts "is the only thing that matters!"[43] Critics likewise hailed the matchmaker in the 1907 performance of Friedrich Smetana's opera *The Bartered Bride* as "a figure of overwhelming comedy."[44]

There were more sympathetic portrayals of matchmakers, to be sure, but these were mostly limited to the informal matchmaking efforts of friends or family members. For example, in C. Weßner's short story "Ein Weiberfeind" ("A Misogynist"), Karl slyly arranges a weekend getaway between his friend, a self-avowed misogynist, and a young woman who does, in fact, melt the friend's cold heart and spur him to propose marriage.[45] Indeed, the advice column of the *Berliner Lokal-Anzeiger* responded to a reader's question about whether the matchmaking business was shady by defending the efforts of the "women who, in their circle of friends, feel obligated to take on this role." "But the whole thing becomes rather distasteful," it continued, "when it is carried out commercially as a source of income for the matchmaker."[46] It was indeed the combination of matchmaking and business that was disreputable, and, on balance, most matchmakers probably hewed closer to the oft-publicized and derided type whose swindles and rip-offs filled the crime sections of Berlin's newspapers.[47]

Of course, it was often not the matchmakers themselves who cheated their customers but rather the men and women—whose ill-fated unions matchmakers cobbled together as quickly as possible so as to profit from their nuptials—who swindled each other. Such cases usually followed the script of the 1901 case of "The man with eight brides," as the headline read, where a man used matchmakers to put him into contact with eight eager brides, whom he then swindled to the tune of DM 25,000.[48] Other times, the line between swindler and agent was blurry, as when would-be swindlers posed as matchmakers and then bilked their clients out of their dowries, savings, or both. In the highly publicized 1905 case against the matchmaking service Veritas, for example, the sixty-three-year-old owner, Ferdinand Gombert, was charged with lying to potential clients, leading them to believe he was using their questionnaires (and accompanying fees) to arrange marriages with his many other wealthy clients, and then disappearing and pocketing his profits. This rather clever method allowed him to ensnare at least forty-three men and women and to make off with over DM 1,000.[49] In his trial, Gombert claimed that the self-proclaimed victims had simply lacked patience and had "jumped off" the business model too soon. He was nevertheless found guilty and sentenced to a lengthy prison sentence. Others would, in later years, follow in his footsteps with similar schemes aimed at getting Berliners to buy into a system that, in truth, did not exist beyond an attractive sales prospectus.[50]

Their bad reputation notwithstanding, matchmakers had, by the first few years of the twentieth century, become a popular tool for Berliners to navigate and imagine metropolitan life. Newspapers ran sketches of quaint little matchmaking bureaus that were opening as cooperatives around Germany, and they described chance encounters at cafés and even mental hospitals using the language of matchmaking.[51] In this last instance, where a doctor at an insane asylum unintentionally played matchmaker between two patients, the *Berliner Morgenpost* caught readers' attention with the headline, "Not a matchmaking bureau."[52] Other cases of fortuitous encounters spun as matchmaking—for example, a traffic accident that ultimately brought the driver into contact with the injured man's wife—were, it seems, attempts to cast the city itself as a sort of matchmaker.[53] For that matter, the *Berliner Lokal-Anzeiger* editors found themselves being asked to become unwitting matchmakers when someone wrote into the advice column requesting the name and address of a teenage girl who had written for advice about kissing a few weeks earlier. "We are not that indiscreet!" the advice columnist balked. "As a matter of principle, we do not engage in matchmaking between the people who write to us for advice."[54]

Matchmaking became so widespread that Berlin authorities eventually developed a set of laws to regulate it. And while the rules about fees and percentages remained confusing enough that the advice columns of Berlin newspapers were filled with questions—from clients and matchmakers alike—about what was legal and what was not, the machine of matchmaking gradually began to run more smoothly.[55] To be sure, there were still people like Margarethe Bornstein, who repeatedly tried to open legitimate matchmaking offices but were turned down by the police, but there were many more who succeeded in running their own full-time matchmaking businesses.[56]

Matchmaking, in some form or another, had naturally existed for centuries, but narratives of matchmaking in Berlin around 1900 reworked existing tropes of love into something more practical and modern, not to mention something for more or less all Berliners.[57] Matchmaking was a direct response to Berliners' obsession with fortuitous encounters and love at last sight, a rejection of the chasm between imagined love and all-too-real loneliness and isolation. The Backhauses observed unromantically the fact that "fate" only rarely brought compatible couples together; and one news article about a freelance—or nonlicensed—matchmaker made sure to point out in her sales pitch to potential customers that she could arrange a "coincidental" meeting with the man or woman of their liking.[58] An exposé on matchmakers similarly observed dryly that "love at first sight" is rare and that most successful matches are the result of careful, calculated matchmaking efforts.[59] This was very different from the faith so many Berliners put in Cupid's arrows and the possibility that their soulmate might be walking down the street next to them, and it is interesting that the idea of waiting for that same chance was now considered impractical, even if its allure was so powerful that matchmakers still used the idea of fortuitous encounters to market their services.[60]

More importantly, there is evidence that matchmakers actually provided a useful service to Berliners who were otherwise struggling to make connections in the big city. Berliners who made use of matchmaking services were, as a short story suggested, both happier and, crucially, more modern. Indeed, Hermann Heinrich's 1902 short story "Furcht vor der Ehe" ("Fear of Marriage") features an aging bachelor professor who never married but who, through the ostensibly "fortuitous" but actually carefully orchestrated occasion of a dinner evening with friends, meets the thirty-something, old-maid "aunt" Julchen, who enchants him and causes him to abandon his aversion to marriage. The joy he experiences in his newfound love cures his long-standing health problems, and he even starts to dress stylishly and use mustache wax, a quintessentially modern grooming technology.[61] This brazenly intentional matchmaking, joked about by the matchmakers as "fate," brings even the most hardened of bachelors—not to mention the old-maid "aunt"—to embrace love, intimacy, and "modern" life.

Critics of matchmakers objected to what they saw as an overemphasis on practicality and argued that this often came at the expense of creating true love matches.[62] Historians, too, have generally positioned matchmaking (i.e., "arranged" marriages) as opposite to or wholly different from so-called love marriages.[63] On the other hand, matchmakers believed that modern life rendered this continuum, this binary of arranged and love, outdated and irrelevant; as they put it, the reality of the modern world required one to be practical, to know from the outset where one stood financially, and to make decisions about marriage accordingly. "Matchmaking institutes have in modern life become a social requirement," Fritz Podszus, owner of a mammoth matchmaking firm (allegedly Germany's largest and oldest), argued. "[It] is a characteristic symptom of our time, one that no cultural historian will be able to ignore."[64] Hans Ringlau, who worked for

Podszus, argued in the company's promotional material that smart people use a matchmaking service because it saves them the "embarrassing question" of their financial readiness for marriage. Matchmaking services, he continued, do not try to make decisions of the heart for their clients, for it remains "up to them to search for the answer to the most important question as to whether their characters are right together and whether each other's cultural style, views, and approach to life match their long-held expectations."[65] Matchmaking services thus packaged their services as practical necessities in a turbulent, busy, and financially precarious modern world.

Another pitch for Podszus's company presents Theodor—the author's "family doctor"—whose medical training has taken a very long time, leaving him little opportunity "to take part in society and see if he couldn't perhaps find a wife who would make him happy." But Theodor is not interested in the services of a matchmaker, and he tells the author that "having a wife selected for you by a matchmaker demeans and cheapens marriage. . . . If I get married at all, I will only marry a woman I have found on my own and only after I am convinced that our life together will make us both happy." The author and salesman naturally has a response ready: a matchmaker only sets you up with a group of women who want to get married. It is still up to the client to pick one who "fulfills the desires of the head as well as the heart." Theodor brings up the frequent swindles and the disreputable practices of sleazy matchmakers, but the salesman retorts, "You can't throw out all solid, respectable matchmakers just because of a few crazy women." Theodor's final resistance is to argue that he has "such a high, noble opinion of marriage" that he would never want to connect it to anything having to do with business or money, and here the salesman reaches his closing argument in stride:

> We are in complete agreement, especially when you consider the fact that no one is going to ask to you get married except when your heart has spoken. Consider further that marriage, in addition to its ideal nature, also has a legal and financial side. . . . I advise you not to wait until an extraordinary fortune falls into your lap. . . . For that you're too old, [and] you've had as little opportunity to meet enough women on your own as I did. So take the services of a specialist.[66]

Matchmakers, especially matchmaking services, bureaus, and so-called institutes, thus presented themselves as professional problem-solvers, experts who understood that modern metropolitans had neither time

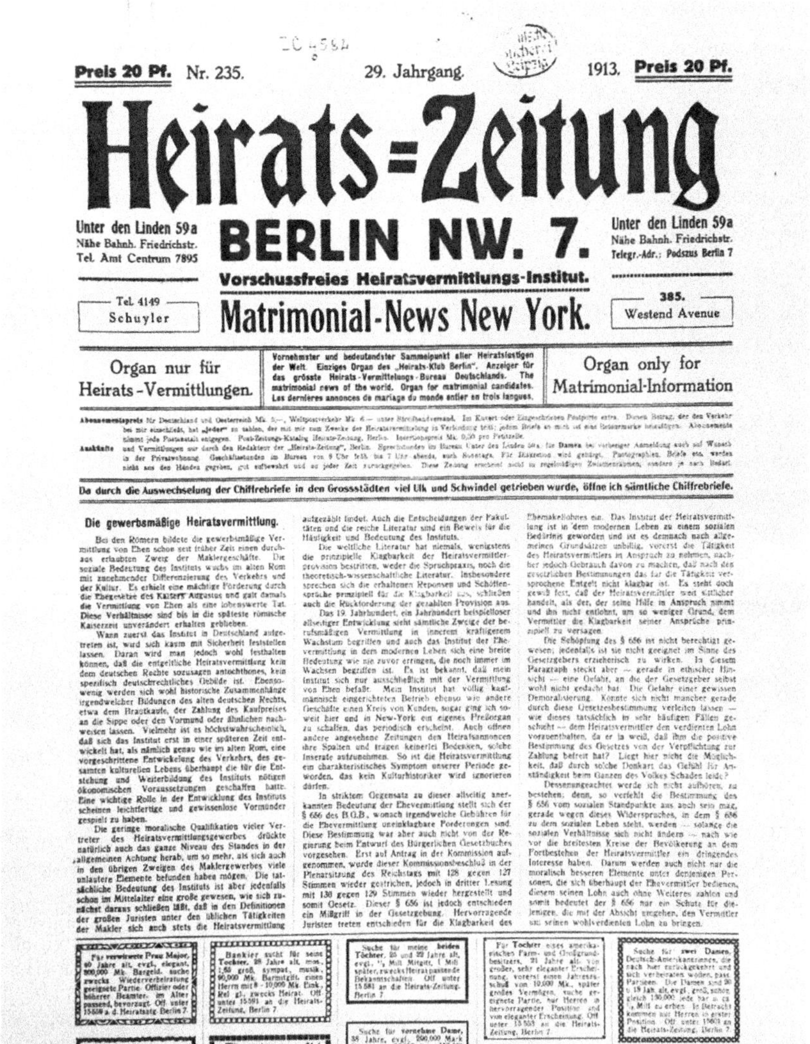

FIGURE 4.15 Fritz Podzsus's *Heirats-Zeitung*, published in New York under the title *Matrimonial-News*, 1913

Source: *Heirats-Zeitung* 29, no. 235 (1913), 1.

nor money to meet the old-fashioned way and whose carefully designed systems, metrics, and databases could be relied upon for a successful trip to the altar. Indeed, as another matchmaking service advertised, "The changing realities in our current go-getting time have created a variety of new institutions [that allow one to] attain a goal quickly and directly. An honest marriage institute counts among the most important of these conveniences." This particular owner then cited her "refined understanding, tactfulness, and tenacity," pointed to her "unique system," and, instead of asking for three easy payments, noted that she ran her business solely on "free-will donations" by happy customers.[67]

THERE IS NO record of how long this woman's "pay as you like" matchmaking service lasted, but its existence underscores the fact that, because of what lawmakers saw as a slippery slope between matchmaking and prostitution, matchmakers were forced to operate within fairly narrow legal boundaries. Offering one's services as a matchmaker exposed her to a degree of risk and liability, not least because matchmakers had such a poor reputation. For that matter, there were also risks involved in using a matchmaker to find love or marriage or both, not only because one might get swindled, but also because it meant going public with one's loneliness, one's desperation at finding someone, one's failure to make the traditional methods work. There was something embarrassing and slightly distasteful about handing over control of one's intimate future to a stranger. On the other hand, not a few Berliners reached the point where the traditional methods had not worked and where they grew willing to employ other means of finding a mate. If only there were a way to preserve the anonymity, the respectability of that loneliness while, at the same time, working against it!

This, it seems, is the best way of situating and understanding the rise of newspaper personal ads as a modern technology of love.[68] Personal ads were already well over a century old, but, until the late 1890s and early 1900s, they remained an obscure and mostly ignored method of finding love that was so rare that Berlin police suspected they were nothing more than advertisements for prostitution and investigated individual ads to determine whether the author should be punished. Indeed, when Berlin's mayor became of aware of a personal ad in the June 17, 1837, edition of the *Berliner Intelligenz-Blatt*, he sent a copy to the chief of police and asked him to consider training the attention of the police's censorship office on what he feared was a growing problem. "[Such ads] make it nearly impossible," he wrote, "for a father to be able to read newspapers to his children."[69] This may have been an overreaction, but the ad indicates why Mayor Baerwald was so troubled:

> The respectable gentlewoman, who, in responding to the ad from Saturday, wished to rendezvous on Tuesday at 6:00 p.m. at the agreed-upon place in front of the Brandenburg Gate, is asked sincerely to suggest another because it was impossible for the sender to appear.[70]

Berliners were using the pages of a respectable Berlin newspaper to set up their amorous rendezvouses, and while the language was completely aboveboard and chaste, it smacked too much of love for sale. The chief of police did nothing about the ad in question, but the police did continue to monitor Berlin's few newspapers for any particularly seditious or offensive ads.[71] Thirteen years later, the police file that contained these letters back and forth between the mayor, the chief of police, and the Ministry of the Interior was reopened to include several new ads of interest to the police. This time, the police actually took action, probably because the author of the ad was so brazen in his search for love, intimacy, or sex:

> A young, independent, respectable man yearns to start a liaison with a young woman, married or not. He only wishes not to receive less than he offers. Interested gentlewomen are asked to arrange the details via the address A. D. Z.[72]

Once the police located the "young, independent, respectable man," they fined him fifty thaler, despite his unconvincing protestations that he had written the ad for someone else.[73]

Interestingly enough, the man's ad was sandwiched between one placed by a Berliner looking to marry any widow who was emigrating to America and another apologizing "a thousand times" for missing a rendezvous with the author of an ad titled "Je vous salue, Mademoiselle!," but the police seemed content to leave these authors unmolested.[74] Police and mayoral interest in individual personal ads is nevertheless striking, for it points to the fact that personal ads existed and were perhaps even growing more popular in the nineteenth century but remained on the periphery of Berlin life.[75] Of course, it is possible that ads might have exploded earlier than they did, or that the need for that particular technology of love already existed in the 1850s. But personal ads relied on newspapers, and these did not take off in Berlin until the very late nineteenth century. Papers like the *Berliner Intelligenz-Blatt* existed, but their readership was small and their distribution extremely limited.[76] Classified sections in newspapers of the 1870s and 1880s—compared with those of the first two decades of the twentieth century—show that marriage ads were not terribly common and certainly not as ubiquitous as they would become a generation later.

The Berliners who snatched up daily newspapers and made them such a vital part of the city were, if not using ads themselves, completely fascinated by them and found them impossible to overlook. An 1899 piece about what Berliners read when they sat in cafés, for example, observed that while most readers were interested in politics and economics, even those who craved only this serious fodder "naturally read the ads, too."[77] Max Pollaczek's article a year later attempted to document the variety of ways in which Berliners read the newspapers. There were those who went through the paper systematically from front to back, others who "snacked" on various parts of it, and still others—women, he said—who, no matter what, went straight for the engagement announcement section of the ads and only then turned to the feuilleton ("especially the serial novel") and local news, in that order.[78] When the *Berliner Morgenpost* described the sights and sounds of life on the famous Friedrichstrasse in a sketch in 1901, it could not help but include the shouts of a street vendor hawking "the *Heirats-Zeitung*! Organ for all who want to marry rich and happy!"[79] In a telling anecdote from Berlin nightlife, the *Berliner Lokal-Anzeiger* reported on a masquerade ball put on by the Society of the Deaf and took special care to describe the most interesting costume: someone came dressed as a Litfaßsäule—one of the immensely popular advertising pillars that stood on most street corners throughout Berlin. "[The costume pillar] is covered from top to bottom with interesting ads," Maximilian Wolff described. "Everyone surrounds it, everyone wants to study the ads."[80]

Berliners consumed personal ads by the thousands. They were cut out, circled, and passed along to others, and many of the surviving copies of the turn-of-the-century newspapers display the telltale marks of their ads having been read and cut out. The few Berliners who were not reading ads found themselves hounded by newspaper columnists exhorting them to be sure to do so. Max Pollaczek, in his piece on how Berliners read newspapers, asserted that the ads were far more interesting than anything else in the entire newspaper—"for thoughtful readers, at least." "What's in the ads section," he wrote, "is real life." "The social relationships of the population play out with extreme fidelity in the columns of the ads," he continued, "and whoever has a bit of fantasy could form from two-, three-, and four-lined ads a novel more striking and gripping than any bit of fiction—and it would hold very close to the truth."[81] The *Berliner Lokal-Anzeiger*'s weekly columnist, the Berlin Observer, penned several similarly rhapsodic columns on the personal ads and called them a piece of Berlin cultural history worth reading, studying, analyzing, and appreciating. "Nearly every ad," he wrote, "forms a note in this symphony [of life]."[82] People now browse newspapers, he wrote in 1910, only for the special announcements and the ads. Most telling of all was the fact that "other than the news," even he—the public voice of the newspaper editors—counted the ads "as the most important page of the newspaper."[83]

Literature, too, shows Berliners devouring ads. For example, in Rudolf Hirschberg-Jura's short story "Ein Zeitungsausschnitt" ("A Newspaper Snippet"), the protagonist, while going about his morning routine of eating breakfast and reading the newspaper, notices immediately that someone has cut an ad out of his paper. "By habit his eyes glanced over the ads, when suddenly his attention was grabbed by a nothingness, to wit, an empty, square, cut-out place in the middle of that most beloved column in which the marriage ads, box-number greetings, and anonymous escapades are all gathered together."[84] Personal ads also made their way into the theater, as in Rudolf Schwarz's 1909 comedy, *Liebesleute* (*Lovers*), which showed Berliners reading ads, even if, in this case, the sheer volume of ads could be frustrating. "Nine—ten—eleven sections and nothing but ads!" exclaims the cantankerous father of a young man who has just written an ad.[85] There was also Richard Kessler and A. Stein's comedy *Die Heiratsannonce* (*The Personal Ad*), where Annchen thwarts her father's attempt to marry her off through a personal ad by intercepting the responses and disguising her country-bumpkin boyfriend, "Bummel," as the refined, monocle-wearing cavalier her father had selected for her.[86]

Turn-of-the-century literature also reveals countless Berliners not just reading but actually using ads. The Berlin novelist Dora Duncker wrote a lengthy collection of short stories that each started with a personal ad and then imagined the responses and experiences the author enjoyed because of it.[87] Karl Escher's 1911 short story "Die Verlobungseiche" ("The Engagement Oak") features Anny, who has just had a fight with her fiancé and decides to post a personal ad saying she wants to get married and will be walking by a well-known oak tree on Easter Sunday. As it happens, there is beautiful weather on Easter and many people are out walking. The dozens of men who show up to meet the eager young bride end up finding mates in the women who have unwittingly made their way to the rendezvous point. Anny's fiancé shows up, as well, and the two use the opportunity to patch things up.[88] In

FIGURE 4.16 One of the many pages of ads that are riddled with holes

Source: Berliner Lokal-Anzeiger, March 16, 1906, Nr. 137, accessed via microfilm at the Zentral- und Landesbibliothek Berlin.

still another story, Martha, a woman entering her forties still unmarried, decides she will post a personal ad and try to find her own bit of happiness. From the responses she receives, she selects that of Friedrich Müller, whose letter seems very proper and lacks spelling and typographical errors. When they finally meet at Aschinger's on Alexanderplatz, she falls for him immediately and accepts his marriage proposal, only to discover too late that he has been swindling her of her modest but hard-earned savings.[89]

Even commercial advertisers seized on the popularity of personal ads. Paul Burow's furniture store, for example, regularly ran advertisements that made use of a clever pun on the word *Ehe* (both "marriage" and the preposition "before"): "Before you buy furniture, take a look at Paul Burow's furniture shop." Placed near the engagement announcements and designed to look like a personal ad, these advertisements were meant to catch the eyes of those looking for love.[90] There was also the news story of the businessman who wanted to jump-start his new venture, a café, and decided to use the personal ads to do so. He posted two ads in the newspaper, one as the daughter of a factory owner looking to find a husband, the other as a wealthy bachelor finally ready to get married, and answered the many responses he received by arranging a rendezvous at his very own café on the day of its grand opening. Needless to say, dozens of Berliners came to the café that afternoon with hopes of meeting their dream spouses, only to find that the whole thing had been a ruse meant to drum up business. The *Berliner Morgenpost*'s report of the spectacle nevertheless mused that "perhaps a few hearts did actually find each other while they were waiting; perhaps some of the men decided they could live without the [rich] father-in-law, the women without the sizable wealth of their future husband, and were content with the attainable." The café owner, in any case, did a booming business that day.[91] Not surprisingly, the *Berliner Morgenpost* ran a fictional retelling of the event a few years later, though in this case the café owner decided to repeat his ploy each night. Consequently, the café grew into a rather popular locale for single Berliners looking to get married—a "marriage café."[92]

By 1901, personal ads had established such a critical mass among classifieds, more generally, that newspapers felt the need to create an entire section for "marriages" alongside jobs for men, jobs for women, housing, services, items for sale, and so on.[93] There was no single "type" of Berliner who used personal ads, and a quick glance through the thousands upon thousands of ads reveals ads from every class, confession, background, and financial situation.[94] Men generally wrote more ads than women (at a rate of two to one), and most ads were written by Berliners in their early thirties.[95] Posting an ad was easy and

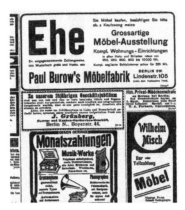

FIGURE 4.17 Paul Burow's clever use of a convenient pun as a way to move some product
Source: Berliner Lokal-Anzeiger, March 11, 1905, Nr. 119.

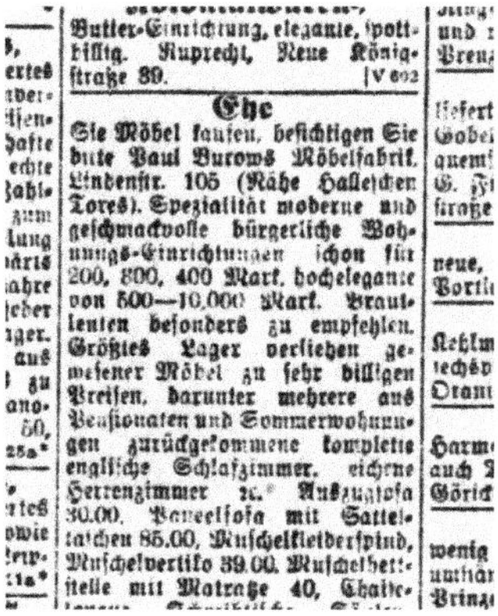

Butter-Einrichtung, elegante, spottbillig. Ruprecht, Neue Königstraße 89. V 692

Ehe

Sie Möbel kaufen, besichtigen Sie bitte Paul Burows Möbelfabrik, Lindenstr. 105 (Nähe Halleschen Tores). Spezialität moderne und geschmackvolle bürgerliche Wohnungs-Einrichtungen schon für 200, 800, 400 Mark, hochelegante von 500—10,000 Mark. Brautleuten besonders zu empfehlen. Größtes Lager verliehen gewesener Möbel zu sehr billigen Preisen, darunter mehrere aus Pensionaten und Sommerwohnungen zurückgekommene komplette englische Schlafzimmer, eichene Herrenzimmer ꝛc. Auszugsofa 30.00, Paneelsofa mit Satteltaschen 85.00, Muschelkleiderspind, Muschelvertiko 39.00, Muschelbettstelle mit Matratze 40, Chaise-

FIGURE 4.18 Another example of Paul Burow's punning
Source: Berliner Lokal-Anzeiger, January 11, 1906, Nr. 18.

was relatively anonymous, but it was not free. Most newspapers charged by the word. The *Berliner Lokal-Anzeiger*, for example, charged fifteen pfennigs per word, as did the *Berliner Morgenpost* and the *Berliner Tageblatt*. Bolded titles cost an extra forty to fifty pfennigs, depending on the paper, and words with more than fifteen letters counted double. The average personal ad ran about twenty-five words and, in most cases, required a title, which meant that one commonly paid just over DM 4 for an ad. This was no small sum for single Berliners. Frieda Kliem's ad, for example, which ran just thirteen words, would have cost her DM 2.35, which represented a rather sizable portion of her meager DM 30 monthly income. Some ads were much longer—the one directly below Frieda's would have cost the "well-situated gentleman" who wrote it over DM 14—and many ads appeared several days in a row (or longer).[96] These costs added up, and there was thus a practical limit on the extent to which one could make use of them, depending on her financial situation.

Ads usually followed a pattern of listing one's basic attributes— approximate age, profession, and a cryptic statement about wealth—and then specifying the corresponding qualities of the desired mate.[97] But each ad was different. Some listed a religious affiliation (or lack thereof), though the relative infrequency of this information suggests that confession was perhaps no longer so central (or, inasmuch as ads were billed by word count, economical) in the search for love in the modern city;[98] others explained their particular plight (typically a lack of family connections or opportunity) and justified why they had decided to use "this no longer uncommon method" to find a spouse; still others cited very specific traits they were looking for, often a special domestic skill, a preferred hair color, or, most commonly, especially in ads written by men, a level of savings or income that had to be present. This last bit was particularly frustrating to the many Berliners who quite simply did not have any money, as one woman lamented to her fellow newspaper readers. The woman mentioned ads most of whose requirements she met ("honorable, loving, thrifty") but was finally excluded by "because I don't have any 'assets.' It's surely the same for many others, too." "Should we all become old maids?" she asked.[99] Her letter set off such a firestorm of similar letters to the *Berliner Lokal-Anzeiger* that the editors, who kept trying to stop the debate, finally, after over a month of argument, told readers that they would throw any additional responses in the garbage.[100]

The proviso of "assets" was particularly frustrating for women, for while men and women largely wrote similar ads, women, as Joachim Werner concluded in his 1908 study of several thousand personal ads in Berlin newspapers, rarely requested savings but nearly always referred to their own, if they had any.[101] Men, on the other hand, usually requested savings but often did not reveal how much they had.[102] As statistician F. Bartholomäi put it cleverly in his 1874 study of ads: whereas men on average "offered" 34,959 thaler (of their own wealth) and demanded 15,963, women offered 16,383 thaler and demanded practically nothing.[103]

There were other differences, too, things men and women each tended to emphasize. Women, as the columnist Dorothee Goebeler complained after she had helped a man go through some 263 responses to an ad he had posted, all emphasized their "inner life," which she derided as simply a meaningless "fad," a poor substitute for real, genuine expressions of personality and intellect. "Women of the twentieth century" nevertheless all advertise it, she wrote, from the teenager to the mother with grown children, the telephone operator to the rich, for "it is for the soul what the slit skirt was for the leg . . . : the latest novelty!"[104]

Men, too, had their go-to lines, the most popular of which mentioned "discretion" and "honor." Nearly all men closed their ads with the assurance that "discretion is a matter of honor," which, especially when they were also requesting a photograph (as most did), was apparently meant to guarantee respondents that they would not expose them for having used personal ads. They also quite frequently wrote that "anonymity is pointless" (or simply "no anonymity"), as one woman protested in a 1908 reader letter to the *Berliner Lokal-Anzeiger*. "Why do men insist on this condition?" she asked, arguing that such stipulations only delegitimized the entire medium of the personal ad. "A woman from [better] circles and, in my opinion, such a man, too, cannot simply throw about her name by immediately providing it to an anonymous ad."[105] This, of course, was the inherent risk of personal ads, and the focus on inner life, discretion, honor, and the most common personal ad term of all, respectability, says a lot about the nature of this emerging technology of love. Personal ads were without a doubt becoming a prominent part of the modern metropolis, but, their popularity notwithstanding, they stood in tension with dominant middle-class respectability.

BERLINERS WHO CONSIDERED posting personal ads had to weigh the considerable costs to their reputation against the potential benefits. For one, there was the problem of anonymity. Women, who were so often required to send photographs along with their responses to anonymous ads, faced the potential embarrassment of having those pictures made public if the correspondence never amounted to anything. One distraught woman wrote for advice to the *Berliner Lokal-Anzeiger* about how to get her photograph back, and the response she received can hardly have been very comforting. "Try to get the name of the person behind the ad to whom you sent your photograph with a request to the newspaper delivery office," the advice columnist wrote. "Once you have that, demand your photograph back. You may ultimately have to go to the police."[106] Picking up the responses to one's own ads often proved difficult, too, as the editors of the *Berliner Lokal-Anzeiger* acknowledged in response to a letter written by a woman complaining that someone had picked up all of the responses her ad had generated. "[This kind of thing] is unfortunately a very common occurrence," the editors acknowledged, noting that the delivery office was not required to verify people's identities when picking up responses. Some Berliners had apparently taken to ripping a numbered streetcar ticket in half, including one half with the ad order, and requesting that the delivery office require the person picking up the responses to show the other half—but "this doesn't always help," they admitted.[107] Indeed, the delivery office workers themselves were often dishonest and used their access to names and ads for devious ends, as happened in a 1902 case.[108] Swindlers used ads, as well, and even those Berliners who were especially cautious about revealing anything about savings and valuables or rendezvousing with the respondents all too often found themselves bamboozled, blackmailed, or worse, like Emma Schäfer and Frieda Kliem.[109]

Information about Berliners using ads, however it was obtained, was potentially very damaging, especially to those in positions of prominence. Count Paul von Hoensbroech, a writer, public figure, and former priest who rose to prominence after a very public exit from the Jesuit order, discovered this painful truth in what was probably the most publicized, sensational case involving personal ads before World War I. The count was named the defendant in a highly charged civil case brought by a matchmaker—a Polish man by the name of L. Pokorny—claiming that von Hoensbroech had used his services and then refused to pay. In and of itself, this was hardly front-page news, for matchmakers and their clients were frequently in court bickering about whether one had paid or swindled the other. Indeed, Fritz Podszus, the owner of Berlin's largest matchmaking service and publisher of the personal-ad-only newspaper *Die Heirats-Zeitung / Matrimonial-News*, published in both Berlin and New York, was involved in quite a few court cases at the turn of the century.[110] This case was different, though, because von Hoensbroech's respectability as a public and religious figure was beyond reproach, and he had been caught posting a personal ad. Once the ad was discovered, he repeatedly denied that he had ever published one. Even when both the police and newspapers got hold of the ad and reprinted it, von Hoensbroech stuck to his story, which sounded less convincing each time he told it. The ad itself, which ran in the *Berliner Tageblatt* in 1894, was not particularly damning, though parts of it were perhaps embarrassing:

> **Marriage**. A German cavalier from the high nobility, 40 years old, very distinguished and nice appearance, impeccable past, meager savings but completely free of debt, wishes to marry a rich woman

of any confession so long as she has an enlightened religiosity. Any sort of matchmaking—other than by her parents or guardians, is out of the question: anonymous replies will not be considered. Seeker plays a prominent role in political life and is in every way capable of establishing a happy family life. Responses are asked under K. 1687 on the delivery office of this newspaper, Berlin SW. Utmost discretion is a matter of honor.[111]

Count von Hoensbroech may have been a little too eager to cover up his use of a personal ad, and his attempts to explain it only fanned the flames even further. Von Hoensbroech was the editor of Berlin's *Tägliche Rundschau*, a relatively small daily newspaper, and he used his editorial power to publish several statements in the paper that repeated his innocence and claimed he could not talk about the case for reasons "that, as they have to do with my religious past, are subject to my oath of priestly secrecy, which I consider inviolable."[112] When pressed further, von Hoensbroech revealed that he had paid Pokorny a small sum so that he might "just have a little peace" and be rid of the "intrigue" against him, but he continued to stay silent about a variety of embarrassing letters that had been published and that showed him reminding the matchmaker about his various language skills and the fact that he had been given important tasks by the kaiser himself. "It is not necessary for me to give a statement as to the authenticity or inauthenticity of the letters, and for obvious reasons," he wrote in another piece in the *Tägliche Rundschau*.[113] The case might again have faded away, but von Hoensbroech seemingly could not help himself from commenting on it further. He remained evasive about the personal ad and even claimed in his memoir that the whole thing had been a setup, a ploy by the ultramontanists meant to punish him for leaving the Jesuits and joining the Protestant church.[114] In a later trial, Pokorny announced he could prove that von Hoensbroech had written the ad himself, but the entire case was dismissed because of the statute of limitations.[115] From then on, Count Paul von Hoensbroech slowly faded from prominence, and one of his final flashes of relevance came in a news article reporting on a lecture he gave that had to be broken up because members of the audience were throwing rotten eggs and beer steins at him.[116]

Somewhere along the way, the von Hoensbroech scandal may have become more about the spectacle itself than the revelation that a prominent Berliner and political friend of the kaiser had used a personal ad, but the incident nevertheless points to the fact that the use of personal ads and matchmakers carried significant risk. Placing an ad was not illegal, but it brushed up against the boundaries of what respectable, discreet, middle-class Berliners did, no matter how much each ad writer claimed to possess these same qualities.[117] "Looking for a husband or wife with a personal ad," Hans T., a Berlin postal worker wrote in 1911, "is still counted by many as a little indecent." When they told others how they met their spouses, he wrote, users of personal ads generally received "an ironic, somewhat disdainful smile."[118] Indeed, when a man posing as a German lieutenant in his ads was revealed to be nothing more than a swindler, the newspaper remarked that "readers of the ad should have known that a member of our officer corps would never write an ad of this sort."[119] Others observed that, in general, the problem with personal ads was that they conflicted with "good morals" and had "too much of a businesslike character" with their sterile, "cold words" and stipulations about money.[120] This was essentially the response of Helene Kuërs's boss, Friedrich, when she suggested that he use personal ads to find a wife. "[He said] these ways of finding a wife didn't suit him," she wrote in her diary.[121] Ida Susemaus, the staid, traditional aunt who represents "old Berlin" in Leo Leipziger's *Der Rettungsball* (*The Rescue Ball*), similarly gets upset when another character jokes that Ida reminds her of someone who would write a personal ad.[122] There was even a hint of unmanliness in writing ads. When Annchen's father tries to marry her off by using a personal ad in the 1910 play *Die Heiratsannonce* (*The Personal Ad*), his wife chastises him, saying, "If you were a man, you wouldn't need an ad to get our child married. But you're not one."[123] Bartholomäi, the statistician, himself could not resist the jab that many ads were plainly pathetic, depraved, and, for men, embarrassingly unmanly. Noting that a good half of ads were written by "businessmen [and businesswomen]," he opined that "neither figure reflects particularly well on the respective social classes." Reading them "makes one a feel a little uneasy," he wrote.[124]

Personal ads struck Berliners as an affront to the idea that "marriage is made in heaven," as they so often liked to say.[125] For women, advertising for love was too easily linked to selling sex. The related conflation of men advertising for love and men buying love, sex, and intimacy from prostitutes rarely seems to have been made, however, and women found themselves confronted with this double standard at every turn.

Yet thousands of men and women used personal ads each month, so there was clearly something that made them worth the risk, worth the cost of flouting the marriage idealism and general aura of respectability that was so compelling for most Berliners. On some level, the use of personal ads was motivated by the modern sensibility regarding love and dating whereby men and women, mostly in their late teens and twenties, embraced fortuitous encounters, sports, dancing, and the workplace as legitimate avenues to connection and intimacy. Personal ads were, in this sense, yet another modern method that Berliners used because it offered some measure of success—however defined—where traditional approaches did not.

But personal ads were different in a number of quite revolutionary ways. Most interesting is perhaps their use by middle-class gay Berliners, who found in personal ads a detour around a legal system and a variety of public prejudices that normally made love and dating so difficult. Gay Berliners of the working class could regularly gather in Berlin's numerous gay bars and mingle without fear of being discovered by authorities.[126] But, as Magnus Hirschfeld pointed out in a 1904 article, "the vast majority" of gay Berliners lived "completely withdrawn, and even those who did attempt to find others (or even take part in a sort of ad hoc matchmaking service) in the bars, cigarette stores, and private lofts often found those places discovered by authorities and their usefulness thus destroyed.[127]

The beauty of gay personal ads was that they could be written relatively anonymously and in coded language such that one had a legitimate shot at finding a "like-minded" (as the phrase went) man or woman and avoiding much of the risk associated with semipublic meetings or casual rendezvouses in places like the Tiergarten and the Kaiser-Passage shopping area. Aware that ads that were potentially offensive could be investigated by police, gay Berliners took steps to camouflage their ads such that they might blend in to the sea of ads filling the newspapers. Paul Näcke, a Berlin sexual scientist, observed as much in his 1902 study of gay personal ads in Berlin newspapers, noting that most said as little as possible that might make them stand out.[128] Näcke noticed that more gay ads mentioned modern activities—bicycling and sports—than was otherwise common, but "[they] have to be similar to [the others] so as not to offend."[129] One did, however, have to leave some clues in the ad so as to find the right partner, and here the term "like-minded"— or "correspondence with the like-minded"—was most useful, for it had little meaning except to "those in the know." Other common terms were "modern," which was at once innocuous and otherwise rare, as well as "lonely" and "energetic." More risky hints included a handful of Latin codes ("Sappho," "Antinous," or "Uranus") and rather overt references to "decadence."[130] Näcke identified the following ads making use of this coded language:

> **Looking for a girlfriend**. Young woman, mosaic, 18 years old, from respectable family, who lacks friends, would like to meet a similar young woman.

A man from the better circles wishes to meet **a bicycle partner**.

Bicyclist, businesswoman, 25, looking for connection to women for short excursions. Letters under number "69."

Young, intelligent man looking for **colleague**. Letters requested under "Lonely."

Married, energetic woman wishes to start friendly interaction with married, well-situated women since husband is often away.

Decadent, hypermodern naturalist young man wishes . . . to start correspondence with thoughtful, distinguished gentleman.

Educated Christian (22) looking for interaction with freethinking, debonair women. Letters treated with discretion . . . .

Looking for a **friend**. Intelligent gentleman looking for intelligent, like-minded friend.

Many-sided, educated young woman wishes to start correspondence with those like-minded.[131]

These, according to Näcke, had been printed in various Berlin newspapers in the 1890s, and he estimated that there were many hundreds more.[132] Of course, there were also gay journals and newsletters—for example, Adolf Brand's literary magazine *Der Eigene*—that printed ads, as well. While gay publications were constantly being shut down and censored, they also allowed gay Berliners to be slightly more specific about the type of partner they wanted to find. This holds up based on just two ads from the back of a 1904 issue of *Der Eigene*:

Student, from the best circles, raised in the spirit of antiquity, manifold artistic interests, wishes to start a correspondence with a like-minded fellow student. . . . Letters under "Hellas" to the editors of [*Der Eigene*].

Aristocrat, young, belonging to the oldest noble family of Hungary, independent but bound by the free development of his inner nature by social circumstances, inspired by upstanding sympathies and passionate love for the beauty of nature and art, is looking for connection to a like-minded person as a travel partner, friend, secretary, or reader. . . . Letters under "Byron" to the editors of [*Der Eigene*]. Discretion a matter of honor![133]

The trouble and risk involved in this relatively safe method of finding gay love highlights how difficult it was to form same-sex relationships at the turn of the century, even in what was surely Europe's most gay-friendly city.[134] Still, the fact that so many wrote ads speaks to the promise of personal ads as a way to escape urban isolation.[135] In fact, it might make sense to consider personal ads as the middle-class equivalent of the gay bar, for not only did authors of ads usually cite their isolation, they also sought not casual sex or fleeting intimacy but long-term, stable relationships, which is precisely what both Hirschfeld and Näcke found in their visits to Berlin's numerous working-class gay bars.[136] Personal ads were for middle-class gay Berliners thus an advanced, easier, safer, and essential method of making connections, and, at the turn of the century, they were beginning a steady climb to popularity.[137]

Personal ads were also revolutionary because they promised a complete reimagining of the entire system of meeting potential partners and making decisions about marriage. They transformed the fortuitous encounter from a chaste fantasy, a risky promiscuity, and a marketing tool for matchmakers to a relatively straightforward—if still somewhat unlikely—possibility. In other words, the technology of personal ads convinced Berliners that they just might be a single ad away from seeing "love at last sight" once again. But this was different from the stylized, newsprint obsession with fortuitous encounters, for these missed connections were real and used without ceremony or flourish.

The experiences of Fritz Reinert are revealing in this regard, for Fritz was one of the many Berliners who used personal ads to make a missed connection. Fritz came as a teenager to Berlin in 1902 to take in the sights and sounds of the city but also to train as a printmaker for a year or so before returning to his native Glogau in far eastern Prussia.[138] When he was not working, Fritz indulged in Berlin's myriad nightlife offerings and nearly always ended his evenings playing billiards with his friend Otto at Hering's bar. One Sunday in the late fall of 1902, Fritz and Otto were wandering around the city when two "exquisitely beautiful" young women passed them on their bicycles as they headed toward the popular Schildhorn area of the Grunewald forest. "We smiled at each other. Otto and I were totally flustered," Fritz wrote in his diary that evening, and when they had climbed to the top of the so-called Dachberg hill, they were thrilled to see the two women sitting there as well. "We sat near them," but it soon grew chilly and the ladies moved to the nearby colonnade where there was less wind. Fritz and Otto eventually got up and walked back to the Grunewald train station, but they quickly realized that they "had fallen in love with the girls. We argued with each other as to why we hadn't sat down with them. We talked about them the rest of the day. Since we will probably never see them again, we were really sad."[139] When he woke up the following morning, his "first thoughts were on the two girls," and Fritz

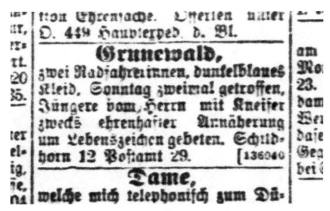

FIGURE 4.19 Fritz Reinert's attempt at making a missed connection
Source: Berliner Lokal-Anzeiger, October 19, 1902, Nr. 491.

wrote that he was unable to get them out of his head the entire day.[140] So, after work the next day, Fritz went straight to the main office of the *Berliner Lokal-Anzeiger* and paid for the following ad:

> **Grunewald**, 2 bicycle riders, dark blue dress, met twice on Sunday, the gentleman with the pince-nez asks the younger for a sign of life for the purpose of an honorable meeting. Schildhorn 12 Post Office 29.

Buying the ad "felt a little strange," Fritz wrote that evening. "That little bit of fun cost me 3.70 Mk. I did it mainly for fun and don't really expect any answer."[141]

Imagine Fritz's surprise when, after work the next day, he stopped by Post Office 29 and was told that his ad, "Schildhorn 12," had a response. "I rushed home and read the letter. But what they wrote was very vague and left the first step toward a meeting up to me."[142] Fritz went directly to Hering's bar, found Otto, and "discussed the matter with [him]. He also got a kick out of it. The whole thing is actually rather amusing." Fritz nevertheless composed a reply early the following morning "and, in it, asked to meet next Sunday."[143] He spent the next few days waiting for a response. After a few more days, he seemed ready to give up hope. "The two girls from Grunewald still haven't answered and I will probably not receive anything more. I don't like it at all; I'd really like to see or at least talk to them again."[144] And yet he went back to the *Berliner Lokal-Anzeiger* a few days later and gave it one last shot. "After much thought, I wanted to try my luck again since I just could not get the bicyclists out of my head":

Grunewald, Schildhorn 12, why no answer, asking for a sign of life. Longing, Post Office 29.[145]

Fritz Reinert never did hear back from the bicyclist in the dark blue dress, and he spent the remainder of his year in Berlin more or less unattached and content to spend his evenings playing billiards and occasionally going to a nightclub or cafés. In early 1903, Fritz was let go from his job with the print-maker and eventually left Berlin.[146] But the brief success he had with a missed-connection personal ad is nevertheless remarkable, and it seems likely that the dozens of other Berliners who used ads for similar purposes each week had experiences similar to his.

Personal ad proselytes recognized the revolutionary nature of ads and argued that they completely changed the way love and dating worked in the modern city. For one, most other "modern" approaches to love at the turn of the century were alike insofar as they fought back against the giant, whirring, anonymous metropolis and sought to make the city smaller, more accessible, and less anonymous. But instead of working against the size and anonymity of the modern metropolis, personal ads could use these qualities to the advantage of single Berliners looking for love. In one of the earliest defenses of personal ads, a 1900 feature piece titled "Marriage through the Newspaper" pointed out that personal ads were groundbreaking because the anonymity of the medium allowed people to be transparent, state exactly what they wanted, what they were like, and where they stood financially. "The anonymity under whose protection these [ads] are written," the author wrote, "makes anything possible." "I can well imagine," he continued, "that people with very particular tastes" are able to find exactly the soulmate they seek. The sheer number of potential romantic interlocutors, in other words, actually made one more likely to find a compatible mate via the personal ads. And the fact that the first contact was written—not among family or friends—removed the necessity of a "personal meeting, which, no matter what, implies a certain moral commitment and makes a later termination of relations embarrassing for both parties." Instead, writing allowed for a longer, more meaningful exchange of "all important questions of life," after which an in-person meeting was not only less uncomfortable but also more likely to lead to something that satisfied both. Personal ads, he concluded, "guarantee a larger freedom of choice" and thus represented a significant improvement over "fortuitous encounters made at parties, in theaters, at balls, etc. or those encounters that are set up by the friendly arrangement of others." And if, he wrote finally, there really are people who are meant for each other even though they might live far away from each other, "It is precisely through the newspaper that they have a real possibility of coming into contact with one another. So there is a poetry to personal ads, which are said to be so prosaic."[147]

But it was not the fact that personal ads made fate any more attainable or wieldy that made them so transformative. Rather, it was the realization that fate and fortuity were unstable and outdated foundations for love in the modern world. As Joachim Werner put it in the introduction to his highly regarded study of personal ads (a study that actually put him in contact with a woman he ultimately married), "We civilized people of the twentieth century leave the matching of two people . . . up to chance. Systematic, intentional searching is nonexistent or exists only outside the bounds of convention"—a convention based, as another Berliner put it, on a "philistine" morality.[148] Werner went on to point out that "the old convention has failed" and a new one must take its place. Personal ads, he wrote, could do this, could facilitate the "greater breadth" and "deeper content" of the modern, "differentiated individual" of the twentieth century.[149]

In this way, personal ads represented not simply a tweaking of earlier methods but a wholesale reimagining of how dating and courting might work in an urban world. By shifting the focus from trying to harness fate to recognizing that fate was an impractical fantasy and attempting instead to accommodate the individual, personal ads were an important step in Berliners' efforts to adjust their lives to the modern, metropolitan world.[150] So, too, was the groundbreaking notion that to be modern with respect to love and dating was to work with the realities of the modern metropolis and create a system that used Berlin's size and anonymity to forge love and intimacy.

As the police were in the middle of their investigation of the death of Frieda Kliem, they received an interesting package from a gentleman named H. Krämer. Krämer had never met Frieda Kliem, nor did he have any information about her murder or disappearance.[151] But Krämer was profoundly interested in personal ads, and that passion had gotten him thinking about what he saw as the biggest problem moving forward: the business of ads. Others had already pointed out the perceived incompatibility of marriage and business, and Krämer understood that the idea of buying ads seemed too much like buying love for most Berliners.[152] He knew, too, that it was the financial aspect of ads that motivated swindlers and generated wealth for newspaper publishers. Either way, someone was profiting from ads, and Krämer apparently started wondering what all of those lines of newsprint added up to. So, in 1913, he undertook a fairly simple study, word for word, of all of the personal ads in just one day in Berlin's three biggest newspapers, the *Berliner Lokal-Anzeiger*, the *Berliner Morgenpost*, and the *Berliner Tageblatt*. Krämer counted 538 ads composed of almost ten thousand words—words that cost 15 pfennigs each—and calculated that, in one day, each newspaper brought in between DM 40,000 and DM 90,000, or over DM 175,000 together. And that was just one Sunday. "If we consider all of the newspapers in Germany, the flood of money from personal ads rises to many million marks each year," Krämer wrote in the newsletter of an organization he founded, the Ehe-, Mutterschul-Mission (Marriage and Mothering Mission). But Krämer's genius was in his idea that the German state, not newspapers or matchmakers, should profit from the millions of marks Germans—and especially Berliners—spent on personal ads each year by taking control of personal ads and creating a state-run dating service. If the state were to mass-produce compatibility questionnaires, distribute them to all Germans, require by law that they fill them out, and then collect the responses in a central database, the entire problem of swindlers—not to mention individuals' fears about asking for help in the search for a spouse—could be eliminated. And the state, Krämer calculated, would make a tidy profit, to boot. Krämer even had an idea for who could oversee the entire operation: the empress.[153]

The police stored Krämer's letter and newsletter with the rest of the Kliem case files even though it clearly was of no help in their ongoing investigation. Krämer, for his part, realized that his idea was a long shot, and his organization and newsletter were essentially his effort—"in the meantime," as he put it—to do what the state might someday want to do.[154] Krämer disappears from the historical record after this, so it is safe to assume that his rather clever idea never got off the ground, but his interest in using personal ads as the building blocks of something greater, more official, and more public is yet another example of Berliners trying to mesh modern approaches to love and intimacy with the existing framework of middle-class sensibilities. It also suggests just how far personal ads had come in just one or two generations. Indeed, if Krämer's organization is set alongside the fact that Berlin's mayor once tried to compel the police censorship office to check each ad either before or after it was published, the astonishing rise of this fundamentally new technology of love becomes even clearer.

Berliners almost universally referred to personal ads at the turn of the century as "this no longer uncommon way," a telling phrase. Personal ads had become a common, "self-evident," as one Berliner put it, method of finding love and intimacy in the modern metropolis—so self-evident, in fact, that they began to blend in seamlessly with other quintessentially modern methods of communication.[155] One newspaper reader described the way he had "advertised" right in the middle of the turn-of-the-century postcard fad and how he and his future wife corresponded at first using only postcards until they decided to meet in person (and then get married).[156] By the beginning of the twentieth century, personal ads had emerged as a "surrogate" for earlier, trusted methods, and one Berliner after another wrote letters to the newspapers reminding her fellow readers how many happy personal-ad couples she knew.[157] Berlin newspapers relayed stories about people receiving dozens, even hundreds of responses to a single ad, and book reviewers gushed about the latest studies and novels that finally gave that "no longer uncommon way" the attention it deserved.[158]

And yet as popular as they had become by the beginning of World War I, there is something unmistakably defensive about the abiding tagline of personal ads: this no longer uncommon way. This is evident, too, in the way those thirty-eight women responded to Paul Kuhnt's personal ad in 1914. Nearly all of them felt compelled to justify their use of ads by calling themselves "mature adults," explaining that they had resorted to ads only because they were widows or without family and thus had no respectable way to get in contact with other men, or couching their response in such reluctant language—"I would not have anything against getting married again," as one woman wrote—that no one would mistake them for loose, dishonorable women.[159] Personal ads could not shake the tinge of disreputability, their perceived incompatibility with a middle-class respectability based on stability, predictability, and knowing where one stood and what one could expect out of life. Indeed, folding personal ads into existing patterns of middle-class life proved exceptionally difficult. This is what made the atmosphere of the turn of the century—especially with regard to love, dating, and intimacy—so sensational and fraught with contradiction.

5

Modern Dating and Respectability on Trial

WALTER BAHN WAS still a very young man when he began practicing law, but neither his age nor his choice of clients could prevent him from becoming the most sensational criminal defense attorney in early twentieth-century Berlin. Although he came from a long line of attorneys, taking over the family business was hardly enough to earn one any fame in the big city.[1] It was, rather, precisely the clients he chose—not to mention his success in defending them—that propelled him to fame. Bahn was just twenty-nine years old when he took the case of Theodor Berger, the Berlin pimp who brutally raped and murdered nine-year-old Lucie Berlin in 1904. Just two years later, he represented Wilhelm Voigt—better known by his Madame Tussaud's wax figure, Carl Zuckmayer play, and unforgettable moniker, "Der Hauptmann von Köpenick"—who stood trial for impersonating an army officer, commandeering a battalion of real soldiers, taking over a Berlin suburb's city hall, arresting the town mayor and treasurer, and making off with more than DM 4,000. If Bahn, whose law office was directly next to Berlin's main criminal court and was, as a 1931 article about Berlin's greatest lawyers put it, "a place of refuge for reprobates of all sorts," needed any additional cases to cement his status as Berlin's premier defense lawyer, he found another in 1910, when he defended Frau von Schönebeck-Weber, who had murdered her husband, an army major, in a fit of jealous rage. She was pronounced legally insane and put in a mental institute.[2]

While Bahn may have made his name by representing these infamous Berliners, it was his interest in taking the cases of the downtrodden, the poor, and the broken that earned him the respect of his peers in the legal world. A 1931 article in *Das Kriminal-Magazin* praised Bahn as one of Berlin's

FIGURE 5.1 Walter Bahn (middle) during a 1932 murder case
Source: Landesarchiv Berlin F Rep. 290-02-06, Nr. 167/1.

"giants of advocacy," a lawyer whose manifold courtroom skills shone particularly bright in the "countless cases in which this people's defender represented the interests of the poor and embattled with an empathetic heart and without regard to external success." "Walter Bahn is an orator of the highest quality," the article continued, "a temperament controlled by a will of purposefulness and quiet, contemplative manliness."[3] Bahn's reputation as the "people's defender" earned him the respect of those interested in Berlin's underworld of crime, prostitution, and poverty, too, and he was asked to contribute to Hans Ostwald's fifty-volume sociological chronicle of metropolitan squalor and crime, the *Großstadt-Dokumente* (*Big-City Documents*). While his volume, *Meine Klienten* (*My Clients*), discussed only the cases of Berger and Voigt, his reflections in it, not to mention his collaboration with Ostwald more generally, suggest that he was probably interested in more than just fame and glory. Indeed, Bahn described in the book's introduction his fascination with criminal defense attorneys and how, as a boy, he "knew no greater pleasure than to sit in the courtroom during sensational trials and follow the battle between defense attorney and state prosecutor." "My sympathies were naturally with the defense attorney," Bahn recalled. "I realized instinctively even back then that he is an indispensable monitoring body for the administration of justice."[4] But he is also more than this: "[The defense attorney] stands in constant contact with the people and thus knows better than anyone the struggle for daily bread; [he] knows that one must keep in mind the famous saying, 'To understand is to forgive,' when considering the temptations that come from the difficult struggle for existence." These defendants, he concluded, need solid representation in front of judges who are prejudiced against them.[5]

Bahn's description of his motivation for defending Berlin's poor and delinquent is compelling, but his comments on criminal justice and the modern world are far more relevant and interesting, for it is here that Bahn touched on the confrontation between middle-class respectability and the modern world. Bahn wrote in the introduction to *My Clients* that while Berlin's judges were "no doubt thinking, objective men who try to discover the truth to the best of their abilities," they nevertheless ran up against the problem of perspective. Bahn pointed to the fact that the truth looks different according to one's perspective and worldview. Just as judges and legal thinkers, for example, once believed in witches and sentenced defendants accordingly, he wrote, "So also is our justice system a product of our time, even though it suffers by continuing to drag along a heap of decaying viewpoints."[6] In Bahn's view, a defense attorney was thus "there to bring modern . . . viewpoints to bear" on the court, such that those living in the modern world might not be subject to such outdated and prejudicial notions of right and wrong.[7]

A few years after his book was published, however, Bahn did something that throws this image of a man aligning the court to the modern world into question: he took the case of Paul Kuhnt, the forty-nine-year-old retired pharmacist charged with the murder of Frieda Kliem.

Bahn's choice to defend Paul Kuhnt was actually wholly consistent with his modus operandi as a criminal defense attorney in Berlin. After all, Kuhnt was destitute, his repeated professions of innocence had been ignored by the police, who had held him in jail during the yearlong investigation and discovery period, and the case itself was a highly publicized sensation. It was instead Bahn's methods, his witnesses, and, more generally, his theory of the case that contrasted so interestingly with the legal ethos he put forward in *My Clients*. By shifting the focus from Paul Kuhnt's obvious culpability to Frieda Kliem's questionable respectability, Bahn devised a defense strategy that threatened to derail the seemingly straightforward argument of the prosecution, as well as redefine the trial in terms of hegemonic femininity, middle-class respectability, and modern approaches to love and intimacy. Accordingly, Kuhnt's trial offers a fascinating window onto the clash between the values of traditional, middle-class society and Berliners' attempts to find love in the turn-of-the-century metropolis.

FROM THE SEARCH for the killer, the sting-like capture of Kuhnt, and the colorful characters and revealing evidence put forward to the centrality of personal ads in the case and the presence of a high-profile defense lawyer like Walter Bahn, the criminal trial of Frieda Kliem's murderer had all the makings of a sensational cause célèbre on par with the Frau von Schönebeck-Weber, Wilhelm Voigt, and Theodor Berger cases. But the timing of Frieda Kliem's murder was also notable. The initial reports of a body having been found in the Falkenhagen forest appeared in the newspaper on June 28, 1914, just one day before every newspaper ran an unforgettable headline about the assassination of Archduke Franz Ferdinand.[8] Indeed, while, in the past, normal news stories continued to run alongside momentous and earthshaking national and international news events, the run-up to war in July and August 1914 was such big news that Berlin's daily newspapers all but ignored the day-to-day happenings on the continent and in the city. The local news section of the *Berliner Lokal-Anzeiger*, for example, completely disappeared at the beginning of the war, and it is remarkable that newspaper editors expended any ink at all covering the discovery of a corpse in a suburban forest. What little about the murder that did appear in the newspapers petered out after no clear suspect could be found, and, other than speculating about the "mysterious letter" Frieda had been waiting on and advertising the police's DM 1,000 reward for her killer, there was not much more to be said.[9] Frieda Kliem, who burst onto the main stage of Berlin life in those final days of June 1914, was thus just as quickly ushered off to make room for world war.

So it was that Berliners had mostly forgotten about Frieda Kliem when Walter Bahn entered his appearance on behalf of Paul Kuhnt on October 18, 1915.[10] The police investigation had been going on for well over a year at that point, and Kuhnt had spent that entire time in jail. His long detention prompted his wife, Margarethe, to write in more than once to the police and ask when her husband's trial would actually begin. His family needed him, she wrote, not least because her two boys had volunteered for the war and were fighting "in the east."[11] Margarethe also tried to keep her husband up to date on the state of his defense. Back in December 1914—just a few months after his arrest—she wrote him to say that she had met with Walter Bahn, who apparently expressed an early interest in the case, and that she was anxious for Paul to come back home. "Each day I wait for your return home," she wrote.

"This endless waiting is tiring and dull—that surely shows in my letters. Will you be with us for Christmas? . . . [If not, it] will be a day like any other, then, one that must be endured, one that will come to an end. But I can't believe that this could take several more weeks still."[12]

Like the German soldiers who thought they would celebrate Christmas 1914 in front of the hearth and not on the front line, Kuhnt and his wife would be disappointed. The investigation and pretrial matters were complicated and seem to hit every possible snag. There was, for one, the matter of witnesses, and there were many who had something to say about Frieda Kliem. But by the time witness summons were sent out, many witnesses had conflicting commitments or simply could not be located. Dr. Paul Jeserich, for example, who was the medical expert the state would rely on in establishing Frieda's cause of death, wrote to say that he could not come to Berlin the day of the trial and would send his assistant, Dr. Paul Müller, instead.[13] Ernst Krause, the forester who found Frieda's corpse, was also unable to come to the trial (though he was allowed to give a deposition).[14] And a variety of other witnesses never received their witness summons, which the police discovered when they received more than a few of them—which had been sent via certified mail—marked "return to sender."[15]

There were also the numerous witnesses Walter Bahn wanted added to the witness list, and it is here that his defense strategy starts to become clear. Bahn's first move was to try to establish the respectability and trustworthiness of his client, and to do so he petitioned to add Kuhnt's wife, Margarethe, to the witness list, hoping she might soften the edges of what the prosecution would surely claim was evidence showing Kuhnt to be an adulterous lecher who used personal ads to swindle women.[16] Bahn also made contact with two of Kuhnt's friends—Max Blumensaat and a man named Euschmann—and was apparently convinced that they would serve as useful character witnesses for the defense, knowing Kuhnt as they did to be "a man of honor."[17] Here was an invocation of the oft-bandied-about and always amorphous concept of honor, and Bahn was clearly intent on framing his client as a paragon of middle-class virtue and respectability. To this end, he also added Professor Kolbe of the Royal Museum of Natural Sciences in Berlin, who, he claimed, knew both Kuhnt's "personality" and "the scientific importance and work of the defendant."[18] Kuhnt, as it turned out, cultivated an interest in insects alongside his career as a pharmacist and belonged to two scientific societies: the German Entomological Society and the Berlin Entomological Society.[19] At some point, he became the club librarian and later member of the editorial board for the former, and, in addition to his frequent participation in lively debates at society meetings, he wrote book reviews, contributed articles on various insect types to the society's journal, the *Deutsche Entomologische Zeitschrift*, and, in 1912, published a 1,138-page handbook on German beetles that was both well reviewed and frequently cited by other scholars.[20] All of this was character information that Bahn wanted the jury to hear, and it supported—rather impressively—the "honorable" portrait he wanted to paint of Paul Kuhnt.

But playing up Paul Kuhnt's credibility as a respectable, honorable, middle-class Berliner was only half of the legal defense Bahn was putting into place. The other half was even more important, for Bahn was planning a full-out assault on Frieda Kliem's character, indeed, her own honor and respectability as a middle-class woman. To do so, he requested complete access to the police's copious notes on their investigation into Frieda's past, friends, and personality. This was a smart move, for the police had expended considerable effort interviewing anyone who had anything to say about Frieda—all, of course, hoping to find some clue about who might have had a motive to kill Frieda. The police had been particularly intent on finding anything related to her amorous and intimate connections, an investigatory tack they presumably would not have taken if Frieda had been a man. Bahn's request was granted, and he waded through the dozens of police statements and focused on five strands of testimony in particular that portrayed Frieda as a promiscuous, dishonest, and disreputable woman who could have been killed by one of the former lovers, jealous types, and violent vagabonds who were part of her shady milieu. The first thread was about Otto Mewes, Frieda's *Verhältnis*, who had left the Berlin-Brandenburg area but nevertheless remained one of Frieda's closest friends. Nearly every one of the friends and neighbors interviewed by the police had something to say about Mewes, and since no one but Frieda and Mewes knew the extent of their intimacy and the witnesses could thus only speak about it in vague, speculative ways, the relationship appeared perhaps more scandalous or indecent than it really was. After all, as a single woman, Frieda hardly received the benefit of the doubt when it came to male friends and visitors. Mewes himself apparently acknowledged—either to the police or directly to Bahn—that he had "intimate relations" with Frieda, "often spent the night with her," and had a spare key to the apartment.[21] Frieda had left what little belongings she had to Mewes (and Antonie Köhler) in her will, and, upon learning of her death, Mewes apparently felt justified in cleaning out their joint bank account. But as suspicious as all of this sounded, Mewes had been in Switzerland and France in the months before, and the month of, Frieda's death. Playing up Mewes in the trial was thus motivated exclusively by Bahn's desire to make Frieda seem like a loose, disreputable woman. The police had seemingly been compelled by this line of reasoning, and so, Bahn thought, would a judge and jury.

The second thread Bahn followed had to do with the many men Frieda's friends and neighbors claimed to have seen around her place both before and after her disappearance. The fact that no one knew anything concrete about these men or why they were there fed the suspicion Bahn wanted to plant in jurors' minds. Otto Westphal, for example, told investigators that he often saw Frieda on the street or in front of her apartment door with various men. When he asked who they were, Frieda claimed they were her cousins.[22] Her neighbor, Marie Schönemann, gave a similar report, saying that when Frieda had visitors, "it was always cousins . . . or uncles," such as the tall, lean man she saw peering at her doorbell with a magnifying glass.[23] Another neighbor, Hulda Sello, said she once saw Frieda with a man on a Sunday afternoon. He was tall and skinny, wore a gray suit, and had a blonde mustache. They were coming from a bicycle ride, she thought, and the man left his bicycle in the courtyard and went with Frieda into her apartment, only to leave ten minutes later holding a roll of fabric.[24] Even Otto Westphal's wife remembered seeing a man in a blue suit go up to Frieda's apartment one afternoon. He was also tall and skinny, but had a dark mustache and wore eyeglasses.[25] But there were more curious incidents, too. Another friend told police that she once rang Frieda's doorbell but received no answer even though she could hear a man's voice inside.[26] Otto Seiffert, too, claimed to have heard from Marie Schönemann that she had watched as Frieda, who was walking down the stairs, passed by a man with a goatee walking up the stairs and immediately grew red in the face. As the man passed her, he turned around and said, "Oh, Frau Kliem!" to which Frieda responded by turning around and following him back up the stairs. After a while Frieda came back downstairs and told Marie that the experience had been embarrassing enough that she had wanted to hide.[27] Who were these men? Why were their appearances in and around Frieda's apartment so strange and secretive? There were some who conjectured that Frieda was renting out a room and that this explained the men moving in and out of her living space; but no one could say for sure, and this, of course, only made things seem worse.[28] And of course the fact that her friends and neighbors had noted and remembered these details in the first place suggests something about the vulnerable position of single women like Frieda, whose comings and goings—amorous or not—seemed always to be shrouded in ignominy and degradation.

It was precisely this uncertainty and lack of information about her "real" activities and motives that Bahn wanted to emphasize, and even though his material consisted primarily of scraps and fragments that seemed suspicious only because Frieda had been killed, this made no difference and, in fact, strengthened his point. So it was that hazy, almost entirely uninformed statements like that of the elderly Westphals—"The word is that [Frieda's friend, Antonie Köhler] is a prostitute"—for which they admitted to having no proof, were particularly useful for the defense.[29] So also were long-shot connections like the statement of Max Jaworr, who ran a manufacturing business and had once overheard one of his employees saying that he was going to "his Friedel on Franzstrasse," where he would spend the night. Once again, while it was unlikely that "Friedel" was Frieda Kliem (who did live at Franzstrasse 5, though there were at least two Franzstrasses in Berlin), the mere whiff of plausibility served Bahn's purpose of attacking her status as an upstanding woman. The fact, moreover, that Jaworr had given his testimony in the form of a deposition from the battlefields of World War I highlighted the contrast between masculine respectability and duty, on the one hand, and feminine promiscuity, on the other.[30]

Then there was the mysterious behavior of Hermann Selka, the belligerent husband of Frieda's friend, Anna. The Selkas' marriage had, as Anna told the police, been "sad from the start," primarily because Hermann was constantly without work and generally preferred to rely on his wife's earnings. He tried to compel her—first with angry words, then with fists—to let him use her savings (a considerable DM 10,000), and her unwavering refusal led not only to arguments, but also to domestic violence from which Anna sought refuge in Frieda Kliem's apartment. The Selkas had gotten to know Frieda on their many bicycle rides, though Anna claimed her husband never liked Frieda.[31] After Anna moved out of their shared apartment for good in April 1914, filed for divorce, and temporarily moved in with Frieda, Hermann started to show up at Frieda's apartment and ask about his wife, whom he wanted back. Frieda, Anna remembered, had simply stopped answering the door, and even after Anna left Berlin altogether, Hermann continued to come by to try to retrieve his wife's things. Frieda told her neighbors that she was afraid of Selka, for he had threatened to go to the police and to rough her up the same way he had his wife. Frieda also told them that she felt Selka was stalking her, not least because he often appeared out of nowhere when she was bicycling.[32] Selka, for his part, told the police that he had run into Frieda in early June 1914 while bicycling near the Falkenhagen forest (where Frieda was later killed). The two discussed Anna's whereabouts and then rode back into the city together, whereupon they went their separate ways. One

of them—presumably Selka—proposed that they ride again the following
Sunday and meet at the same place, but Frieda apparently never showed up.
Selka spent the next few days asking about Frieda around her apartment, and
when her neighbors confirmed that she had disappeared, he made the odd
comment that she was likely lying dead up in her apartment.[33] He also paid
an unexpected visit over the lunch hour to Robert Adam, their mutual friend
from the bicycle rides. Selka apparently asked him where his wife, Anna, had
escaped to, and when Robert lied and said he did not know, Selka responded
suddenly, "Have you heard the latest? Miss Kliem has disappeared. She was
surely lured into the forest and is now dead." "I told him he was crazy," Robert
recalled, but "as I [later] read about Kliem's murder, it occurred to me that
Selka had referred to the probability of her having been murdered."[34] Around
that same time, Selka went to the police and filed a missing person report,
though the neighbors figured he did this only as a way to get the police to give
him a peek inside Frieda's apartment so he could retrieve some of his wife's belongings. The police had naturally been quite interested in Selka as a murder
suspect, especially after the mailman claimed a man had approached him
about Frieda's mail and, when told she had disappeared, remarked offhand-
edly, "Well, she's for sure not coming back."[35] The mailman could not identify
Selka as the man who said this, but there was nevertheless enough suspicion
surrounding Selka that this line of testimony—from both Selka and the other
witnesses—undoubtedly influenced the jury as they formed an opinion of
Frieda Kliem and her shady circle of acquaintances.

The final thread of testimony Bahn was intent on highlighting had to do
with a comment Otto Mewes made to the police in a letter he sent them just a
few weeks after Frieda's murder. Mewes, presumably fearful that he would become a suspect, used the letter to explain his relationship with Frieda and de-
tail the items he had received from her recently. Frieda had sent Mewes a letter
the day before her disappearance and included a variety of items that seemed
odd in light of her subsequent death, most notably a birthday present, even
though his birthday was still two months away, and a variety of family papers,
which, as Mewes put it, "even Frau Köhler couldn't understand." Mewes was
not sure what to make of the letters, and he wrote to police that "if the conclusion of the doctors were not so strongly indicative of murder, one might
think instead of a suicide, especially since she often told me that she thought
about sticking the gas hose [from the stove] in her mouth and putting an end
to her difficult existence."[36] This did not fit with the reports of Frieda's other
friends, who all said they had never seen any indication that Frieda might be
suicidal, and the police apparently put little stock in the idea.[37] But Walter

Bahn nevertheless raised the question of a possible suicide, not just to sow seeds of doubt in the minds of the jurors, but to cast Frieda in an unflattering light. After all, while suicide—especially by poor, single women—was exceedingly common in Berlin at the turn of the century, it carried a stigma of shame, a lack of fortitude and character, and a sort of vague criminality.[38] It was, in other words, just one more reason a solid, middle-class Berliner like Paul Kuhnt could hardly have had anything to do with Frieda.

WHEN PAUL KUHNT entered the courtroom on November 25, 1915, he did so with confidence, bolstered by Walter Bahn and his carefully designed defense strategy. However, the state had, during his thirteen months in jail, discovered a few additional details about his life that might have made him—and his counsel—a bit uneasy. For one, the police had put Kuhnt's alibi to the test, and they found it to be full of holes. Kuhnt claimed that he had been in Leipzig on the day of the murder to meet with a publisher about his zoological publications, and he offered as proof the claim that he had been in a particular bakery at a particular time of the day to buy a cheesecake to take back to his family in Berlin.[39] The Leipzig police could find no record of Kuhnt's visit, and Kuhnt had been unable to produce as much as a train ticket or hotel bill.[40] Kuhnt's response was that he had traveled to Leipzig under a false name, which trapped him in a larger lie about his identity. Kuhnt admitted to having altered the name on his birth certificate to "Kalinder," and while this gave his alibi a small shot at believability, it also raised important questions about whether Kuhnt was perhaps living a "double life"—a near certainty considering his relationship with Anna Piegors and his use of personal ads as a married man.[41] The police had also had time to probe into Kuhnt's employment and financial history, and their findings there were damning. Kuhnt had always stated that he was a retired pharmacist, but this, according to the German Pharmacists' Society, was only partially true. Kuhnt, in fact, had no training as a pharmacist and had simply purchased a pharmacy and hidden his lack of credentials and expertise.[42] While Kuhnt sold the pharmacy business and lived off of the rent he received as the building owner, various letters to the court showed that he had a staggering number of outstanding debts to doctors in and around Berlin, and a telegram from a creditor to the police confirmed that Kuhnt was trying to borrow against his existing debts.[43]

Between his escapades under the name "Kalinder," his outstanding debts, and his shaky alibi, Kuhnt's credibility as a man of scientific importance and middle-class respectability was crumbling as the trial began. Reporters for the daily newspapers were present at the trial and published a selection of the testimony so Berliners would not miss any details.[44] And the case opened with some early fireworks. Before the twelve-member jury was selected and the witnesses sworn in, Chief Judge Arthur Hesse, who often questioned the defendant directly, launched an attack on Kuhnt's flimsy explanations for his proximity to the world of Frieda Kliem.[45] He began with the simple but important question of whether Kuhnt knew Frieda Kliem:

KUHNT: I don't know her at all.

CHIEF JUDGE HESSE: But there is very compelling evidence that you do. You have already been caught telling various lies, and if you defend yourself dishonestly and untruthfully, it might make an unfavorable impression on the jury. This whole case is already full of mysteries. You have lived a sort of double life; you now have the opportunity to give an explanation for things, and I urge you to stick to the truth.

The judge then questioned Kuhnt about his finances, whereupon Kuhnt explained that his father was extremely wealthy and had helped him buy his pharmacy on Bülowstrasse. But he also earned money of his own; for example, the royalties from his scientific publications amounted to an incredible DM 2,000 per year. This was admittedly a lot of money, but the judge suspected that it had not been enough for Kuhnt and that his use of personal ads was financially motivated.

CHIEF JUDGE HESSE: It is rather curious that you used a false name to post newspaper personal ads and look for marriage opportunities, isn't it?

KUHNT: I cannot deny that.

CHIEF JUDGE HESSE: Your marriage ad read: "Senior teacher, Dr., widower, no children, 51 yrs., looking for spouse." You received a lot of responses to this ad. What did you plan to do with this ad?

KUHNT: I wanted to meet women so I could write a novel. These kinds of encounters always make women tell about their experiences.

CHIEF JUDGE HESSE: That is hardly believable. You recently lost a lot of your savings; couldn't the thought of making some money have motivated your decision to write personal ads?

KUHNT: No, not at all.

CHIEF JUDGE HESSE: So it was completely harmless? Did you tell anyone about this completely harmless plan, perhaps your wife?

KUHNT: No, my wife would have laughed at me if I had told her I was writing a novel.

The judge then asked Kuhnt why he had used a false name and tried to forge his birth certificate, to which Kuhnt replied that he thought personal ads were not anonymous and that one had to show proof of identity to pick up the responses. And he continued to deny that money had anything to do with his use of ads.

CHIEF JUDGE HESSE: So you met Frieda Kliem this way?

KUHNT: I am sure I did not.

CHIEF JUDGE HESSE: Think carefully before answering. This answer in particular could have serious implications.

KUHNT: No, I don't know Kliem.

CHIEF JUDGE HESSE: Kliem was an older [single] woman who lived alone on Franzstrasse. Just like you, she posted personal ads. A piece of writing that was found at her place is signed by Adolf Mertens and was most certainly written in your hand.[46]

Surely this would trip up Paul Kuhnt, for the writing was clearly identical, as the court handwriting expert himself confirmed.[47] But Kuhnt was well coached by Walter Bahn and found a way to wriggle around the state's clearest link between Paul Kuhnt and Frieda Kliem:

KUHNT: [after being shown the piece of writing] It is very similar to my handwriting; but I have never used the name Adolf Mertens.

CHIEF JUDGE HESSE: The writing is quite obviously yours; you cannot contest that!

But Kuhnt was unwavering in his claims to know neither Frieda Kliem nor Adolf Mertens, and the judge, presumably exasperated at Kuhnt's steadfast denial of apparent and obvious facts, moved on to the matter of what he called Kuhnt's "double life."

CHIEF JUDGE HESSE: It is a very strange thing indeed that you traveled to Leipzig using a false name. You are leading a double life. You undertake odd things under a false name. Anyone can see it. There is clearly something going on here.

Kuhnt, as the *Berliner Tageblatt* reporter put it, once again "gave a convoluted answer that the chief judge again called completely unintelligible." So, too, was Kuhnt's claim to have forgotten about Kliem's silverware and other valuables, which he "found" in a commuter train and then put in a hiding place in his home.

CHIEF JUDGE HESSE: Didn't you tell anyone at home about this strange find?
KUHNT: No.
CHIEF JUDGE HESSE: That is also very remarkable. Didn't you feel obligated
    to take the packet to the station manager or the police? That would have
    been the simplest and most natural thing to do. A man in your position,
    your education, a married father with grown children does exactly that.
KUHNT: I can't explain it either.

This was where Kuhnt started to give answers, presumably because Bahn had told him not to fight the charge of theft. Kuhnt admitted that, around the time of the bank incident with Anna Piegors, he had fallen on hard financial times because his rental income had dropped off due to the war. He was worried that he would not be able to pay his mortgage, and he suddenly thought of the bankbook he had found. He figured the bank account would be frozen, but he planned to have a girl he knew present herself as Frieda Kliem, thereby convincing the bank that the account should be unfrozen and that the balance of the account should be paid out.[48]

Kuhnt, at this point, had apparently admitted as much as he intended to, and the remainder of the morning found him denying having heard about Frieda's death or seen the reward posters, acting strange when arrested, trying to commit suicide on the way to the police station, and even being in Berlin on the day of the murder. The chief judge again pointed to the gaps in Kuhnt's Leipzig alibi, and with that the morning session of the trial was concluded.[49] The chief judge's interest in poking holes in Kuhnt's story and credibility, however, was not. The afternoon session began with the topic of how Kuhnt had met Anna Piegors on the street and initiated an intimate relationship with her.[50] Here, again, was the fortuitous street encounter that so fascinated Berliners, and its role in the chief judge's questioning of Kuhnt reinforces the point that Paul Kuhnt had done more than look or fantasize about fortuitous encounters on busy streets, and the intimacy he enjoyed as a result of it proved damaging to his public character.

A seasoned defense attorney, Walter Bahn took the opportunity to re-emphasize Kuhnt's scientific credentials before pulling a trick out of his sleeve and reminding the jury of the uncertainty surrounding the discovery of Frieda's body. Because over a week had passed between her death and the forester's discovery of her body, ascertaining a cause of death had been exceedingly difficult. Based on what was available for forensic examination, one might have classified the death as a suicide if there had not been so many other suggestions of murder. The medical experts admitted that they could not rule out a natural death, and while, absent any evidence of deadly blunt trauma to the body, poisoning was probably the most likely cause of death, they had been unable to recover any traces of poison. In light of this fact, as Bahn pointed out to the jury, the state attorney had initially been prepared to drop the murder charges against Kuhnt and proceed only with the charges of theft. This was, of course, a bombshell, and Bahn, aware that this was his best chance of an acquittal, stated for the record that he re-served the right to call the state attorney himself as a witness to this fact at some point in the trial. Of course, there was no getting around the fact that Kuhnt possessed various poisons—including a small quantity of cyanide, which Dr. Jeserich, the court chemist, suggested might have been strong enough to kill Frieda without leaving any trace elements—as part of his zo-ological and entomological studies, and the chief judge took pains to bring this to the attention of the jury. But Bahn no doubt saw this as acceptable collateral damage.[51]

The remainder of the afternoon was spent discussing Kuhnt's shaky alibi, his claims to have found Frieda's valuables in the commuter train, and the basic details of Frieda's circle of friends and potential love interests. Bahn also put Kuhnt's wife, Margarethe, on the stand, where she confirmed her husband's alibi and, more importantly, testified to his respectability as a mar-ried father of five. The session ended with Bahn's request for three additional witnesses (among others, Otto Mewes) to be called, a request that the court granted. Since Bahn's proposed witnesses did not live in Berlin, the court de-cided to take Friday off and resume the case on Saturday.[52] This would prove unnecessary, for the witnesses apparently could not be located, and the chief judge was then left to decide whether the trial should be postponed until they could be found. The state attorney rather surprisingly argued in favor of this, reasoning that the court and jury needed to consider all of the important evi-dence before deciding on a verdict. Bahn, for his part, requested only that his client be released from jail in the meantime since he had been locked up for over a year and could hardly endure another delay. The chief judge ultimately decided in favor of continuing the trial at a later date, but not before issuing some harsh words to the defendant:

CHIEF JUDGE HESSE: You cannot simply dismiss the fact that there is very compelling evidence against you. You are clearly trying to hide something; can you not shed some light on this darkness?

KUHNT: As far as the murder goes, I have nothing to hide. I can only repeat
     that I did not know Kliem.
CHIEF JUDGE HESSE: But this assertion is very improbable. Can you really
     not explain any of this?
KUHNT: The claim is that it is suspicious that a piece of paper was found in
     Kliem's apartment with the words "Mertens, you will marry me." This can
     be explained, as has been proven, by the fact that Kliem had an oracle
     book and got these words from it.

It is unclear what Kuhnt was referring to here when he suggested that it had
somehow been proven that Frieda had conjured the name "Adolf Mertens"
from some sort of occult power or why Bahn coached his client to make this
assertion. The chief judge, though, was apparently willing to play along with
this absurd notion, perhaps attempting to prove Kuhnt wrong even in his
own fantasy:

CHIEF JUDGE HESSE: But she still would have to have known Mertens since
     she was in contact with him. Defendant, I would like to give you the op-
     portunity to come clean.

At this point, Walter Bahn stepped in and shifted the discussion to save his
client:

BAHN: I disagree with His Honor's assertion. There are no compelling
     theories of the murder, not least because we don't even know the cause
     of death.

Bahn's tactic was clearly successful, for members of the jury then asked
Kuhnt to describe exactly how he had found Frieda's valuables in the commuter train—a line of questioning that missed the larger point of Kuhnt's
obvious guilt for the smaller, minute details of how he found the valuables
and to which authorities he might have reported them missing. Bahn, a genius at spinning questions of character and respectability, was even able to
turn a potential negative—Kuhnt's decision to keep the valuables instead of
turning them in as lost—into a positive, asserting as he did that his client,
as a "scientifically educated man from a good family," must have had a "bad
conscience" from having stolen the items and thus hid them away because
he was so ashamed of what he had done in an "unfortunate" moment of
weakness.[53]

The court denied Kuhnt's request to be released from prison during the trial recess, and, as it turned out, it was almost five months before he entered the courtroom again.[54] In the meantime, Otto Mewes made his way from Switzerland to Berlin for the trial, though not before writing the police to see if he might instead give a deposition from afar so as not to aggravate what he referred to as his respiratory problems. The police denied this request, but they did agree to send him—per his insistence—the train fare for his journey, which, as he characteristically complained in yet another letter to the police, had not been enough because of tiny fluctuations in the exchange rate between marks and Swiss francs.[55] Antonie Köhler also aborted her vacation and came to Berlin to serve as a witness, and Walter Bahn seemed particularly interested in her testimony about Frieda's desperation to find a husband, for it offered him yet another chance to impugn Frieda's character and respectability.

As the trial began anew on March 9, 1916, a full twenty months after Frieda's murder, it did so with a new state attorney at the helm, as the original attorney—Fuhrmann—had been called up to fight the war. He was replaced by state attorney Gerhard Mix, who was no doubt thrilled to see one of Walter Bahn's new witnesses, Kuhnt's own father, dismissed because he had more or less disowned his son after the arrest in October 1914 and had nothing to say on the matter. In some ways, this set the tone for the first day of the new trial. As Kuhnt took the stand once again, there was little new to be said or asked. Of interest was Kuhnt's admission to having used matchmaking services in addition to personal ads—also, as he claimed, as a means to gather material for his novel. The chief judge once again questioned Kuhnt's stated intent in this "stupidity" (Kuhnt's words), arguing that, in the dozens of responses Kuhnt received, there was not a single "atom" of material for novels or fiction. If his intent really had been to find material for his novel, the chief judge continued, Kuhnt would have realized that this method was useless and stopped. Instead, as Kuhnt admitted, he met with at least two women who had responded. Kuhnt continued to deny having ever met or corresponded with Frieda Kliem, though, and the rest of the day's questioning never emerged from the tangled web of details about where he found Frieda's valuables, what he claimed to have done in Leipzig on the day of the murder, and how he decided to drain her account when he fell into financial difficulty.[56]

The next morning followed a similarly unremarkable pattern, though Bahn, whose client was not on the witness stand, now homed in on the strongest arguments for his client's innocence. Bahn first sought to establish that Kuhnt was not actually in financial trouble around the time of the murder, and here Kuhnt's significant earnings from his scientific publications served as useful proof, for they underscored his credibility as a respectable man of science. Bahn then turned to what remained the most significant hole in the state's theory of the case—the cause of death—and drove home the point that, absent a clear cause of death, any discussion of a murder (and, more importantly, a murderer) was based solely on speculation and uncertainties. The medical experts called as witnesses admitted that one could at most speak in terms of possibilities and probabilities, and to this end they suggested that there were three possible theories: death by poisoning, death by choking, and death by violent trauma. They were in agreement that these last two were the least likely, and while there were no traces of poison found in Frieda's body, the deputy court chemist did point out that this did not rule out poisoning as a cause of death. Bahn, careful not to let this line of questioning end in such a way, was clever enough to get the witnesses to agree to the possibility of a natural death (by heart attack) before allowing the court to turn to a different topic. Unfortunately for him, that happened to be the matter of the cards and letters found in Frieda's apartment bearing Kuhnt's handwriting. Kuhnt eventually admitted to having written them but claimed he must have forgotten. In any case, he granted, Frieda may have been one of the many women with whom he corresponded, but he never met her personally.[57]

After a midday break, Bahn turned his attention to the fact that both Frieda's neighbors and the police were initially considering several other men as possible suspects. The most important of these was Otto Mewes, who, as a known lover of Frieda Kliem, had long been the police's (and later Bahn's and the newspapers') greatest interest. Bahn was unable to get anything particularly useful out of Mewes's testimony, though. Mewes did admit that Frieda had spoken of suicide, but he also pointed out that she loved life (especially bicycling and music) and was fit and healthy, thereby throwing into serious question the possibility of death by natural causes. Bahn's questioning of Mewes, Frieda's neighbors, and Antonie Köhler was far from disappointing, however, for it allowed him to dredge up the colorful story of Frieda's attempt to find love by any means necessary. It was on this note that the questioning of witnesses ended for good. The court took a short recess before starting closing arguments.[58]

Walter Bahn actually had the final say, but by the time the state attorney finished his closing statement, there was little Bahn needed to do. In what was without a doubt the most shocking, unbelievable twist in both the investigation and trial, state attorney Gerhard Mix asked the jury to find Kuhnt guilty of only theft, not murder. To be sure, there was plenty of evidence against Kuhnt, and Mix spent the majority of his closing argument discussing it, reminding the jury that a suicide was unlikely if not impossible, as was a natural death; that Frieda was killed not by a random passerby but by someone she knew and was in contact with through her personal ads; and that Kuhnt was clearly leading a double life, had posted personal ads, was having financial trouble, had been in correspondence with Frieda, was found to be in possession of her valuables, and acted suspiciously when arrested. Taken together, this was extremely compelling evidence for jurists, he said, and even more so for laypeople; but he could not recommend to the jury that they find Paul Kuhnt guilty of murder.[59]

The fact that Mix's colleague in the state attorney's office had originally asked to withdraw the charge of murder against Kuhnt makes this rather astonishing turn of events slightly less surprising. However, the state had ultimately decided to charge Kuhnt with the murder and had expended considerable effort preparing for the trial, so it is hard to see what happened during the trial that could have convinced Mix to change his mind at the last second. Indeed, by all accounts, the trial had gone well for the prosecution.

It is impossible to know what was behind this decision. It is equally hard to guess at the state attorney's reasoning for putting together a solid case, trying it twice, and then, when a guilty verdict was, in all likelihood, just moments away, asking the jury to convict Kuhnt of only the most obvious charge of theft. This sudden change is so baffling that one is left to wonder if the change in state attorney might have had something to do with it.[60] Perhaps Mix had never believed in Kuhnt's guilt and had tried to persuade Fuhrmann to drop the murder charges. Or maybe he, too, had been convinced by Bahn that the case was not about Kuhnt's guilt—which even the chief judge clearly considered to be self-evident—but rather about the mysteries and uncertainties surrounding Frieda's allegedly questionable and disreputable behavior. Indeed, it is possible that Frieda's own advocate—the state—had turned against her on account of the disreputable, desperate, degenerate single woman the defense had made her out to be.

Whatever the reasons, when Walter Bahn stood up to give his closing argument, his job as the defense attorney was done. He used this last opportunity to address the jury to put the trial into the context of his lengthy and storied legal career, pointing out that he had never in his life seen such a convoluted and mysterious case. Everything was in a sort of fog, he said. There were, he admitted, suspicious facts against his client, but none of these had, under closer inspection, held up and proven that Paul Kuhnt had anything to do with this terrible murder. The jury must only, Bahn concluded, find the defendant guilty of theft—and not murder.[61] In lieu of iron-clad proof, it was Kuhnt—a married, middle-class man—who deserved the benefit of the doubt.

Bahn had reason for optimism, for murder convictions were becoming rare in early 1900s Berlin according to a variety of judicial statistics and metrics— figures Bahn would have known quite well. Between 1890 and 1900, for ex- ample, there had been seventy-seven murders in Berlin. Of those, thirteen were deemed unsolvable; ten cases were scrapped because the defendant was pronounced insane; seventeen cases were aborted when the defendant died in the interim (fifteen of these committed suicide); two cases were dropped because of a lack of evidence; and five defendants were acquitted because of mitigating circumstances. Just thirty murder investigations (just under 39 percent) ended with a guilty verdict: twenty-eight defendants were given prison sentences, and two were sentenced to death.[62] And in 1914, when Berlin murders peaked, just three people were convicted of homicide.[63] More to the point, Berlin's criminal justice system had been growing ever more le- nient toward offenders. With the exception of sensationally violent and sa- distic murders like that of Lucie Berlin by Bahn's client Theodor Berger, a variety of political forces were converging to liberalize criminal laws, view lawbreakers as products of their problematic surroundings, and base verdicts and sentencing on new psycho-criminological theories, particularly those re- garding insanity. The left-liberal press was also quick to make a public spec- tacle of judges and prosecutors for their decisions, and so they adjusted their judicial and prosecutorial actions accordingly.[64]

In his closing remarks, Bahn thus had no need to refer once again to his client's sterling reputation as a middle-class, family man of science, nor was there any sense in reminding the jury of Frieda's ostensibly "loose" lifestyle and unsavory friends, since the state had dropped the murder charge. What he did do, however, was advise Kuhnt to make one final statement to the jury before they began deliberating. Whether these were rehearsed words written by Bahn or spontaneous thoughts of Kuhnt himself, we cannot know; but they fit so perfectly with Bahn's entire defense strategy that it is not hard to guess. Paul Kuhnt, addressing the jury for the last time, appealed to them, as he put it, to restore his family's "honest name." He was not, he said, "such a monster" that he could have ever committed murder.[65]

Here, one final time, were what had become the central themes of the entire case: respectability, character, reliability, and stability. To be sure, when the jury left the courtroom to deliberate, their ultimate product would be a verdict form indicating their decision about whether Paul Kuhnt was guilty of the murder of the thirty-nine-year-old seamstress, Frieda Kliem. At its core, however, what they were actually debating behind those doors was the conflict between middle-class respectability and the modern world that threatened to destabilize it with its individualistic ethos, nontraditional methods for finding love, and enterprising, tradition-eschewing women. During the trial, the questioning and evidence mapped vaguely onto the facts and theories of the case, but what each side kept returning to was the question of the two protagonists' credibility as respectable, middle-class Berliners. Bahn had pushed his point hard, emphasizing time and again the ways in which Paul Kuhnt checked the boxes of traditional respectability as a family man, a scholar, and an honorable member of his many societies and social circles. Frieda, on the other hand, had failed repeatedly to conform to the world of tradition and refused to embrace grandfather and grandmother's way. Her casual dating, her personal ads, and the very fact that she loved bicycling and did so with unmarried friends and lovers alike marked her as a modern woman, an unstable, unpredictable, dishonorable old maid who certainly did not deserve the sad fate she ultimately received, but who also did not deserve the benefit of the doubt over an established family man whose story was full of holes and whose own parents had disowned him, but who nevertheless hewed closely enough to the ideals of middle-class comportment.

The daily newspapers recorded with a telling lack of fanfare and surprise the announcement that the jury had returned a verdict of not guilty on the murder charge. As expected, the jury found Kuhnt guilty of theft, which carried a jail sentence of six months. Kuhnt had already spent almost three times that sentence in jail while awaiting trial, so he was promptly released from custody and sent back to his wife, Margarethe, and five children, two of whom, as Bahn had reminded the court throughout the trial, were fighting for the German fatherland.[66] Once out of jail, Kuhnt was forced to confront his mounting debt. He sold off his pharmacy and scientific collection and spent the next twenty-three years working odd jobs in pharmacies around Berlin. He retired in 1939 and moved in with his daughter in the Berlin suburb of Mahlow, where he died in 1944 at the age of seventy-eight. His obituary in the *Pharmazeutische Zeitung* (*Pharmaceutical Journal*) does not mention the trial.[67]

Fragen an die Geschworenen

in der Strafsache

gegen

den

Rentner Paul Kuhnt
========

Fragen.	Antworten.
	Dabei sind die §§ 307, 308 der Strafprozeßordnung zu beachten:
	§ 307. Der Spruch ist von dem Obmanne neben den Fragen niederzuschreiben und von ihm zu unterzeichnen.
	Bei jeder dem Angeklagten nachteiligen Entscheidung ist anzugeben, daß dieselbe mit mehr als sieben Stimmen, bei Verneinung der mildernden Umstände, daß dieselbe mit mehr als sechs Stimmen gefaßt worden ist. Im übrigen darf das Stimmenverhältnis nicht angegeben werden.
	§ 308. Der Spruch ist im Sitzungszimmer von dem Obmanne kund zu geben. Der Obmann spricht die Worte: „Auf Ehre und Gewissen bezeuge ich als den Spruch der Geschworenen" und verliest die gestellten Fragen mit den darauf abgegebenen Antworten.

1. Ist der Angeklagte

   Paul Kuhnt

   schuldig, im Juni 1914 im Forst
   zu Finkenkrug vorsätzlich die
   unverehelichte Frieda Kliem
   getötet zu haben, und zwar
   indem er die Tötung mit Ue-
   berlegung ausführte ?

   Nein! Paul Schlentz.

2. Für den Fall der Vernei-
   nung der Frage zu 1 :
   Ist der Angeklagte Paul
   Kuhnt schuldig, im Juni 1914
   im Forst zu Finkenkrug die

St. P.
*Nr. 120. Fragen an die Geschworenen (§§ 293 ff. St.P.O.).

FIGURE 5.2 The first page of the verdict form, signed by the jury foreman, indicating the jury's response—"Nein"—to the question of whether Kuhnt was guilty of murder

Source: Landesarchiv Berlin A Pr. Br. Rep. 030-03, Nr. 927, Bl. 248.

THE TRIAL OF Paul Kuhnt brought no justice for Frieda Kliem, but it forced suspects and witnesses to investigate and reflect upon themselves, their neighbors, and their friends in a court of law. Were people what they claimed to be? Did everyone have a hidden identity? Who was living a double life?

Identity, presented either authentically or as an illusion, indeed became supremely relevant in the modern metropolis, where the ubiquity of strangers, new faces, and mysterious crimes shaped the way city people searched for love and intimacy.[68] As they saw it, the anonymity of the big city made crime more likely and life riskier. Love seemed so often linked to murders and swindlings, whether a groom whose happy bride was blissfully unaware of his existing marriage, a woman murdered by her jealous lover, or a prominent man blackmailed by his mysterious paramour. Indeed, Berliners, who so loved to talk about their city, discussed love using a dramatic lexicon made up of words like deception, danger, and masks. Modern, urban love was said to be difficult, even risky, and the notion that navigating urban relationships came down to one's ability to avoid being duped, to don a mask, and to snatch love out of the jaws of danger became quite prevalent in both newspapers and literature at the turn of the century. In his 1910 novel *The Notebooks of Malte Laurids Brigge*, for example, Rainer Maria Rilke takes readers into the mind of his protagonist, who struggles to acclimate himself to the modern urban environment. The sounds of the late-night electric trains keep him up, as do the many automobiles, pedestrians, and city noises. He writes that he is "learning to see" in a new way, and one of the first things he realizes is "how many faces there are. There are tons of people but even more faces, for each person has more than one."[69] Rudolf Lothar, the insightful columnist for the *Berliner Lokal-Anzeiger*, made a similar point when he noted that love itself had become nothing more than "colloquialisms, conversational artifice, and masked games." It had become fashionable, he said, to be deceptive. "The person who told the truth in today's society," he concluded, "would play a sad role" or, in other words, be unsuccessful and lonely.[70] Georg Simmel, for his part, viewed deception as an essential feature of modern—and especially urban—life, part and parcel of the way modern people navigated the modern world.[71] In Rilke's novel, Lothar's column, and Simmel's scientific work, masks at once plagued and assisted the modern urban dweller. To eschew masks or lay one's identity bare was to be old-fashioned, traditional, and out of sync with the times.

At the same time, Berliners who embraced modern techniques most often found themselves at odds with hegemonic middle-class respectability. This was especially true in matters of love and intimacy, for while Berliners almost universally harbored a fascination for modern methods like street encounters and casual dating, it was another thing altogether to accept the arm of a stranger on a streetcar or on the sidewalk. This dissonance between the bliss of imagined love and the strictures of normative masculinity and femininity played out in the Paul Kuhnt trial, where the life of Frieda Kliem, who used modern methods to bridge the gap between her middle-class aspirations and the realities of turn-of-the-century Berlin, was as much on trial as the defendant. Walter Bahn probed at the issue of her identity and emphasized that she was not what she said she was. Her fake wedding rings, her "widow" personal ad, her "uncle" boyfriend—these were masks, tools for navigating modern intimacy. Using them made her modern; it also made her decidedly suspect.

Paul Kuhnt himself was taken to task for wearing a mask. The chief judge, in his very direct questioning of the defendant, kept returning to the fact that Kuhnt had been leading a double life and had been caught trying, unsuccessfully, to hold in balance the trappings of middle-class respectability and the adventure of modern (if extramarital) love via personal ads. Walter Bahn was observant enough to realize that the case hinged on proving his client's stability, authenticity, and predictability. Accordingly, he did his utmost to persuade the jury that Kuhnt was a model of consistency, arguing even that Kuhnt had been so predictable and so firmly attached to the rails of respectability that when he stole Frieda's valuables from the commuter train in a moment of weakness, he quickly locked them away because he was too ashamed to profit from them in any way.

Bahn, in other words, did everything he could to put Frieda's masks on full display and remove the masks from his client. And the jury had, in the end, been less willing to forgive Frieda's inconsistencies, her fake rings, her masks. Put simply, women like Frieda Kliem were less likely to receive the benefit of the doubt when it came to questions of authenticity and respectability. Their tethers to middle-classness and to the stability it afforded were cracked and threadbare and could not bear the strain of inauthenticity put on them by newspaper personal ads or an individualistic, enterprising, entrepreneurial approach to dating, sex, and intimacy, more generally.

Would Paul Kuhnt have been convicted of murder if Frieda's many masks had gone undiscovered, if the Frieda who posted ads and dated casually had been "Friedrich," or if Walter Bahn had allowed the state attorney and chief judge to trump up Kuhnt's double life and myriad masks without challenge or rebuttal? It all certainly seems plausible, for while sports, office and apartment building romances, street encounters, casual dating, and free-love unions were without a doubt on the rise at the turn of the twentieth century, stability remained the bedrock of hegemonic norms of respectability, especially with regard to femininity. Indeed, stability, not love, was the reigning ideology of the time. One columnist even dug up an ostensibly scientific term—misoneism—to describe turn-of-the-century society's distrust of "the new."[72] Masks, insofar as they represented a more fleeting, short-term, individualistic, and independent approach to love, family, and community, were precisely the unsettling and mysterious part of modern life that so offended the established and authoritative power that was the middle class.

Personal ads, too, cut against the grain of stable, middle-class identity, but in a slightly different way. They represented the wholesale reimagining of a system of love and dating, one that derived its effectiveness from the size and movement of the city itself. They actually thrived on masks. Where other modern methods aimed in some way at removing masks by shrinking the big city, making many small towns (in apartment buildings, in offices, on Berliners' daily routes to work) out of a single metropolis and thus making strangers more familiar, to use personal ads was to accept of the reality of masks, acknowledge that all city dwellers wore them, and then sort through various masks and decide which one was most appealing. This was, then, not the outright rejection of masks, not even the acceptance of fewer masks, but the very practical embrace of a modern world filled with masks and the individualistic decision to pick from among them.

Frieda Kliem appears to have made her choice about which mask she found most pleasing when she arranged her rendezvous in the forest with the man she thought was Adolf Mertens. She had, in fact, fallen in love with the mask that was Adolf Mertens. Her words in that final letter to Otto Mewes—where she describes bicycling to the suburbs, swimming in a lake, lying in a hammock, and taking in the scents of the flowering acacias along the way home—belie a tranquility that is remarkable for Frieda's personality and uncommon for her experience of the modern metropolis. Things had not been particularly easy for Frieda; she spent much of her life searching for love, intimacy, and connection, only to come up perpetually short. And even though Frieda's tragic end fed the narrative of modern urban love as a sort of macabre masquerade—one where men and women shrugged off tradition and adopted the modern methods, thereby exposing themselves to deception, danger, and disaster—her experience of love at the turn of the century is best understood in terms of that last letter. Frieda Kliem at last embraced the big city, the problem of masks and stable identity, and the radically new technology of personal ads; she abandoned tradition and embraced modern love; and she found, if only for a characteristically fleeting moment, love in the big city.

Epilogue

FRIEDA KLIEM'S BERLIN still exists. It shows up at various points throughout the city: the Landwehrkanal, which saw the desperate and weary faces of Berliners worse off than Frieda before they threw themselves in it, still flows, lined in some neighborhoods by turn-of-the-century villas that have not been destroyed or renovated; giant industrial complexes like the famous Elizabeth-Hof on Erkelenzdamm, which housed not only a number of turn-of-the-century factories but also the meagerly paid, fed, and clothed Berliners who worked there, still dot the city; and Franzstrasse 5, where Frieda lived in her last apartment, appears only minimally changed. Turn-of-the-century landmarks like the Tiergarten and Friedrichstrasse are still there, too, though Segways have replaced horse-drawn buggies in the former and international retailers now line the latter.

For the most part, however, the Berlin of the late nineteenth and early twentieth centuries is gone.[1] In a way, that city actually lives on in this disappearance, as a lack of permanence was one of its most remarkable traits. Berlin was for Berlin-born journalist Arthur Eloesser a city "without memory, without tradition, without a sense of duty to the past."[2] Indeed, as Eloesser wrote, to live in Berlin at the turn of the century was to "swim toward a shoreless future."[3] This metaphor appears time and again, whether in the longing of Gertrud Steinbach's protagonist, who runs into a lake toward the seemingly limitless horizon as an expression of her yearning for independence from the man who waits for her on the shore, or in the sense that not a few Berliners left the stable shores of tradition and ran headlong into the rough waters of a modern sensibility and a new approach to love.[4] This process was far from easy, for the waves of the big city crashed hard upon women like Frieda Kliem, nor was it necessarily permanent, for the tides of modern life and middle-classness swept and pulled one back in unpredictable and disorienting ways.

If the experiences of Frieda Kliem and the many others who have appeared in these pages indicate anything, it is that this transition from stable land to a shoreless future is, in fact, part of the modern condition. Metropolitan Berlin offered a bewildering array of choices and outlets for individualism, but these routes to another shore were tenuous at best. There were some Berliners, as historian Andrew Lees describes, who praised the fact that, in the modern metropolis, "men and women were on their own [and needed] to assert themselves in order to achieve success" and that this "strengthened the larger collectivities of the nation and the state."[5] But no matter how true this was for Germany's economic development, the lives under consideration in this book suggest that the compulsion to act on one's own in matters of love and intimacy was anything but constructive or simple. Modern, middle-class life was adorned with the apparent freedom of sidestepping the conventions and perceived strictures of tradition, of marriage, of meeting within the "four walls" of the parents' home; and yet the very fabric of life in the city at the peak of industrialization was threadbare enough that most Berliners—especially women—simply needed marriage to achieve the status of middle-class respectability.[6] The turn-of-the-century city, in other words, offered women like Frieda Kliem the chance to make it on their own, to break with convention and order their lives—and, importantly, their intimate relationships—according to their individual fancies. And yet this freedom was bundled with the grim imperative of the "struggle for existence," in which one had to make it or else drown.

This coupling of marriage and respectability comes into even greater relief when compared to the Berlin (and Germany) of a century later, when there is a decidedly strong trend away from marriage. Indeed, in an article that recalls the early 1900s promotional articles of matchmaking giant Fritz Podszus's *Heirats-Zeitung*, Germany's largest online "matchmaker," Parship, recently published the results of its study of Europeans' interest in marriage under the title, "Marriage? Not That Important." Of the 52 percent of European singles currently looking for a long-term relationship, Parship claims, only a third are interested in getting married. Germans—especially those living in big cities like Berlin—are even less eager to tie the knot, Parship says, with only 20 percent reporting that they hope to get married.[7]

The contrast with turn-of-the-century Berlin reveals an important point about the triangular relationship between marriage, the middle class, and the turn-of-the-century individual. A century ago, Berliners were quite taken with the liberating potential of an individualistic approach to love and dating, but while individualism had been on a steady rise for well over a century at that point, it seems that turn-of-the-century Berliners were hardly confident in the stability or reliability of the unfettered individual and instead believed that they needed marriage to establish themselves in the modern world. Marriage was still firmly entrenched in metropolitan society as the dream of middle-class life, the ultimate status-maker, stability-creator, and respectability-generator of even the self-consciously modern generation of 1900—and especially so for women.

One must therefore resist the urge to believe entirely turn-of-the-century Berliners when they decried the "men who don't marry," "modern types of women," and the "modern aversion to marriage."[8] These were not characters and trends invented purely out of thin air, but were also the products of Berlin and, as such, as much tasty narrative as oppressive reality. Indeed, the way Berliners built upon these narrated realities is suggestive of their thinking about love, marriage, and risk in turn-of-the-century Berlin. The fortuitous encounter was thus critically important, for it was at heart a middle-class fantasy through which Berliners balanced their irresistible attraction to the freedom of the modern world with the ever-present awareness of the risks associated with it.

Masks, another idée fixe of turn-of-the-century Berlin, were also laden with the tension of fascination and risk that characterizes the experience of the modern city. The importance of masks at the turn of the century was not primarily their use in a temporary fantasy that turned the world upside down. Masks were instead convenient shorthand for the inauthenticity that at once liberated and unsettled middle-class Berliners, and their complex relationship with them is evidence of how contested the notion of individualism became in the modern city.

This, it seems, is what was so discomfiting about the potential liberation of modern methods, approaches, and sensibilities: to act selfishly—indeed, in one's own self-interests—vis-à-vis love, marriage, and intimacy was to distance oneself from a community of values, traditions, and middle-classness. The associated risks of this trade were great, as women like Frieda Kliem knew all too well. Indeed, Frieda frequently bent the truth (about being a widow, about her "uncle") as part of a difficult and ultimately unsuccessful decision to give up authenticity in order to gain stability. The fact that some succeeded in reaching the opposite shore only ratcheted up the tension of modern metropolitan life. While the opposite shore seemed closer than ever, the defense of middle-classness, and its emphasis on knowledge, stability, and opacity, grew fiercer in response.[9]

Living and loving in the modern metropolis meant confronting these tensions, uncertainties, and instabilities—a fact not lost on Baudelaire in nineteenth-century Paris.[10] And yet where Baudelaire's aesthetic was founded on the ability to feel at home in the flux of the modern city, turn-of-the-century Berliners were anything but comfortable with the ephemeral, impermanent world around them. To be sure, there were those who used these qualities of modern life to their advantage. It is not inconsequential that Walter Bahn, when appealing to the jury for his client's innocence, referred to the "fog" that characterized, he argued, the whole situation. Swindlers of all sorts played on Berliners' uneasiness about the tensions of the modern city to great success, and these swindlings, in turn, only fed the narrative of danger, risk, and masks. But as much as Berliners were fascinated by the fleeting, fugitive, and impermanent, the private, intimate, emotional lives of the Berliners in this book suggest that they were, in fact, quite uncomfortable with these abiding themes of urbanity in the turn-of-the-century city.

Looking just a decade past the Berlin under study here—to the Weimar era—reveals a resolidification of many aspects of the modern city, not the least of which was the strikingly robust individualism that characterized the 1920s. To be sure, Weimar Berlin had its own disorienting blend of anxiety and elation, but the unsettling aspects of this period—hyperinflation, political instability, the Great Depression, even the rise of fascism—had clearer, more distinct outlines. If, as historian Detlev Peukert famously argued, the Weimar era let loose or liberated "classical modernity" and was "a brief, headlong tour of the fascinating, and fateful, choices made possible by the modern world," then the resolidification of the somewhat fragile individualist ethos of the turn of the century and the explosion of a broader variety of sexual identities and approaches to love and intimacy in the 1920s is easier to understand.[11] The inherent tensions of turn-of-the-century individualism, in other words, had been at least partially released. Of course, it was not simply the birth of a new decade or even necessarily the disposal of the political system of imperial Germany that set free the full development of modernity but rather, as historian Eric Weitz puts it, "war and revolution" that, among other things, "caused a tectonic shift in moral and sexual values."[12]

The best way to understand the dramatic difference between 1900 and 1920 is thus not simply in the visibility and popularity of alternative sexualities and moralities, but, more generally, in the robustness of individualism in the 1920s and the extent to which Berliners were more content with the flux of the modern city and less anxious about the place of tradition and stability in the modern world. The exchange of a community of values for an intimate community was, in other words, less fraught in the Weimar Republic than it had been at the turn of the century, and approaches to love and intimacy in Weimar-era Berlin were thus much different.[13]

This is not to say that love in 1920s Berlin was necessarily any easier, deeper, or longer lasting. The fabric of Weimar society offered its own unique set of potential challenges to finding love, intimacy, and meaningful connections, as have subsequent eras.[14] Indeed, nowadays one is bombarded with commercials and advertisements for the twenty-first-century equivalent of the newspaper personal ad or matchmaking service: online dating services. Parship, Match.com, and eHarmony nearly always contain testimonials of (now-happy) men and women observing that modern life leaves one no time for dating, that it is difficult to meet people outside of one's circle of work colleagues, and even that cities and what might be called the virtual metropolis of online interaction are so large and impersonal that finding a meaningful relationship is all but impossible.[15] These complaints are, of course, precisely the problems and concerns that attracted so much attention at the turn of the twentieth century.

It may be that love and meaningful connections are inherently elusive. Or perhaps this is simply the narrative of love in modern world. Raymond Carver's short story "What We Talk about When We Talk about Love," seems to make a similar point, as the characters gravitate irresistibly and naturally toward violence, drama, and heartache when describing past and present relationships and talking about love, more generally.[16] On the one hand, the emplotment of love as difficult, scarce, and fleeting picked up with the birth of the metropolis because it underscored in the most intimate of ways the larger and more powerful urban trope of instability, impermanence, and uncertainty. On the other, the heartache of Berliners like Frieda Kliem and the insecurity of would-be husbands like Ernst Schwarz was very real, and the flourishing of personal ads, casual dating, and more individualistic approaches to love and marriage reveals undeniable rifts with the "when grandfather took grandmother" world of the nineteenth century.

We might, therefore, conclude that the modern world—epitomized by the modern metropolis—not only exacerbated some of the long-standing and inherent risks of love, intimacy, and marriage, but also created a whole new set of them. This book registers the tensions of Berliners coming to terms with these risks and, in some cases, creating paths around or through them, but it is clear that there was and is no panacea. The story of love in the big city at the turn of the century is, in many ways, our own story as well.

Notes

INTRODUCTION

1. Being murdered was and is, of course, exceedingly rare, but while violent crime was somewhat less common in Berlin than in Paris and London (because Berlin had virtually no organized crime), murders in fact rose sharply after 1900 and reached their zenith in 1914, when Frieda herself became such a statistic. Frieda's tragic fate was, strictly speaking, therefore uncommon, but her murder nevertheless crystalizes a whole panoply of trends peaking in 1914. On violent crime in Berlin, see Andreas Roth, *Kriminalitätsbekämpfung in deutschen Großstädten, 1850–1914: Ein Beitrag zur Geschichte des strafrechtlichen Ermittlungsverfahrens* (Berlin: Erich Schmidt Verlag, 1997), especially 290; Hans-Ulrich Wehler, *Deutsche Gesellschaftsgeschichte, 1849–1914* (Munich: C. H. Beck, 2006), especially 521.

2. On modernity and its inherent liminality, see Marshall Berman, *All That Is Solid Melts into Air: The Experience of Modernity* (New York: Penguin, 1982); Ulrich Beck, *Risk Society: Towards a New Modernity*, trans. Mark Ritter (London: Sage, 1992); David Frisby, *Fragments of Modernity: Theories of Modernity in the Work of Simmel, Kracauer, and Benjamin* (Cambridge: Polity Press, 1985).

3. On bourgeois cultural hegemony, see Andreas Schulz, *Lebenswelt und Kultur des Bürgertums im 19. und 20. Jahrhundert* (Munich: Oldenbourg, 2005), especially 22ff.

4. Ute Frevert, *Men of Honour: A Social and Cultural History of the Duel* (Cambridge: Polity Press, 1995); Hansjoachim Henning, "Soziale Verflechtungen der Unternehmer in Westfalen, 1860–1914," *Zeitschrift für Unternehmensgeschichte* 23 (1978): 1–30.

5. Hansjoachim Henning, *Das westdeutsche Bürgertum in der Epoche der Hochindustrialisierung, 1860–1914* (Wiesbaden: F. Steiner, 1973).

6. On middle-class cohesion, see Dolores L. Augustine, "Arriving in the Upper Class: The Wealthy Business Elite of Wilhelmine Germany," in David Blackbourn and Richard Evans (eds.), *The German Bourgeoisie* (New York: Routledge,

1991), 46–86; Karin Kaudelka-Hanisch, "The Titled Businessman: Prussian Commercial Councillors in the Rhineland and Westphalia during the Nineteenth Century," in Blackbourn and Evans, *The German Bourgeoisie*, 87–114; Dick Geary, "The Industrial Bourgeoisie and Labour Relations in Germany, 1871–1933," in Blackbourn and Evans, *The German Bourgeoisie*, 140–161; Frevert, *Men of Honour*; Hartmut Kaelble, "Wie feudal waren die deutschen Unternehmer im Kaiserreich?," in Richard Tilly (ed.), *Beiträge zur quantitativen vergleichenden Unternehmensgeschichte* (Stuttgart: Klett-Cotta, 1985), 148–171.

7. *Die Wandlung* 3 (1948): 69–70; Lothar Gall, "'. . . Ich wünschte ein Bürger zu sein': Zum Selbstverständnis des deutschen Bürgertums im 19. Jahrhundert," *Historische Zeitschrift* 245, no. 3 (December 1987): 601–623.

8. Manfred Hettling and Stefan-Ludwig Hoffmann, "Zur Historisierung bürgerliche Werte," in Manfred Hettling and Stefan-Ludwig Hoffmann (eds.), *Der bürgerliche Wertehimmel: Innenansichten des 19. Jahrhunderts* (Göttingen: Vandenhoeck & Ruprecht, 2000), 9.

9. This nexus of middle-class hegemony and intimacy has largely been ignored by historians. To be sure, social historians have examined the selection of spouses in imperial Germany, but the talk there is mostly about the rise or fall of the love marriage, the role of parents in choosing spouses, and the importance of money and dowries. See, for example, Andreas Gestrich, *Geschichte der Familie im 19. und 20. Jahrhundert* (Munich: Oldenbourg, 1999); Marion Kaplan, "For Love or Money: The Marriage Strategies of Jews in Imperial Germany," *Women & History* 10 (1985): 121–164; Catherine Dollard, *The Surplus Woman: Unmarried in Imperial Germany, 1871–1918* (New York: Berghahn Books, 2009); Sylvia Schraut, *Bürgerinnen im Kaiserreich: Biografie eines Lebensstils* (Stuttgart: W. Kohlhammer, 2013). Gender relations of the German middle class have also received significant attention, though, again, the nexus of middle-class hegemony and intimacy in these studies is only implicit. See, for example, Peter Gay, *The Bourgeois Experience: Victoria to Freud*, vol. 2, *The Tender Passion* (New York: Oxford University Press, 1986); Ute Frevert (ed.), *Bürgerinnen und Bürger: Geschlechterverhältnisse im 19. Jahrhundert. Zwölf Beiträge* (Göttingen: Vandenhoeck & Ruprecht, 1988); Frevert, "Bürgerliche Familie und Geschlechterrollen: Modell und Wirklichkeit," in Lutz Niethammer et al. (eds.), *Bürgerliche Gesellschaft in Deutschland: Historische Einblicke, Fragen, Perspektiven* (Frankfurt am Main: Fischer-Taschenbuch-Verlag, 1990): 90–98; Hettling and Hoffmann, *Der bürgerliche Wertehimmel*.

10. Schulz, *Lebenswelt und Kultur*, 23–24.

11. Beck, *Risk Society*, 127–128.

12. See, especially, Ulrich Beck and Elisabeth Beck-Gernsheim, *The Normal Chaos of Love*, trans. Mark Ritter and Jane Wiebel (Cambridge: Polity Press, 1995), 3–8.

13. Beck, *Risk Society*, 133.

14. Karin Hausen's recent volume of essays is an excellent example of this point. Karin Hausen, *Geschlechtergeschichte als Gesellschaftsgeschichte* (Göttingen: Vandenhoeck

& Ruprecht, 2012). More basically, one might refer to Joan Scott's now practically immortal essay, "Gender: A Useful Category of Historical Analysis," *American Historical Review* 91, no. 5 (1986): 1053–1075.

15. Georg Simmel, *On Women, Sexuality, and Love*, trans. Guy Oakes (New Haven: Yale University Press, 1984), 159; Marianne Weber, *Die Frauen und die Liebe* (Königstein im Taunus: Karl Robert Langewiesche Verlag, 1935), 10.

16. Edward Ross Dickinson, "'A Dark, Impenetrable Wall of Complete Incomprehension': The Impossibility of Heterosexual Love in Imperial Germany," *Central European History* 40 (2007): 488–489.

17. See, among others, Elaine Showalter, *Sexual Anarchy: Gender and Culture at the Fin de Siècle* (New York: Viking, 1990).

18. On the explosion of alternative (sexual) identities in the city, see Robert Beachy, *Gay Berlin: Birthplace of a Modern Identity* (New York: Knopf, 2014); Florence Tamagne, *A History of Homosexuality in Europe: Berlin, London, Paris, 1919–1939* (New York: Algora, 2006); George Chauncey, *Gay New York: Gender, Urban Culture, and the Making of the Gay Male World, 1890–1940* (New York: Basic Books, 1994); Klaus Tenfelde, "Urbanization and the Spread of Urban Culture," in Friedrich Lenger (ed.), *Towards an Urban Nation: Germany since 1780* (Oxford: Berg, 2002), 30–31; Margot Finn, "Sex and the City: Metropolitan Modernities in English History," *Victorian Studies* 44 (2001): 25–32; Sherwin Simmons, "Ernst Kirchner's Streetwalkers: Art, Luxury, and Immortality in Berlin, 1913–1916," *Art Bulletin* 82 (2000): 117–148. Of course, as Mark Steinberg points out in his study of St. Petersburg, it was more the urban press—most notably newspapers—and a growing body of sexual scientific literature than the city itself that made alternative masculinities and femininities so visible and ripe for public comment. Prostitution, of all of the seemingly bourgeoning examples of "decadence" and a quickly fading sense of urban propriety, was without a doubt the favorite of city newspapers and feuilletonists, just as it was the most concerning to city magistrates, police commissioners, and pastors. Mark Steinberg, *Petersburg Fin de Siècle* (New Haven: Yale University Press, 2011), 185–189.

19. Gottfried Korff, "Mentalität und Kommunikation in der Großstadt: Berliner Notizen zur 'inneren' Urbanisierung," in Theodor Kohlmann and Hermann Bausinger (eds.), *Großstadt: Aspekte empirischer Kulturforschung* (Berlin: Staatliche Museen Preussischer Kulturbesitz, 1985), 343–361.

20. "Liebe," *Meyers grosses Konversations-Lexikon*, vol. 12, 6th ed. (1905), 526.

21. Dickinson, "Dark, Impenetrable Wall," 481.

22. Julie Abraham, *Metropolitan Lovers: The Homosexuality of Cities* (Minneapolis: University of Minnesota Press, 2008); Tamagne, *History of Homosexuality*; Chauncey, *Gay New York*; Beachy, *Gay Berlin*.

23. The gender theorist R. W. Connell has in some ways taken the first steps in this sense with regard to masculinity—or masculinities in the plural, as Connell famously proposed. Rather than writing a history of gay men as entirely distinct

from the history of straight men, Connell has, in a variety of contexts, modeled analyzing the multifaceted experience of men in terms of constellations of masculinities that evolve in intertwined and reflexive ways. R. W. Connell, "A Very Straight Gay: Masculinity, Homosexual Experience, and the Dynamics of Gender," *American Sociological Review* 57, no. 6 (1992): 735–751; R. W. Connell., *Masculinities*, 2nd ed. (Berkeley: University of California Press, 2005).

24. Peter Fritzsche, *Reading Berlin 1900* (Cambridge, MA: Harvard University Press, 1996), 1–2.

25. Peter Fritzsche, "Vagabond in the Fugitive City: Hans Ostwald, Imperial Berlin and the *Grossstadt-Dokumente,*" *Journal of Contemporary History* 29, no. 3 (1994): 385.

26. Fritzsche, *Reading Berlin 1900*, 1. See also Steinberg, *Petersburg Fin de Siècle*, 34–35.

27. As Iain Boyd Whyte and David Frisby point out, narratives of Berlin "became transposed into urban imaginaries that drew out largely negative features of the new metropolis within which were embedded the dystopian dimensions of a threatening urban modernity." Iain Boyd Whyte and David Frisby (eds.), *Metropolis Berlin, 1880–1940* (Berkeley: University of California Press, 2012), 10.

28. As such, this is a strikingly different register of Berlin life than what appears in, say, dime store novels or pulp fiction (so-called *Trivialliteratur*), where the worlds portrayed are not so much those of workers and the petit bourgeoisie as of those with money and power. Pulp fiction is tailored to the appetites and fantasies of its readers, and in the strictly censored publishing environment of imperial Germany, this genre was further complicated by the necessity of avoiding run-ins with the censors. So series like "Intimate Stories" ("Intime Geschichten") and "Pillow Talk" ("Was man nicht laut erzählt")—the former of which appears in chapter 2— contorted their salacious-sounding tales to titillate using the lexicon of a prudish political regime. Indeed, pulp fiction authors took to transposing the sex and desire of their plots to chauvinism and even militarism as a way of appealing to the censors. And yet pulp fiction at the turn of the century appealed to the many Berliners, who snatched up copy after copy, offering a flip side to the world they inhabited. After all, Berliners perhaps needed to dream and fantasize about topics like love, sex, intimacy, and marriage. As Peter Pütz writes, "When readers no longer want or need to dream, they stop buying dime store novels." Peter Pütz, "Die Kiosk ist die Schule der Nation: Trivialliteratur und Demokratie," *Gießener Universitätsblätter* 7, no. 2 (1974): 62–63. See also Kaspar Maase, *Die Kinder der Massenkultur: Kontroversen um Schmutz und Schund seit dem Kaiserreich* (Frankfurt am Main: Campus, 2012), 73.

29. Fritzsche, *Reading Berlin 1900*, 114, 162; see also Josef Mooser, *Arbeiterleben in Deutschland, 1900–1970: Klassenlagen, Kultur und Politik* (Frankfurt am Main: Suhrkamp, 1984), 50.

30. See, for example, Zhao Ma, "Down the Alleyway: Courtyard Tenements and Women's Networks in Early Twentieth-Century Beijing," *Journal of Urban History* 36 (2010): 151–172; Sharon Marcus, *Apartment Stories: City and Home*

in Nineteenth-Century Paris and London (Berkeley: University of California Press, 1999); Finn, "Sex and the City"; David Harvey, *Paris: Capital of Modernity* (New York: Routledge, 2003); Joachim Schlör, *Nights in the Big City: Paris, Berlin, London, 1840–1930* (London: Reaktion, 1998); Carl Schorske, *Fin-de-Siècle Vienna: Politics and Culture* (New York: Knopf, 1980).

31. Walter Benjamin, "Paris, die Hauptstadt des XIX. Jahrhunderts," in *Das Passagen-Werk*, vol. 5.1 (Frankfurt am Main: Suhrkamp, 1982), 45–59.

32. In turn-of-the-century St. Petersburg, for example, a massive part of the population left the city and returned to the country villages; and Parisians, for their part, were less mobile and often did not stray far from the neighborhoods and enclaves in which they worked and had family connections. Steinberg, *Petersburg Fin de Siècle*. See also Schorske, *Fin-de-Siècle Vienna*; Scott Spector, *Prague Territories: National Conflict and Cultural Innovation in Franz Kafka's Fin de Siècle* (Berkeley: University of California Press, 2000). For further discussion of Berlin's exceptional and emblematic newness, see Fritzsche, "Vagabond," 386.

33. Of course, not all observers (or Berliners) were quite so happy about the explosion of old Berlin into a modern metropolis, and the late nineteenth and early twentieth centuries featured no small amount of antiurbanist literature. Andrew Lees, *Cities, Sin, and Social Reform in Imperial Germany* (Ann Arbor: University of Michigan Press, 2002); see also Andrew Lees, *Cities Perceived: Urban Society in European and American Thought* (New York: Columbia University Press, 1985), especially 82–90.

34. Police report, Landesarchiv Berlin, A Pr. Br. Rep. 030, Nr. 16927. More generally, see Lees, *Cities, Sin, and Social Reform*.

35. For example, Leo Ou-fan Lee, *Shanghai Modern: The Flowering of a New Urban Culture in China, 1930–1945* (Cambridge, MA: Harvard University Press, 1999); Shu-mei Shih, *The Lure of the Modern: Writing Modernism in Semicolonial Shanghai, 1917–1937* (Berkeley: University of California Press, 2001); Adriana Bergero, *Intersecting Tango: Cultural Geographies of Buenos Aires, 1900–1930* (Pittsburgh: University of Pittsburgh Press, 2008); David Crowley, "Castles, Cabarets, and Cartoons: Claims on Polishness in Kraków around 1905," in Malcolm Gee, Tim Kirk, and Jill Steward (eds.), *The City in Central Europe: Culture and Society from 1800 to the Present* (Brookfield, VT: Ashgate, 1999), 101–117.

CHAPTER I

1. "Berliner Verkehrszahlen," *Berliner Lokal-Anzeiger*, April 15, 1902, Nr. 174.

2. Statement by Frau Dr. Selma Fischer, Landesarchiv Berlin A Pr. Br. Rep. 030-03, Nr. 1425, Bl. 22.

3. Ibid.

4. *Berliner Adressbücher*, 1905. Zentral- und Landesbibliothek Berlin, 999.

5. *Berliner Adressbücher*, 1902–1904. Zentral- und Landesbibliothek Berlin.

6. *Berliner Adressbücher*, 1902. Zentral- und Landesbibliothek Berlin, 1395; statement by Frau Dr. Selma Fischer, Landesarchiv Berlin A Pr. Br. Rep. 030-03, Nr. 1425, Bl. 22.

7. Sewing was, in fact, one of the most common occupations for poor women in the turn-of-the-century city. Robyn Dasey, "Women's Work and the Family: German Garment Workers in Berlin and Hamburg before the First World War," in Richard Evans and W. R. Lee (eds.), *The German Family: Essays on the Social History of the Family in Nineteenth- and Twentieth-Century Germany* (London: Croom Helm, 1981), 221–255, especially 228ff.

8. Based on the consumer price index (which roughly measures purchasing power), one mark in 1900 is equivalent to right around seven US dollars in 2018. Deutsche Bundesbank, "Kaufkraftäquivalente historischer Beträge in deutschen Währungen," https://www.bundesbank.de.

9. Statement by Frau Dr. Selma Fischer, Landesarchiv Berlin A Pr. Br. Rep. 030-03, Nr. 1425, Bl. 22.

10. *Berliner Adressbücher*, 1907, Zentral- und Landesbibliothek Berlin, 1143; statement by Frau Dr. Selma Fischer, Landesarchiv Berlin A Pr. Br. Pr. 030-03, Nr. 1425, Bl. 22.

11. ——er, "Was lehrt uns die Ehestatistik?," *Berliner Lokal-Anzeiger*, August 4, 1905, Nr. 378.

12. One thinks of the lower-middle-class clerk Pinneburg in Hans Fallada's 1932 novel, *Little Man, What Now?* Throughout the novel, Pinneburg struggles to accommodate his middle-class taste and aspirations with his ever-diminishing income.

13. Werner Ladenbauer includes silver as one of the classic elements of the middle-class home (alongside paintings, old clocks, pretty table settings, sculptures, rugs, etc.) in his autobiographical study of bourgeois families in the nineteenth and twentieth centuries. Werner Ladenbauer, "'Blut ist dicker als Wasser'—Die Wiener Familie Ladenbauer," in Hannes Stekl (ed.), *Bürgerliche Familien: Lebenswege im 19. und 20. Jahrhundert* (Vienna: Böhlau, 2000), 97. See also Schulz, *Lebenswelt und Kultur*, 20–21.

14. Statement by Oskar Seibeke, Landesarchiv Berlin A Pr. Br. Rep. 030-03, Nr. 1425, Bl. 50.

15. Quoted in Alfred Kelly, *The German Worker: Working-Class Autobiographies from the Age of Industrialization* (Berkeley: University of California Press, 1987), 73.

16. Memorabilia belonging to Frieda Kliem, Landesarchiv Berlin A Pr. Br. Rep. 030-03, Nr. 1425, Bl. 95.

17. Statements, Landesarchiv Berlin A Pr. Br. Rep. 030-03, Nr. 1425, Bl. 8–14, 23, 40–41, 43–45, 50–51, 58, 63–70, 103–110; letter from Otto Mewes to police, Landesarchiv Berlin A Pr. Br. Rep. 030-03, Nr. 1425, Bl. 95.

18. Statements, Landesarchiv Berlin A Pr. Br. Rep. 030-03, Nr. 1425, Bl. 33–37, 51–52, 67–70, 110–113.

19. Ulrich Beck and Elisabeth Beck-Gernsheim, "Passage to Hope: Marriage, Migration, and the Need for a Cosmopolitan Turn in Family Research," *Journal of Family Theory & Review* 2 (December 2010):, 411.

20. Ibid.

21. A further distinction vis-à-vis emotional motives—the desire to marry for "internal" (e.g., feelings of belonging, closeness, intimacy) or "external" (e.g., as evidence to others of one's status, desirability, etc.)—is tempting but probably not tenable, impossible as it is to weigh these against each other. Cf. Gabriele Thießen, *"Da verstehe ich die Liebe doch anders und besser": Liebeskonzepte der Münchener Boheme um 1900* (Nordhausen: Verlag Traugott Bautz, 2015), especially 114ff.

22. Kathy Peiss, *Cheap Amusements: Working Women and Leisure in Turn-of-the-Century New York* (Philadelphia: Temple University Press, 1986).

23. Hartmut Dießenbacher phrases the question the other way around, to wit, from the side of city organizers and officials: "A steadily decreasing death rate stood alongside a steadily growing birth rate, which raised new problems. What will become of the 'surplus' population? Where should they live? Where to work? Above all: how should they feed themselves?" Hartmut Dießenbacher, "Soziale Umbrüche und sozialpolitische Antworten: Entwicklungslinien vom 19. ins frühe 20. Jahrhundert," in Gesine Asmus (ed.), *Hinterhof, Keller und Mansarde: Einblicke in Berliner Wohnungselend, 1901–1920* (Hamburg: Rowohlt, 1982), 10–11.

24. Eva-Maria Schnurr, "Teenage Angst: Berlin's Turn of the Century Growing Pains," *Spiegel Online International*, November 22, 2012, http://www.spiegel.de/international/germany/the-late-19th-century-saw-the-birth-of-modern-berlin-a-866321.html.

25. Mark Twain, "The Chicago of Europe," *Chicago Daily Tribune*, April 3, 1892, 33.

26. Ibid.

27. By comparison, London grew 145 percent during this period; Paris (158 percent) and Vienna (277 percent) grew at greater rates but still could not match Berlin. Christiania, Norway (present-day Oslo) did have Berlin's 351 percent beat, having grown between 1850 and 1900 at the staggering rate of 714 percent; but it nevertheless remained in 1900 a very small "big city." Thomas Hall, *Planning Europe's Capital Cities: Aspects of Nineteenth-Century Urban Development* (London: Spon, 2005), 300.

28. Lutz Niethammer and Franz Brüggemeier, "Wie wohnten Arbeiter im Kaiserreich?," *Archiv für Sozialgeschichte* 16 (1976): 84.

29. Albert Südekum, *Großstädtisches Wohnungselend*, vol. 45 of Hans Ostwald (ed.), *Großstadt-Dokumente*, (Berlin, 1908), 17; Eugen Baumann, "Die zunehmende Beweglichkeit der Bevölkerung," 14, quoted in Hugh McLeod, *Piety and Poverty: Working-Class Religion in Berlin, London, and New York* (New York: Holmes & Meier, 1996), 11.

30. G. E., "Oktober-Umzug," *Berliner Morgenpost*, September 13, 1900, Nr. 214. On the spectacle of moving day and the role of the daily newspapers in covering them,

see Fritzsche, *Reading Berlin 1900*, 120. Moving day also counts as one of Johannes Trojan's "One Hundred Snapshots" of Berlin life from 1903. Johannes Trojan, *Berliner Bilder: Hundert Momentaufnahmen* (Berlin: Grote, 1903), 216–219.

31. Sylvester, "Berlin bei Nacht," *Berliner Morgenpost*, February 25, 1899, Nr. 48.

32. "Ueber den Potsdamer-Platz," *Berliner Zeitung*, October 12, 1905, Nr. 240.

33. Dorothee Goebeler, "Berlin auf der Strasse: Der Potsdamer Platz," *Berliner Lokal-Anzeiger*, July 1, 1913, Nr. 337.

34. E. G., "Nachtleben der Großstadt," *Berliner Lokal-Anzeiger*, October 24, 1900, Nr. 498.

35. Stefan Zweig, *The World of Yesterday: An Autobiography*, trans. Harry Zohn (Lincoln: University of Nebraska Press, 1964), 1–27.

36. Even if Berlin was widely recognized as having the most fantastic and colorful night-life, this does not mean its dynamics were atypical or unrepresentative of big cities at the turn of the century. All of the problems and opportunities of the modern me-tropolis were, in greater or lesser form, present in other so-called first- and second-rank cities around 1900. See, for example, McLeod, *Piety and Poverty*, xx; Heidrun Homburg, *Rationalisierung und Industriearbeit: Arbeitsmarkt—Management—Arbeiterschaft im Siemens Konzern Berlin 1900–1939* (Berlin: Haude und Spener Verlag, 1991), 91.

37. Karl Baedeker, *Berlin and Its Environs*, 5th ed. (Leipzig: Karl Baedeker, 1912), v.

38. M. L., "Wenn Fremde nach Berlin kommen: Vergnügungen und Enttäuschungen," *Berliner Morgenpost*, March 28, 1906, Nr. 73.

39. Agnes Harder, "Briefe einer Provinzialin aus Berlin. II," *Berliner Lokal-Anzeiger*, July 12, 1910, Nr. 347. Johannes Trojan, too, fantasizes about a newcomer being so confused that he mistakenly takes the train back out of town when he means to go to the city center. Trojan, *Berliner Bilder*, 66–69.

40. Frisby, *Fragments of Modernity*, 39.

41. Georg Simmel, "The Metropolis and Mental Life," (1903) in Gary Bridge and Sophie Watson (eds.), *The Blackwell City Reader* (Malden, MA: Wiley-Blackwell, 2002), 11.

42. Ibid., 13.

43. Ibid., 12–13.

44. Ibid., 14.

45. Ibid., 15.

46. For that matter, as William Cronon demonstrates so brilliantly with regard to turn-of-the-century Chicago, the metropolis lives and breathes through its rural surroundings. William Cronon, *Nature's Metropolis: Chicago and the Great West* (New York: Norton, 1991). On the urban/rural dichotomy, more gener-ally, see Charles T. Stewart Jr., "The Urban-Rural Dichotomy: Concepts and Uses," *American Journal of Sociology* 64, no. 2 (1958): 152–158; Tony Champion and Graeme Hugo (eds.), *New Forms of Urbanization: Beyond the Urban-rural*

Dichotomy (Aldershot: Ashgate, 2003); Norton Ginsburg, Bruce Koppel, and T. G. McGee (eds.), *The Extended Metropolis: Settlement Transition in Asia* (Honolulu: University of Hawaii Press, 1991); Jeremy Porter and Frank Howell, "On the 'Urbanness' of Metropolitan Areas: Testing the Homogeneity Assumption, 1970–2000," *Population Research and Policy Review* 28, no. 5 (2009): 589–613.

47. Moritz Föllmer, *Individuality and Modernity in Berlin: Self and Society from Weimar to the Wall* (Cambridge: Cambridge University Press, 2013). See also Moritz Föllmer, "Suicide and Crisis in Weimar Berlin," *Central European History* 42 (2009): 195. Luisa Passerini also speaks of European cities in terms of isolation. Louisa Passerini, *Europe in Love, Love in Europe* (New York: New York University Press, 1999), 38–39.

48. Judith Walkowitz, *City of Dreadful Delight: Narratives of Sexual Danger in Late-Victorian London* (Chicago: University of Chicago Press, 1992), 17.

49. Schlör, *Nights in the Big City*.

50. Anthony McElligott, *The German Urban Experience 1900–1945: Modernity and Chaos* (London: Routledge, 2001), 186.

51. Ibid., 75.

52. "Momentbild von der Strasse," *Berliner Lokal-Anzeiger*, July 16, 1902, Nr. 327.

53. Julius Knopf, "Straßenbahnskizzen," *Berliner Morgenpost*, August 22, 1912, Nr. 230.

54. "Gespräche im Stadtbahncoupé," *Berliner Tageblatt*, June 8, 1907, Nr. 285.

55. One journalist went as far as to suggest that Berlin was so different from small towns—where gossip and nosey neighbors reigned supreme—that people often moved to Berlin to get away from this and live quiet, isolated lives. This is quite interesting, though hardly representative. Most Berliners found the isolation heartbreaking and oppressive. M. C., "Einsam gestorben in der Großstadt," *Berliner Lokal-Anzeiger*, January 29, 1908, Nr. 51.

56. "Öffentliche Meinung: Einsame Mädchen," *Berliner Lokal-Anzeiger*, November 11, 1900, Nr. 530.

57. "Öffentliche Meinung: Einsame Damen," *Berliner Lokal-Anzeiger*, November 18, 1900, Nr. 542.

58. Dr. A. Römer, "Das Rendezvous am Potsdamer Platz: Ein heiteres Strassenbild mit ernstem Hintergrund," *Berliner Morgenpost*, December 28, 1902, Nr. 303.

59. Friedrich Lenger, "Grossstadtmenschen," in Ute Frevert and Heinz-Gerhard Haupt (eds.), *Der Mensch des 19. Jahrhunderts* (Frankfurt am Main: Campus-Verlag, 1999), 291.

60. Trojan, *Berliner Bilder*, 103–106.

61. Maria Janitschek, "Weihnachtsspaziergang eines Einsamen," *Berliner Lokal-Anzeiger*, December 25, 1900, Nr. 602.

62. Maurice Level, "Einsamkeit," *Berliner Morgenpost*, April 30, 1913, Nr. 117, 1.

63. Ibid.

64. Ibid., 2.

65. Dagobert v. Gerhardt-Amyntor, "Die Gefahren der Einsamkeit," *Berliner Lokal-Anzeiger*, January 5, 1902, Nr. 7; "Einsam bin ich und verlassen," *Berliner Lokal-Anzeiger*, July 28, 1901, Nr. 349.

66. Walter Benjamin, *Illuminations*, trans. Harry Zohn (New York: Schocken Books, 1968), 169.

67. Armand Ernesti, "Im Strudel der Hauptstadt verloren," *Der Eigene*, June 1903, 424.

68. Hugo Klein, "Furcht vor der Liebe," *Berliner Morgenpost*, April 26, 1904, Nr. 97.

69. Heinrich Teweles, "Aller Liebe Anfang," *Berliner Morgenpost*, August 1, 1908, Nr. 179.

70. Aimée Gaber, "Sehnsucht," *Berliner Morgenpost*, October 23, 1910, Nr. 291; A. Burg, "Fritz Wendekamp's Jugendliebe," *Berliner Morgenpost*, September 3, 1907, Nr. 206.

71. "Der Photograph als Heiratsvermittler," *Berliner Lokal-Anzeiger*, August 22, 1906, Nr. 425.

72. "Das Bild des Zukünftigen," *Berliner Morgenpost*, February 5, 1907, Nr. 30.

73. Aimée Gaber, "Sehnsucht," *Berliner Morgenpost*, October 23, 1910, Nr. 291; "Eine Bekanntschaft auf dem Kirchhofe," *Berliner Lokal-Anzeiger*, May 3, 1910, Nr. 221.

74. Th. Ebner, "Von der Strasse: Momentbilder," *Berliner Morgenpost*, March 8, 1904, Nr. 57.

75. Aribert, "Die Liebessprache," *Berliner Morgenpost*, August 16, 1905, Nr. 191.

76. Reinhold Ortmann, "Wiedersehen," *Berliner Morgenpost*, September 6, 1904, Nr. 209.

77. Lenelotte Winfeld, "Begegnung," *Berliner Morgenpost*, November 6, 1910, Nr. 305.

78. *You've Got Mail*, DVD, directed by Nora Ephron (Burbank, CA: Warner Home Video, 2001).

79. In an interesting and fortuitous twist, this pairing of "Encounter" and *You've Got Mail* is perhaps not so odd or uncommon: Nora Ephron's film was, in fact, an adaptation of Berliner Ernst Lubitsch's 1940 film, *The Shop around the Corner*, which, like "Begegnung" from 1910, used letters and not email or chatrooms as the mode of communication between the two lovers. Whether or not Lubitsch was familiar with Winfeld's "Encounter" is unclear, but given Lubitsch's Berlin-based youth (around 1910) and the ubiquity of daily newspapers, it is tantalizing to think that *You've Got Mail* might, in some distant way be based on Lenelotte Winfeld's "Begegnung."

80. Georg Lomer, *Liebe und Psychose* (Wiesbaden: Bergmann, 1907), 12–13.; Pascal, "Ein Buch über die Liebe," *Berliner Lokal-Anzeiger*, June 15, 1907, Nr. 299.

81. M. Warwar, "Straßenbekanntschaften," *Berliner Morgenpost*, October 3, 1909, Nr. 257.

82. Ibid.

83. "Das Publikum: Straßenbekanntschaften," *Berliner Morgenpost*, October 10, 1909, Nr. 264.

84. Ibid.

85. "Das Publikum: Das Ansprechen auf der Strasse," *Berliner Morgenpost*, May 1, 1904, Nr. 102.

86. "Das Publikum: Das Ansprechen auf der Strasse," *Berliner Morgenpost*, May 12, 1904, Nr. 111.

87. "Briefkasten: Konditorei," *Berliner Lokal-Anzeiger*, May 8, 1904, Nr. 215.

88. In fact, I stopped counting after finding well over one hundred cases of swindlers who had played on Berliners' eagerness to end their loneliness. Each story was more or less the same with just the names and places differing from case or case. Some were quite bizarre, though; for example, a man posing as a doctor found various "patients" in the hospital who believed love had found them. "Eine Bekanntschaft von der Strasse," *Berliner Morgenpost*, January 6, 1903, Nr. 4.

89. For example, "In die Berliner Eheverhältnisse," *Berliner Morgenpost*, December 31, 1898, Nr. 87. "Berliner Eheschliessungen," *Berliner Lokal-Anzeiger*, January 7, 1901, Nr. 10.

90. Pessimistic contemporary takes on Berlin's marriage rates include Friedrich Prinzing, "Heiratshäufigkeit und Heiratsalter nach Stand und Beruf," *Zeitschrift für Sozialwissenschaft* 6 (1903): 546–559; Prinzing, "Die Wandlungen der Heiratshäufigkeit und des mittleren Heiratsalters," *Zeitschrift für Sozialwissenschaft* 5 (1902): 656–674. More recently, John Knodel and Mary Jo Maynes argued that urban marriage rates were much lower in Berlin than elsewhere. John Knodel and Mary Jo Maynes, "Urban and Rural Marriage in Imperial Germany," *Journal of Family History* 1 (1976): 129–168. Catherine Dollard's argument is that Prinzing, Knodel, and Maynes misinterpreted the statistical data available and bought into the compelling narrative of a national crisis of a massive surplus of unmarried German women. Dollard, *The Surplus Woman*, 79.

91. Dollard, *The Surplus Woman*, 79.

92. "Die Statistik der Liebe: Die Myrte blüht," *Berliner Morgenpost*, January 12, 1904, Nr. 9.

93. ——er, "Was lehrt uns die Ehestatistik?," *Berliner Lokal-Anzeiger*, August 4, 1905, Nr. 378.

94. On the matter of marrying for the purposes of an apartment lease, see "Die Ehe gegen die Arbeitslosigkeit," *Berliner Morgenpost*, May 2, 1901, Nr. 102. Statistics from Berlin's statistical office back this up. See *Statistisches Jahrbuch der Stadt Berlin* (Berlin: P. Stankiewicz' Buchdruckerei, 1908–1911), 85.

95. Helene Lange and Gertrud Bäumer (eds.), *Handbuch der Frauenbewegung* (Berlin: W. Moeser, 1902), vol. 4, *Die Deutsche Frau im Beruf*, by Robert Wilbrandt and Lisbeth Wilbrandt, 22.

96. Dollard, *The Surplus Woman*, 86. See also Rolf Gehrmann, "German Towns on the Eve of Industrialization: Household Formation and the Part of the Elderly," *History of the Family* 19, no. 1 (2004): 13–28; Paul Puschmann, Per-Olof Grönberg, Reto Schumacher, and Koen Matthijs, "Access to Marriage and Reproduction among Migrants in Antwerp and Stockholm: A Longitudinal Approach to

Processes of Social Inclusion and Exclusion, 1846–1926," *History of the Family* 19, no. 1 (2004): 29–52.

97. *Statistisches Jahrbuch der Stadt Berlin* (Berlin: P. Stankiewicz' Buchdruckerei, 1905), 17; *Statistisches Jahrbuch der Stadt Berlin*, 1908–1911, 85.

98. K——tsch, "Die Neigung zum Heirathen," *Berliner Lokal-Anzeiger*, May 1, 1901, Nr. 202.

99. Hermann Schwabe, *Betrachtungen über die Volksseele von Berlin* (Berlin: Guttentag, 1870), 12.

100. Dora Duncker, *Reelles Heiratsgesuch etc.: Inserat Studien* (Stuttgart: Carl Krabbe, 1888), 2.

101. Dorothee Goebeler, "Einsame Frauen," *Berliner Lokal-Anzeiger*, December 22, 1912, Nr. 651.

102. Ibid; Lenger, "Grossstadtmenschen," 270.

103. Letter to Adolf Mertens, Landesarchiv Berlin A Pr. Br. Rep. 030-03, Nr. 1232, "Mord; darin Zeitungsausschnitte, Briefe, Abschriften von Annoncen," Bl. 39.

104. "Öffentliche Meinung: Drei Bräute und ein Mann," *Berliner Lokal-Anzeiger*, November 13, 1904, Nr. 535.

105. "Öffentliche Meinung: Gnädige Frau?," *Berliner Lokal-Anzeiger*, August 12, 1900, Nr. 374.

106. Schwabe, *Betrachtungen über die Volksseele*, 12ff.

107. For diaries revealing the heartache of this parting, see, for example, Else Behrens, *Tagebuch 1898–1903*, Deutsches Tagebucharchiv, Signatur 1314 / I.1–1314 / I.2; also Fritz Reinert, *Tagebuch 1902–3*, Deutsches Tagebucharchiv, Signatur 1929.

108. "Öffentliche Meinung: Warum Junggeselle bleiben," *Berliner Lokal-Anzeiger*, December 29, 1907, Nr. 659.

109. "Der Weg zur Ehe," *Berliner Morgenpost*, August 6, 1911, Nr. 214.

110. "Das Publikum: Wie kommt man zu einer Frau?," *Berliner Morgenpost*, November 12, 1911, Nr. 312.

111. On the other hand, and to hear Frau Hoffmann of rural Brandenburg describe it, A. G. may not have been so far off. Engagements, she wrote, are "very simple. The man says to his future wife, 'I'm going to marry you. Take care of everything, we'll have the wedding on such and such a day.' There's no special engagement party. How can there be for poor people? He works and she works. Also they're not called fiancés; more likely people say, 'He's going with her; he's going to marry her.' If you're of age, you don't have to ask your parents for permission to marry; and you don't ask. In the other case the parents are asked when children want to marry. Permission is always given." Quoted in Kelly, *The German Worker*, 361.

112. "Das Publikum: Wie kommt man zu einer Frau?," *Berliner Morgenpost*, November 12, 1911, Nr. 312.

113. Ibid.

114. Ibid.; emphasis added.

115. Jens Flemming, "'. . . von Jahr zu Jahr ein Sorgen und Bangen ohne Ende': Einkommen, Lohn, Lebensstandard," in Wolfgang Ruppert (ed.), *Die Arbeiter: Lebensformen, Alltag und Kultur von der Frühindustrialisierung bis zum "Wirtschaftswunder"* (Munich: C. H. Beck, 1986), 139.

116. Kelly, *The German Worker*, 27ff.

117. Statement by Marie Schönemann, Landesarchiv Berlin A Pr. Br. Rep. 030-03, Nr. 1425, Bl. 10.

118. Quoted in Kelly, *The German Worker*, 72.

119. "Verzweiflung," *Berliner Morgenpost*, August 9, 1905, Nr. 185, quoted in Fritzsche, *Reading Berlin 1900*, 121.

120. *Statistisches Jahrbuch der Stadt Berlin*, 1905, 305.

121. Carola Lipp, "Sexualität und Heirat," in Ruppert, *Die Arbeiter*, 191–192.

122. "Die Frau im Kampf ums Dasein: Zur Einführung," *Berliner Morgenpost*, December 11, 1898, Nr. 71.

123. "Die Frau im Krampf ums Dasein," *Berliner Morgenpost*, February 14, 1899, Nr. 38.

124. Carola Lipp points out, for example, that sex often served as a substitute for marriage because working-class men and women simply could not afford to get married. Lipp, "Sexualität und Heirat," 193.

125. Ibid., 192.

126. "Das Liebesdrama in der Weinhandlung," *Berliner Lokal-Anzeiger*, February 16, 1908, Nr. 85.

127. Th. Ebner, "Von der Strasse: Momentbilder," *Berliner Morgenpost*, March 8, 1904, Nr. 57.

128. "Sonderbare Brautpaare (Aus dem Tagebuch eines Standesbeamten)," *Berliner Morgenpost*, May 2, 1909, Nr. 105.

129. Sadly, Berlin's statistical office kept no record of employment status on arrival in the city. *Statistisches Jahrbuch der Stadt Berlin*, 1905, 82–83.

130. Ibid.

131. Ibid., 81.

132. Ibid., 21.

133. Paul Puschmann and Arne Solli, "Household and Family during Urbanization and Industrialization: Efforts to Shed New Light on an Old Debate," *History of the Family* 19, no. 1 (2004): 1–12. Indeed, as Puschmann et al. point out, the literature on this topic is filled with methodological problems, and "evidence is searched in order to proof [*sic*] that urban in-migrants indeed got into deep trouble upon arrival in the city [or, alternatively, that they thrived]." Puschmann et al., "Access to Marriage," 30. There have been a variety of efforts to determine the presence of extended family networks for city-bound migrants, whether via the growth and decline of the nuclear family, as in Steven Ruggles, *Prolonged Connections: The Rise of the Extended Family in Nineteenth-Century England and America* (Madison: University of Wisconsin Press, 1987); the size of extended

families, more generally, as in Michael Anderson, *Family Structure in Nineteenth-Century Lancashire* (Cambridge: Cambridge University Press, 1971), 152–160; the cohabitation of the elderly with their offspring, as in Rolf Gehrmann, "German Towns," 13–28; the marriage rates of newcomers, as in Katherine Lynch, "The European Marriage Pattern in the Cities: Variations on a Theme by Hajnal," *Journal of Family History* 16 (1991): 79–95; Michel Oris, "The Age at Marriage of Migrants during the Industrial Revolution in the Region of Liège," *History of the Family* 5 (2000): 391–413; and degrees of social inclusion and average time to marriage and childbirth for newcomers, as in Puschmann et al., "Access to Marriage"; and Lynch, "European Marriage Pattern," 83. Frans Van Poppel arguably gets closest to a definitive measure of social networks for newcomers in his study of sixty thousand marriage certificates in thirty cities in the nineteenth- and early twentieth-century Netherlands. His conclusion, like the others, as Puschmann et al. summarize, is that "the fact that newcomers initially did not have a large number of friends and acquaintances at the place of settlement made it more difficult to meet potential partners." Frans Van Poppel, "Trouwen in Nederland: Een historisch-demografische studie van de 19e en vroeg- 20e eeuw," PhD dissertation, Wageningen University, 1992, cited in Puschmann et al., "Access to Marriage," 35.

134. "Berliner Beobachter," *Berliner Lokal-Anzeiger*, May 14, 1905, Nr. 230.

135. Puschmann et al., "Access to Marriage," 46.

136. Ibid., 29; Leslie Page Moch, *Moving Europeans: Migration in Western Europe since 1650* (Bloomington: Indiana University Press, 2003); Colin Pooley and Jean Turnbull, *Migration and Mobility in Britain since the 18th Century* (London: Routledge, 1997).

137. David Kertzer and Dennis Hogan, "On the Move: Migration in an Italian Community, 1865–1921," *Social Science History* 9, no. 1 (Winter 1985): 20. See also Clé Lesger, Leo Lucassen, and Marlou Schrover, "Is There Life outside the Migrant Network? German Immigrants in XIXth Century Netherlands and the Need for a More Balanced Migration Typology," *Annales de Démographie Historique* 2 (2002): 29–50.

138. "Öffentliche Meinung: Wer weiß Rat?," *Berliner Lokal-Anzeiger*, April 8, 1906, Nr. 180.

139. "Berliner Beobachter," *Berliner Lokal-Anzeiger*, November 2, 1902, Nr. 515.

140. Jürgen Kocka et al., *Familie und Soziale Plazierung: Studien zum Verhältnis von Familie, sozialer Mobilität und Heiratsverhalten an westfälischen Beispielen im späten 18. und 19. Jahrhundert: Forschungsbericht des Landes Nordrhein-Westfalen* (Opladen: Westdeutscher Verlag, 1980), 47.

141. For example, Rudolf Lothar, "Eine Liebesszene," *Berliner Lokal-Anzeiger*, December 5, 1910, Nr. 617; J. Lorm, "Ehefragen," *Berliner Lokal-Anzeiger*, August 13, 1905, Nr. 395; Paul Kirstein, "Verlobungen: Auch eine Osterplauderei," *Berliner Morgenpost*, March 30, 1902, Nr. 75; "Das Publikum: Das Heiratsalter," *Berliner Morgenpost*, November 29, 1908, Nr. 281.

142. Paul Kirstein, "Verlobungen: Auch eine Osterplauderei," *Berliner Morgenpost*, March 30, 1902, Nr. 75.

143. Wilhelm Brönner, "Der Kampf um die neue Liebe," *Geschlecht und Gesellschaft* 1, no. 1 (1906): 7–14.

144. Fritz Wernicke, "Allerlei Tänze," *Berliner Morgenpost*, December 8, 1908, Nr. 288; K. E., "Tango-Typen," *Berliner Morgenpost*, November 30, 1913, Nr. 328; Rudolf Lothar, "Die modern Wohnung," *Berliner Lokal-Anzeiger*, May 18, 1909, Nr. 304; C. A., "Konditorei—Café—Bar: Ein Stück Berliner Entwickelung," *Berliner Morgenpost*, December 3, 1905, Nr. 284.

145. Kelly, *The German Worker*, 30–31. See also Lynch, "European Marriage Pattern."

146. Quoted in Kelly, *The German Worker*, 361.

147. David Sabean, "Household Formation and Geographical Mobility: A Family Register Study for a Württemberg Village, 1760–1900," *Annales de démographie historique* (1970): 275–294.

148. "Ein modernes Frauenblatt," *Berliner Morgenpost*, January 1, 1910, Nr. 1.

149. E. M., "Wie man Männer fesselt: Möglichkeiten der Liebe," *Berliner Morgenpost*, December 10, 1911, Nr. 339.

150. "Das Publikum: Das Ansprechen auf der Strasse," *Berliner Morgenpost*, April 24, 1904, Nr. 96.

151. Ibid.

152. "Das Publikum: Tanzstundenluxus," *Berliner Morgenpost*, October 18, 1908, Nr. 246. On dance lessons so often leading to marriage, see, for example, Wilh. V. Buttlar, "Aus der Ball-Saison," *Berliner Lokal-Anzeiger*, February 2, 1908, Nr. 59; R. G., "Der letzte Tanzstundenball," *Berliner Morgenpost*, February 28, 1904, Nr. 50; Hans Ringlau, "Gelegenheiten zur Heirat," *Heirats-Zeitung* 30, no. 238 (1914): 1–2; L. Marco, "Tanzstunde," *Berliner Morgenpost*, October 30, 1904, Nr. 256; Paul Kirstein, *Verlobung!* (Berlin: Kühling & Güttner Theaterbuchhandlung, 1894).

153. Rudolf Lothar, "Liebe von heute," *Berliner Lokal-Anzeiger*, March 30, 1908, Nr. 165.

154. "Öffentliche Meinung: Die Liebe höret nicht auf," *Berliner Lokal-Anzeiger*, September 22, 1912, Nr. 484.

155. Dorothee Goebeler, "Versorgte Frauen," *Berliner Lokal-Anzeiger*, January 28, 1914, Nr. 50.

156. J. Lorm, "Ehefragen," *Berliner Lokal-Anzeiger*, August 13, 1905, Nr. 395.

157. Rudolf Lothar, "Liebe von heute," *Berliner Lokal-Anzeiger*, March 30, 1908, Nr. 165.

158. J. Lorm, "Frauen-Sehnsucht," *Berliner Lokal-Anzeiger*, October 13, 1907, Nr. 521.

159. Rudolf Lothar, "Das Geheimnis der Koketterie," *Berliner Lokal-Anzeiger*, January 9, 1909, Nr. 15; S. Wities, "Zur Strategie der Ehe," *Berliner Lokal-Anzeiger*, December 22, 1912, Nr. 651.

160. Rudolf Lothar, "Freundschaft und Geselligkeit," *Berliner Lokal-Anzeiger*, December 31, 1909, Nr. 834.

161. Rudolf Lothar, Eine Liebesszene," *Berliner Lokal-Anzeiger*, December 5, 1910, Nr. 617.

162. Paul v. Schönthan, "Liebesbriefsteller," *Berliner Lokal-Anzeiger*, January 19, 1902, Nr. 31.

163. Oskar Klaußmann, "Liebeserklärung und Heiratsantrag," *Berliner Lokal-Anzeiger*, April 12, 1908, Nr. 189; Rudolf Lothar, "Die Scheu vor dem Gefühl," *Berliner Lokal-Anzeiger*, June 25, 1912, Nr. 319.

164. Dorothee Goebeler, "Der ungalante Mann," *Berliner Lokal-Anzeiger*, October 20, 1912, Nr. 536.

165. Hans Ostwald, "Vom Trauring," *Berliner Morgenpost*, December 29, 1908, Nr. 305.

166. "Der Verlobungsring," *Berliner Lokal-Anzeiger*, September 5, 1913, Nr. 451.

167. "Wenn die Hochzeitsglocken lauten," *Berliner Morgenpost*, April 14, 1907, Nr. 87.

168. Some, such as Johannes Trojan, even thought that this—Cupid, fate, etc.—was the only way two people might *ever* find each other in the city. Trojan, *Berliner Bilder*, 231.

169. O. F., "Berlin nach Elf: Im letzten Stadtbahnzuge," *Berliner Morgenpost*, March 18, 1900, Nr. 65.

170. For example, W. Scharrelmann, "Fräulein Mimi," *Berliner Morgenpost*, November 29, 1912, Nr. 328.

CHAPTER 2

1. F. R., "'Steigen Sie nicht aufs Rad!'" *Berliner Tageblatt*, October 7, 1900, Nr. 510.

2. George D. Bushnell, "When Chicago Was Wheel Crazy," *Chicago History* 4, no. 3 (Fall 1975): 172.

3. Victor Ottmann, "Berliner Radfahrerschmerzen," *Berliner Lokal-Anzeiger*, July 26, 1911, Nr. 375.

4. "Wohin radeln wir morgen?," *Berliner Morgenpost*, June 16, 1900, Nr. 138.

5. Sylvester, "Die Berliner Parks: Der Thiergarten," *Berliner Morgenpost*, June 3, 1899, Nr. 128.

6. Eduard Bertz, *Philosophie des Fahrrads* (Dresden: Verlag von Carl Reitzner, 1900), 8–9, quoted in Elmar Schenkel, "Cyclomanie: Fahrrad und Literatur um 1900," *Literaturwissenschaftliches Jahrbuch* 37 (1996): 214.

7. Beth Muellner, "The Photographic Enactment of the Early New Woman in 1890s German Women's Bicycling Magazines," *Women in German Yearbook* 22 (2006): 1168.

8. As Beth Muellner puts it, "Women's bicycling [was] an almost compulsory activity in the modern women's movement." Ibid., 167. On bicycling and the women's movement, see also Gudrun Maierhof and Katinka Schröder, *Sie radeln wie ein Mann, Madame: wie die Frauen das Rad eroberten* (Zurich: Unionsverlag, 1992); Eleonore Salomon, "Aus den Anfängen des bürgerlichen Frauenradsports

in Deutschland," *Theorie und Praxis der Körperkultur* 14, no. 3 (March 1965): 199–206.

9. Wilhelm v. Berg, *Die Radler-Marie*, vol. 72 of *Intime Geschichten* (Berlin: Berliner Roman-Verlag, 1905), 3.

10. Muellner, "Photographic Enactment," 168. For an excellent discussion of literary and social scientific debates about bicycling in turn-of-the-century America, see Ellen Gruber Garvey, "Reframing the Bicycle: Advertising-Supported Magazines and Scorching Women," *American Quarterly* 47, no. 1 (1995): 66–101. On the bicycle as a beacon and aesthetic feature of modernity, see Glen Norcliffe, *The Ride of Modernity: The Bicycle in Canada, 1869–1900* (Toronto: University of Toronto Press, 2001).

11. "Briefkasten," *Berliner Lokal-Anzeiger*, January 3, 1904, Nr. 3.

12. F. R., "'Steigen Sie nicht aufs Rad!,'" *Berliner Tageblatt*, October 7, 1900, Nr. 510.

13. Dr. Fr. Ranzow, "Radelnde Damen," *Die Welt der Frau* 26 (1905), 411.

14. A. von Wartenberg, "Amor in der Sommerfrische," *Berliner Lokal-Anzeiger*, August 6, 1903, Nr. 364.

15. "Die Entführung auf dem Zweirade," *Berliner Morgenpost*, November 6, 1898, Nr. 42; "Zwei Liebestragödien," *Berliner Lokal-Anzeiger*, August 30, 1905, Nr. 427.

16. Berg, *Die Radler-Marie*, 30.

17. "Die Frau im Krampf ums Dasein," *Berliner Morgenpost*, February 14, 1899, Nr. 38.

18. Charles Foley, "Zu Rad: Novellette," *Berliner Morgenpost*, December 28, 1899, Nr. 304; Berg, *Die Radler-Marie*, 30ff.

19. Statement by Antonie Köhler, Landesarchiv Berlin A Pr. Br. Rep. 030-03, Nr. 1425, Bl. 110–113; statement by Anna Selka, Landesarchiv Berlin A Pr. Br. Rep. 030-03, Nr. 1425, Bl. 8–9.

20. Letter from Otto Buning to Frieda Kliem, July 6, 1904, Landesarchiv Berlin A Pr. Br. Rep. 030-03, Nr. 1425, Bl. 95; statements, Landesarchiv Berlin A Pr. Br. Rep. 030-03, Nr. 1425, Bl. 5–7, 11, 67–70.

21. Statement by Emil Freier, Landesarchiv Berlin A Pr. Br. Rep. 030-03, Nr. 1425, Bl. 63–66.

22. New Year's card from Frieda Kliem to Clara Freier, Landesarchiv Berlin A Pr. Br. Rep. 030-03, Nr. 1425, Bl. 95.

23. Statement by Emil Freier, Landesarchiv Berlin A Pr. Br. Rep. 030-03, Nr. 1425, Bl. 63–66.

24. Statement by Clara Freier, Landesarchiv Berlin A Pr. Br. Rep. 030-03, Nr. 1425, Bl. 67–70.

25. Letter from Paul Schambach to police, Landesarchiv Berlin A Pr. Br. Rep. 030-03, Nr. 1425, Bl. 98–100.

26. Statements, Landesarchiv Berlin A Pr. Br. Rep. 030-03, Nr. 1425, Bl. 8–9, 18–21, 39, 42, 71, 83.

27. Statements, Landesarchiv Berlin A Pr. Br. Rep. 030-03, Nr. 1425, Bl. 11, 78–81; letter from Otto Mewes to police, Landesarchiv Berlin A Pr. Br. Rep. 030-03, Nr. 1425, Bl. 95.

28. Statement by Anna Selka, Landesarchiv Berlin A Pr. Br. Rep. 030-03, Nr. 1425, Bl. 8–9.

29. Letter from Otto Mewes to police, Landesarchiv Berlin A Pr. Br. Rep. 030-03, Nr. 1425, Bl. 95.

30. Letter from Frieda Kliem to Otto Mewes, Landesarchiv Berlin A Pr. Br. Rep. 030-03, Nr. 1425, Bl. 95; letter from Otto Mewes to police, Landesarchiv Berlin A Pr. Br. Rep. 030-03, Nr. 1425, Bl. 95.

31. Letter from Frieda Kliem to Otto Mewes, Landesarchiv Berlin A Pr. Br. Rep. 030-03, Nr. 1425, Bl. 95.

32. Historians have studied apartment-level intimacy in a variety of contexts and agreed that apartments counteracted the isolation one often encountered in the city. See, for example, Ma, "Down the Alleyway"; Marcus, *Apartment Stories*; Alexander von Hoffman, *Local Attachments: The Making of an American Urban Neighborhood, 1850–1920* (Baltimore: Johns Hopkins University Press, 1994).

33. Archiv der Akademie der Künste, Kempowski Bio-Archiv 69, 30–31.

34. "Das Liebesdrama im Tiergarten," *Berliner Lokal-Anzeiger*, October 19, 1909, Nr. 701.

35. "In der Wohnung seiner Geliebten erschossen," *Berliner Lokal-Anzeiger*, January 18, 1901, Nr. 29. For a similar case, see "Zwei Liebestragödien," *Berliner Lokal-Anzeiger*, August 30, 1905, Nr. 427.

36. There was the case, for example, of the young fireman who lodged with a married couple in the summer and fall of 1905 and lent a sympathetic ear to the complaints of the wife about her unhappy marriage. Their "harmony of souls" turned into intimacy and professions of love, and the husband ultimately agreed to a divorce so as to prevent the two from committing suicide together. "Ein liebestoller junger Mann," *Berliner Lokal-Anzeiger*, November 21, 1906, Nr. 593. For other examples, see "Ein Ehebruchsdrama," *Berliner Lokal-Anzeiger*, January 21, 1903, Nr. 34; "Berliner Beobachter," *Berliner Lokal-Anzeiger*, September 26, 1909, Nr. 655; "Ein eifersüchtiger Ehemann," *Berliner Lokal-Anzeiger*, November 10, 1909, Nr. 742; "Eine Hochzeit mit Hindernissen," *Berliner Morgenpost*, October 6, 1899, Nr. 285; "Eine blutige Liebestragödie," *Berliner Lokal-Anzeiger*, January 27, 1904, Nr. 43; "Der Mord an der Alice Ratowski vor Gericht," *Berliner Lokal-Anzeiger*, January 12, 1910, Nr. 19. See also Gerhard Lüdtke, *Mein Leben*, Archiv der Akademie der Künste, Kempowski Bio-Archiv 183, 109. For an example of this type of relationship as the topic of fiction, see Franz Scott, *Die Tanzfee: Das Drama der Treue*, vol. 78 of *Intime Geschichten* (Berlin: Berliner Roman-Verlag, 1905). Lodgers, it should be noted, also occasionally found potential intimacy thwarted by this same method, for landladies often objected to the presence of women in their tenants' apartments late at night and sometimes even canceled the lease as a result.

37. "Einsame Strassen," *Berliner Morgenpost*, July 21, 1899, Nr. 169.

38. "Gegenüber: Indiskrete Beobachtungen," *Berliner Lokal-Anzeiger*, September 4, 1910, Nr. 448. Of course, watching/spying on one's neighbors was a common theme of short stories, as well. Mascha von Kretschman wrote in 1913 that while ground-floor tenants lack a balcony, they alone possess a hidden vantage point on others—for example, on the newlyweds who use their balcony for intimacy. Mascha von Kretschman, "Berliner Balkons," *Berliner Morgenpost*, June 19, 1913, Nr. 165.

39. Mascha von Kretschman, "Berliner Balkons," *Berliner Morgenpost*, June 19, 1913, Nr. 165.

40. For example, Emil Peschkau, "Kätchens Mitgift," *Berliner Morgenpost*, November 9, 1898, Nr. 44; Alfred Friedmann, "Zum Maskenball," *Berliner Morgenpost*, February 2, 1907, Nr. 28; Helene-Hanna Kühn, "Liebe," *Berliner Morgenpost*, August 17, 1910, Nr. 191 (Unterhaltungsbeiblatt); A. Burg, "Fritz Wendekamp's Jugendliebe," *Berliner Morgenpost*, September 3, 1907, Nr. 206.

41. Paul Bliß, "Liebe macht erfinderisch," *Berliner Morgenpost*, June 21, 1913, Nr. 167.

42. Stefan Bajohr, "Partnerinnenwahl im Braunschweiger Arbeitermilieu, 1900–1933," *Jahrbuch für Forschungen zur Geschichte der Arbeiterbewegung* 2, no. 3 (2003), 91.

43. "Das Fräulein im Kiosk," *Berliner Morgenpost*, April 2, 1911, Nr. 92.

44. "Erste Liebe," *Berliner Morgenpost*, July 20, 1901, Nr. 168.

45. "Verschmähte Liebe," *Berliner Lokal-Anzeiger*, August 27, 1901, Nr. 400.

46. "Selbstmordversuch eines Liebespaares," *Berliner Lokal-Anzeiger*, March 30, 1903, Nr. 150.

47. "Aus Liebesgram," *Berliner Lokal-Anzeiger*, May 2, 1902, Nr. 203.

48. Frisby, *Fragments of Modernity*, 115; Siegfried Kracauer, *Die Angestellten: Aus dem neuesten Deutschland* (Frankfurt am Main: Frankfurter Societätsdruckerei, 1930).

49. Jill Suzanne Smith, "Working Girls: White-Collar Workers and Prostitutes in Late Weimar Fiction," *German Quarterly* 81, no. 4 (2008): 449–470.

50. "Der Heiratsantrag des Chefs," *Berliner Morgenpost*, February 3, 1910, Nr. 33.

51. "Das Liebesdrama im Tiergarten," *Berliner Lokal-Anzeiger*, October 19, 1909, Nr. 701; "Liebesgeschichten aus der Charité," *Berliner Lokal-Anzeiger*, November 20, 1909, Nr. 759.

52. "Briefkasten: Lottchen," *Berliner Lokal-Anzeiger*, November 18, 1904, Nr. 541; Aimée Gaber, "Seine Braut," *Berliner Morgenpost*, December 3, 1911, Nr. 332.

53. Rudolf Schwarz, *Liebesleute* (Berlin: Berliner Theater-Verlag, 1909) (Landesarchiv Berlin A Pr. Br. Rep. 030-05-02, Nr. 4782); Paul Lehnhard, *Die Liebe im Kontor: Posse mit Gesang in einem Akt* (Mühlhausen i. Thür: Druck und Verlag von G. Danner, 1899).

54. Helene Kuërs, *Aufzeichnungen aus meinem Leben* (1954), Deutsches Tagebucharchiv, Signatur 11581 II.2, 16–17.

55. A. Reitske, "Der Andere," *Berliner Morgenpost*, September 5, 1912, Nr. 244.

56. "Das 'Verhältnis' der Verkäuferin," *Berliner Lokal-Anzeiger*, March 14, 1907, Nr. 143; "Das Liebesverhältnis als Entlassungsgrund," *Berliner Lokal-Anzeiger*, August 27, 1910, Nr. 434.

57. Paul A Kirstein, "Wie sie sich kennen lernen," *Berliner Morgenpost*, November 9, 1902, Nr. 264.

58. A. von Wartenberg, "Amor in der Sommerfrische," *Berliner Lokal-Anzeiger*, August 6, 1903, Nr. 364.

59. Heinz Tovote, "Die Berlinerin: Mädchen aus Berlin W.," *Berliner Morgenpost*, December 25, 1909, Nr. 339.

60. Archiv der Akademie der Künste, Kempowski Bio-Archiv 3931/1-2, 21.

61. For example, Berg, *Die Radler-Marie*; Arthur Zapp, "Die Liebesprobe," *Berliner Morgenpost*, June 1, 1902, Nr. 126; Marin Proskauer, "Der ehrliche Brief," *Berliner Morgenpost*, April 15, 1912, Nr. 103; Hugo von Gießen, "Freds Liebeswerden," *Berliner Morgenpost*, April 29, 1902, Nr. 99.

62. "Nutzen des Sports," *Simplicissimus* 13 (1900), 104.

63. Dorothee Goebeler, "Mütter von gestern und Töchter von heute," *Berliner Lokal-Anzeiger*, September 13, 1907, Nr. 466.

64. "Öffentliche Meinung: Mütter und Töchter von heute," *Berliner Lokal-Anzeiger*, October 13, 1907, Nr. 521.

65. On the contested role of sports in the emancipation of women, see Helen Lenskyj, *Out of Bounds: Women, Sport and Sexuality* (Toronto: Women's Press, 1986); J. A. Mangan and Roberta J. Park (eds.), *From "Fair Sex" to Feminism: Sport and the Socialization of Women in the Industrial and Post-industrial Eras* (London: Frank Cass, 1987); also Kathleen McCrone, *Playing the Game: Sport and the Physical Emancipation of English Women, 1870–1914* (Lexington: University of Kentucky Press, 1988), though her discussion focuses more on sports in women's schools and colleges than the role of sports in unstructured leisure activities.

66. Dorothee Goebeler, "Wie Mädchen altern," *Berliner Lokal-Anzeiger*, April 27, 1914, Nr. 211.

67. Paul A. Kirstein, "Wie sie sich kennen lernen," *Berliner Morgenpost*, November 9, 1902, Nr. 264.

68. El-Correi, "Der Fernsprecher und die — — Liebe," *Berliner Lokal-Anzeiger*, July 20, 1914, Nr. 362.

69. This is different from the much-discussed shift to love marriages. On that shift from arranged marriage to love marriage, see, for example, Marcus Collins, *Modern Love: An Intimate History of Men and Women in Twentieth-Century Britain* (London: Atlantic Books, 2003); Stephanie Coontz, *Marriage, a History: From Obedience to Intimacy, or How Love Conquered Marriage* (New York: Viking, 2005); Christina Simmons, *Making Marriage Modern: Women's Sexuality from the Progressive Era to World War II* (New York: Oxford University Press, 2009), especially chapter 3; Andrew J. Cherlin, *The Marriage-Go-Round: The State of Marriage and the Family in America Today* (New York: Knopf, 2009), chapter 3; Lawrence

Stone, *The Family, Sex, and Marriage in England, 1500–1800* (New York: Harper Torchbooks, 1979); Edward Shorter, *The Making of the Modern Family* (London: Collins, 1976). Others have challenged the notion that marriage—especially the position of women in it—ever really changed all that significantly, pointing out, as does James Hammerton, that "companionate marriage constituted little more than a conditionally attenuated form of patriarchal marriage, part of a transition from one form of patriarchy to another." James Hammerton, "Victorian Marriage and the Law of Matrimonial Cruelty," *Victorian Studies* 33, no. 2 (Winter 1990): 270. Other critiques include Susan M. Okin, "Women and the Making of the Sentimental Family," *Philosophy and Public Affairs* 11 (1982): 65–88; Peter Borscheid, "Romantic Love or Material Interest: Choosing Partners in Nineteenth-Century Germany," *Journal of Family History* 11, no. 2 (1986): 157–168. On the interesting tension between contemporary views about the "marriage of reason" and the "marriage of inclination," see Patricia Mainardi, *Husbands, Wives, and Lovers: Marriage and Its Discontents in Nineteenth-Century France* (New Haven: Yale University Press, 2003).

70. Erich Köhrer, *Warenhaus Berlin: Ein Roman aus der Weltstadt* (Berlin: Wedekind, 1909), 22–23, quoted in Whyte and Frisby, *Metropolis Berlin*, 97–98.

71. Rudolf Lothar, "Wie erobert man eine Frau," *Berliner Lokal-Anzeiger*, September 7, 1908, Nr. 455.

72. Ibid.

73. El-Correi, "Der Fernsprecher und die — — Liebe," *Berliner Lokal-Anzeiger*, July 20, 1914, Nr. 362.

74. Schulz, *Lebenswelt und Kultur*, 12.

75. A. von Eremit's short story "Die erste Balleinladung" ("The First Ball Invitation"), for example, narrates the world of a teenager, Erika, who is finally old enough to attend a ball. "The invitation had been lying on the calling card tray in the parlor for eight days," the story begins. "Erika has already picked it up a dozen times, seeing that it says very clearly, 'Fräulein daughter [is invited], as well.' The invitation to her first ball!" She is, of course, afraid of being a wallflower, of having no one to dance with, and she practices dancing with her brother the night before. "And now it's finally here, the long-awaited ball evening!" The ball begins, Erika finds her dance card immediately filled, and she goes through the various dances—the quadrille, the waltz, the mazurka, the cotillion—as if in a dream. She even tries to wade through the crowd of whirling couples to her mother so she can tell her all about it right in the middle, but there is no time: the next dance is already starting. By the early morning hours, when the dance is winding down and her father is already asleep in the car, Erika has danced with many different men—all true gentlemen—and talks and sings about it all the way home. And at the end of the ball season—referred to simply as "the season"—the ad in the local paper was merely a foregone conclusion: "We are honored to announce the engagement of our daughter Erika to Herrn Max Liebenberg, etc." Everything had gone according to plan and tradition.

A. von Eremit, "Die erste Balleinladung," *Berliner Morgenpost*, January 21, 1913, Nr. 20.

76. Edmund Edel, "Die Zeit der Bälle," *Berliner Lokal-Anzeiger*, January 25, 1909, Nr. 43; Theo von Torn, "Damenwahl," *Berliner Morgenpost*, February 14, 1902, Nr. 38; J. Lorm, "Der Subskriptionsball," *Berliner Lokal-Anzeiger*, February 22, 1903, Nr. 89; Arthur Zapp, "Die Liebesprobe," *Berliner Morgenpost*, June 1, 1902, Nr. 126; Paul A Kirstein, "Die Lösung des Problems," *Berliner Morgenpost*, July 26, 1901, Nr. 173; Rosa Auspitzer, "Eine Ballnacht," *Berliner Morgenpost*, January 26, 1905, Nr. 22; Olga Steiner, *Heiratskandidatinnen; oder: Wie junge Mädchen lieben. Lustspiel in einem Akt* (Berlin: Theater-Buchhandlung Eduard Bloch, 1896); Marie Dabs, *Lebenserinnerungen*, Archiv der Akademie der Künste, Kempowski Bio-Archiv 995; Otto Elster, "Judiths Ehe," *Berliner Lokal-Anzeiger*, October 14, 1910, Nr. 241 (Unterhaltungs-Beilage); Betty Rittweger, "Letzte Liebe," *Berliner Morgenpost*, February 15, 1911, Nr. 46; Elin Ameen, "Nur ein Flirt," *Berliner Morgenpost*, March 5, 1904, Nr. 55; "Verlobt," *Berliner Morgenpost*, February 11, 1899, Nr. 36.

77. A. von Wartenberg, "Saisonanfang," *Berliner Lokal-Anzeiger*, November 14, 1903, Nr. 536; Wilhelmine Buchholz, "Ballmütter in Wahrheit und Dichtung," *Berliner Lokal-Anzeiger*, December 25, 1904, Nr. 605; "Das Heiratsalter moderner Mädchen," *Berliner Lokal-Anzeiger*, January 16, 1902, Nr. 26; Hedwig Neumann, "Berliner Bälle," *Berliner Morgenpost*, February 13, 1910, Nr. 43.

78. "Briefkasten," *Berliner Lokal-Anzeiger*, February 22, 1903, Nr. 89.

79. "Neuheiten für die Ball-Saison," *Berliner Morgenpost*, January 24, 1904, Nr. 20; Martha, "Ball- und Gesellschaftsmode," *Berliner Morgenpost*, February 7, 1904, Nr. 32.

80. There were, after all, so-called *Kinderbälle*, balls for children, even if a vocal few thought this was going too far. H. N., "Der Kinderball," *Berliner Lokal-Anzeiger*, January 17, 1909, Nr. 14; "Das Publikum: Kinderbälle," *Berliner Morgenpost*, February 16, 1913, Nr. 46.

81. The columnist Wilhelm von Buttlar paints a lovely picture of the nerves and hopes tied up in this big moment in a 1908 piece. Wilh. V. Buttlar, "Aus der Ball-Saison," *Berliner Lokal-Anzeiger*, February 2, 1908, Nr. 59. See also Zoë, "'Mit Herren,'" *Berliner Morgenpost*, December 5, 1907, Nr. 285; R. G., "Der letzte Tanzstundenball," *Berliner Morgenpost*, February 28, 1904, Nr. 50; L. Marco, "Tanzstunde," *Berliner Morgenpost*, October 30, 1904, Nr. 256.

82. L. Marco, "Tanzstunde," *Berliner Morgenpost*, October 30, 1904, Nr. 256.

83. "Briefkasten," *Berliner Lokal-Anzeiger*, March 14, 1906, Nr. 133; "Briefkasten," *Berliner Lokal-Anzeiger*, January 25, 1903, Nr. 41; "Das Publikum: Tanzstundenluxus," *Berliner Morgenpost*, October 25, 1908, Nr. 252.

84. R. G., "Der letzte Tanzstundenball," *Berliner Morgenpost*, February 28, 1904, Nr. 50.

85. Schulz, *Lebenswelt und Kultur*, 12.

86. A. von Wartenberg, "Moderne Frauen-Typen," *Berliner Lokal-Anzeiger*, January 1, 1907, Nr. 1.

87. "Berliner Beobachter," *Berliner Lokal-Anzeiger*, October 28, 1900, Nr. 506; Alfred Holzbock, "Mitten in der Gesellschafts-Saison," *Berliner Lokal-Anzeiger*, January 9, 1906, Nr. 14; A. von Wartenberg, "Von der Tanzunlust der Herren," *Berliner Lokal-Anzeiger*, February 10, 1907, Nr. 74.

88. "Öffentliche Meinung: Eine 'Tanzfrage,'" *Berliner Lokal-Anzeiger*, November 7, 1909, Nr. 737.

89. "Öffentliche Meinung: Eine 'Tanzfrage,'" *Berliner Lokal-Anzeiger*, November 14, 1909, Nr. 750.

90. Ch. Täuber, "Auf dem Maskenball," *Berliner Morgenpost*, January 30, 1903, Nr. 25; W. T., "Berliner Maskenball," *Berliner Morgenpost*, February 18, 1906, Nr. 41; "Der Metropol-Theater-Ball," *Berliner Morgenpost*, January 7, 1900, Nr. 5.

91. Alfred Holzbock, "Ballsaison," *Berliner Lokal-Anzeiger*, February 18, 1912, Nr. 89.

92. "Briefkasten," *Berliner Lokal-Anzeiger*, January 15, 1905, Nr. 25.

93. Fritz Reinert, *Tagebuch 1902–3*, Deutsches Tagebucharchiv, Signatur 1929, 89.

94. Max Pollaczek, "Die Maske: Zum Beginn der Ballsaison," *Berliner Morgenpost*, January 19, 1908, Nr. 16.

95. "Das Publikum: Bessere Ideen für Maskenbälle," *Berliner Morgenpost*, March 15, 1914, Nr. 73; "Das Publikum: Oeffentliche Bälle," *Berliner Morgenpost*, January 31, 1909, Nr. 26.

96. M. L., "Die Berlinerin auf dem Ball," *Berliner Morgenpost*, March 1, 1914, Nr. 59; "Berliner Beobachter," *Berliner Lokal-Anzeiger*, January 26, 1902, Nr. 43; "Berliner Beobachter," *Berliner Lokal-Anzeiger*, October 30, 1904, Nr. 511; Alfred Holzbock, "Ballfeste," *Berliner Lokal-Anzeiger*, March 10, 1904, Nr. 117; "Der Wittwenball-Löwe," *Berliner Morgenpost*, February 9, 1904, Nr. 33; Maximillian Wolff, "Maskenball der Taubstummen," *Berliner Lokal-Anzeiger*, March 3, 1901, Nr. 105.

97. Paul Näcke, "Ein Besuch bei den Homosexuellen in Berlin," in Magnus Hirschfeld, *Berlins Drittes Geschlecht* (1904), ed. Manfred Herzer (Berlin: Verlag rosa Winkel, 1991), 172. For other evidence of gay balls, see Magnus Hirschfeld, "Das Ergebnis der statistischen Untersuchungen über den Prozentsatz der Homosexuellen," *Jahrbuch für sexuelle Zwischenstufen mit besonderer Berücksichtigung der Homosexualität* 6, no. 1 (1904): 121; *Eine männliche Braut: Aufzeichnungen eines Homosexuellen* (Berlin: Janssen Verlag, 1996), 90; Hans Ostwald, "Berliner Bilder: Allerlei Kaschemmen," *Berliner Morgenpost*, February 5, 1905, Nr. 31; Arthur Brehmer, "Aus dem dunklen Berlin: Allerlei Bälle," *Berliner Morgenpost*, February 8, 1899, Nr. 33; *Das perverse Berlin* (Berlin: Rich. Eckstein Nachf., 1910), 128–129. See also *Goodbye to Berlin: 100 Jahre Schwulenbewegung. Eine Ausstellung des Schwulen Museums und der Akademie der Künste, 17. Mai bis 17. August 1997* (Berlin: Verlag rosa Winkel, 1997), 72; Jens Dobler, *Von andern Ufern: Geschichte der Berliner Lesben und Schwulen in Kreuzberg und Friedrichshain* (Berlin: Bruno Gmünder Verlag, 2003).

98. "Berliner Beobachter," *Berliner Lokal-Anzeiger*, February 9, 1902, Nr. 67; Martha Hellmuth, "Eliteball in Halensee: Die lieben süssen Mädels," *Berliner Morgenpost*, June 30, 1901, Nr. 151.

99. "Kavaliere—gegen gleich bare Bezahlung," *Berliner Lokal-Anzeiger*, June 19, 1907, Nr. 305.

100. Marion Kiesow, *Berlin tanzt in Clärchens Ballhaus: 100 Jahre Vergnügen—eine Kulturgeschichte* (Berlin: Nicolai, 2013), 10.

101. Marion Kiesow, who has compiled an excellent and lively history of one long-standing Berlin ballroom (the so-called Clärchens Ballhaus), attempts to place Biberkopf (and Döblin himself) in Clärchens at the turn of the century but has to conclude, in the end, that his ballroom of choice must have been another. Ibid., 69.

102. K. E., "Tango-Typen," *Berliner Morgenpost*, November 30, 1913, Nr. 328.

103. Else Krafft, "Tanzstunden . . . ," *Berliner Morgenpost*, March 1, 1908, Nr. 52.

104. Edmund Edel, "Berlin tanzt!," in *Berliner Nächte* (Berlin: Conrad Haber's Verlag, 1914), 77.

105. Ibid., 96.

106. Ibid., 77.

107. Eugen Isolani, "Vom Küssen und von Küssen," *Berliner Morgenpost*, January 31, 1913, Nr. 30.

108. Arthur Brehmer, "Aus dem dunklen Berlin: Die Balllokale," *Berliner Morgenpost*, November 2, 1898, Nr. 38; Alfred Holzbock, "Ballsaison," *Berliner Lokal-Anzeiger*, February 18, 1912, Nr. 89; Dorothee Goebeler, "Der Herr, der tanzt," *Berliner Lokal-Anzeiger*, February 17, 1914, Nr. 87.

109. Arthur Brehmer, "Aus dem dunklen Berlin: Allerlei Bälle," *Berliner Morgenpost*, February 8, 1899, Nr. 33.

110. Alfred Holzbock, "Ein Berliner Roman," *Berliner Lokal-Anzeiger*, September 5, 1912, Nr. 453.

111. Leo Leipziger, *Der Rettungsball* (Berlin: Roland von Berlin, 1912), 22.

112. Ibid., 21–22, 26.

113. Ibid., 24.

114. "Öffentliche Meinung: Moderne Anschauungen," *Berliner Lokal-Anzeiger*, August 6, 1905, Nr. 382.

115. Dorothee Goebeler, "Was ist der Frau erlaubt, wenn sie liebt?," *Berliner Lokal-Anzeiger*, August 24, 1907, Nr. 429.

116. "Öffentliche Meinung: Berufsleben der Frau und Frauen-Sehnsucht!," *Berliner Lokal-Anzeiger*, October 27, 1907, Nr. 547; "Öffentliche Meinung: Moderne Anschauung," *Berliner Lokal-Anzeiger*, August 6, 1905, Nr. 382.

117. "Öffentliche Meinung: Moderne Anschauung," *Berliner Lokal-Anzeiger*, August 13, 1905, Nr. 395.

118. Dorothee Goebeler, "Was ist der Frau erlaubt, wenn sie liebt?," *Berliner Lokal-Anzeiger*, August 24, 1907, Nr. 429.

119. Dorothee Goebeler, "Mütter von gestern und Töchter von heute," *Berliner Lokal-Anzeiger*, September 13, 1907, Nr. 466.

120. Edel, "Berlin tanzt," 99.

121. Else Krafft, "Tanzstunden . . . ," *Berliner Morgenpost*, March 1, 1908, Nr. 52.

122. Sylvester, "Berlin bei Nacht," *Berliner Morgenpost*, February 25, 1899, Nr. 48.

123. Erdmann Gräser, "'Der Tanz erfreut des Menschen Herz . . .' Drei Momentbilder," *Berliner Morgenpost*, February 1, 1914, Nr. 31.

124. Norbert Falk, "Zwei Frauen," *Berliner Morgenpost*, July 2, 1908, Nr. 153.

125. "Berichte über das Tanzlokal 'Mon Plaisir' im Lunapark (1911)," Landesarchiv Berlin A Pr. Br. Rep. 30 Berlin C Titel 610, Th. 3833 Schbg. Th. Nr. 12.

126. Lipp, "Sexualität und Heirat," 192.

127. "Öffentliche Meinung: Sonntagsvergnügen auf der Vorortbahn," *Berliner Lokal-Anzeiger*, October 21, 1900, Nr. 494.

128. Hans Bronnert, "Die Berlinerin: Die Laden-Lady," *Berliner Morgenpost*, December 25, 1909, Nr. 339; "Berliner Beobachter," *Berliner Lokal-Anzeiger*, November 4, 1900, Nr. 518.

129. F. S., "Der Tanz," *Berliner Morgenpost*, February 22, 1899, Nr. 45.

130. Helene Kuërs, *Aufzeichnungen aus meinem Leben* (1954), Deutsches Tagebucharchiv, Signatur 11581 II.2, 16; Öffentliche Meinung: Wie wird jetzt getanzt!," *Berliner Lokal-Anzeiger*, July 31, 1910, Nr. 383.

131. "Die das Lieben fliehen. Der Achtzehnjährige mit den sechs Bräuten," *Berliner Morgenpost*, January 15, 1907, Nr. 12; "Ein gefährlicher Don Juan," *Berliner Morgenpost*, October 15, 1903, Nr. 242; Paul Bliß, "Unter Amors Maske," *Berliner Morgenpost*, November 2, 1898, Nr. 38.

132. "Das Publikum: Ist ein Kuß eine Verlobung?," *Berliner Morgenpost*, February 22, 1903, Nr. 45.

133. "Der junge Don Juan und Schwindler," *Berliner Morgenpost*, June 7, 1906, Nr. 130.

134. "Der traurige Held eines nächtlichen Abenteuers im Thiergarten," *Berliner Lokal-Anzeiger*, September 3, 1902, Nr. 411.

135. "Eine Bekanntschaft vom Tanzboden," *Berliner Lokal-Anzeiger*, January 8, 1909, Nr. 12; "Tanzbodenliebe," *Berliner Morgenpost*, October 6, 1903, Nr. 234; "Das Publikum: Einladung auf einem Ball," *Berliner Morgenpost*, February 5, 1911, Nr. 36.

136. Pipifax, "Das Liebespostamt," *Berliner Morgenpost*, August 15, 1906, Nr. 189.

137. "Berliner Hotels: IV. Die Hotels 'für Ehepaare.'—Die Speziel-Hotels," *Berliner Morgenpost*, January 18, 1905, Nr. 15.

138. Dr. A. Römer, "Das Rendezvous am Potsdamer Platz: Ein heiteres Strassenbild mit ernstem Hintergrund," *Berliner Morgenpost*, December 28, 1902, Nr. 303; Wilhelm v. Berg, *Auf dem Standesamt*, vol. 76 of *Intime Geschichten* (Berlin: Berliner Roman-Verlag, 1905), 44; Peter Berliner, "Ferdinand's Rendezvous," *Berliner Morgenpost*, February 2, 1902, Nr. 28; Hans Levitus, *Von Stufe zu Stufe*, vol. 80 of *Intime Geschichten* (Berlin: Metropol-Verlag, 1905), 8.

139. "Ein Abenteuer in Humboldthain," *Berliner Lokal-Anzeiger*, April 25, 1903, Nr. 191; "Der Tiergarten," *Berliner Morgenpost*, July 15, 1905, Nr. 164; "Tiergartenbummel," *Berliner Tageblatt*, June 19, 1904, Nr. 307.

140. Julius Knopf, "Tiergartenbummel," *Berliner Zeitung*, July 5, 1905, Nr. 153, cited in Fritzsche, *Reading Berlin 1900*, 99.

141. *Das perverse Berlin*, 71–78.

142. Hans Ostwald, "Dunkle Winkel und Menschen," in *Berliner Nächte* (Berlin: Conrad Haber's Verlag, 1914), 2.

143. "Benutzung der Wege und Plätze im Tiergarten und Besprengung derselben (1911)," Landesarchiv Berlin A Pr. Br. Rep. 030, Nr. 18659.

144. A 1997 exhibit at Berlin's Schwules Museum and the Akademie der Künste suggested a similar point, noting that "for homosexuals, who, out of fear of judgment and punishment, were forced to divide their private lives, their apartments, and their circle of close friends from their same-sex desires, anonymous meeting places such as public bathrooms, green spaces in the Tiergarten, or along the city canal at Hallesches Tor offered the only possibility of making contact with other gays." *Goodbye to Berlin*, 73.

145. The editor/publisher of the diary claimed to have received it from its author. This was, of course, also a popular narrative device among authors, so it may or may not be "authentic" in the strictest sense of the word. *Eine männliche Braut*, 32–33, 35.

146. Karl Merz, "Unsre Kolonie," *Der Eigene*, March 15, 1897, 72.

147. "Ein Mann in Frauenkleidern," *Berliner Lokal-Anzeiger*, October 27, 1913, Nr. 546; "Ein Siebzehnjähriger," *Berliner Morgenpost*, November 24, 1904, Nr. 276.

148. Dr. Phil. Max Katte, "Aus dem Leben eines Homosexuellen, Selbstbiographie," *Jahrbuch für sexuelle Zwischenstufen mit besonderer Berücksichtigung der Homosexualität* 2, no. 1 (1900): 305–306.

149. Peter Hamecher, "Drei bescheidene Liedchen für meinen Schatz," *Der Eigene*, January 1900, 326.

150. Dr. Albert Moll, "Wie erkennen und verständigen sich die Homosexuellen unter einander?," *Archiv für Kriminal-Anthropologie und Kriminalistik* 9, nos. 2–3 (1902): 157–160.

151. Josef Kitir, "Eros im Bordell," *Der Eigene*, July 1, 1899, 10–11.

152. Adolf Brand, "Bahnhof Friedrichstrasse," *Der Eigene,* April 1903, 243.

153. Cacsareon, "Es soll—Eine Erinnerung," *Der Eigene*, May 1903, 303–307.

154. Ludmilla von Rehren, "Sonderlicher, den Frauenliebe ist . . . ," *Der Eigene*, April 1903, 234–236.

155. Caesareon, "Brief an eine Mutter," *Der Eigene*, March 1903, 185–188.

156. Norbert Langner, "Echte Liebe: Skizze aus dem Leben," *Der Eigene*, March 15, 1897, 10.

157. Frau M. F., "Wie ich es sehe," *Jahrbuch für sexuelle Zwischenstufen mit besonderer Berücksichtigung der Homosexualität* 3, no. 1 (1901): 308–312.

158. Reinhold Gerling, *Mädchen, die man nicht heiraten soll: Warnungen und Winke* (Oranienburg: Orania, 1917); "Die Freundin der Ehefrau: eine zerrüttete Ehe," *Berliner Morgenpost*, March 19, 1905, Nr. 67.

159. Magnus Hirschfeld, "Sind sexuelle Zwischenstufen zur Ehe geeignet?," *Jahrbuch für sexuelle Zwischenstufen mit besonderer Berücksichtigung der Homosexualität* 3, no. 1 (1901): 40.

160. Ibid., 63.

161. Ibid., 68.

162. Mimosa, "Die weib-weibliche Liebe," *Das Geschlecht: Aufklärung über alle Fragen des Geschlechtslebens* 1 (1904): 3–5.

163. E. Krause, "Die Wahrheit über mich: Selbstbiographie einer Konträrsexuellen," *Jahrbuch für sexuelle Zwischenstufen mit besonderer Berücksichtigung der Homosexualität* 3, no. 1 (1901): 305.

164. Ibid., 306.

165. Edwin Bab, *Die Gleichgeschlechtliche Liebe (Lieblingsminne): Ein Wort ueber ihr Wesen und ihre Bedeutung* (Berlin: Hugo Schildberger, 1903), 52. In the course of my research, I looked specifically for evidence suggesting that some encounters with prostitutes in turn-of-the-century Berlin were perhaps lasting, on-again, off-again relationships—that, in other words, there was more to the relationship than a simple exchange of money for sex—but there is little of record to support such a reading. There is, on the one hand, an Arthur Roessler short story published in 1903 that features a man so lonely, so isolated in the big city that he goes to a prostitute and asks her simply to lie with him "as a sister" and comfort him. But Lelian, the protagonist, is gay, which introduces an entirely different dynamic into the prostitute/client relationship. Arthur Roessler, "Der arme Lelian," *Der Eigene* 1 (1903): 30–42. There are, on the other hand, many instances of single men in Berlin who were lonely and isolated and sought human connection via sex with a prostitute, and in that sense the encounter was, for the client, at least, about more than sex. I was unable to find any evidence, however, that suggested that prostitutes, whether male or female, themselves felt an intimate bond with their clients or derived anything other than income from them. The *Berliner Morgenpost* put it succinctly when it said of the "waitresses" in Berlin's less than reputable night cafés, "They don't sit here for their enjoyment; they sit here so that they can live." "Aus dem dunklen Berlin: Berliner Nachtcafés I," *Berliner Morgenpost*, November 8, 1898, Nr. 43. Hans Ostwald confirms this in his piece on the utter economic despair of Berlin prostitutes. Hans Ostwald, "Notlage oder Trieb? Eine Erwiderung," *Die Neue Zeit* 1, no. 2 (1906–1907): 74–77. Indeed, most prostitute/client encounters were short, one-time, businesslike transactions. Fritz Reinert, the twenty-something printmaker who left his hometown of Glogau and spent a year working in Berlin, described his interactions with prostitutes in his diary with a clearly dismissive, unemotional air: "On the way home jabbered at

by a girl, went in to the apartment, screwed for 3.50, quick amusement, left soon after, didn't really have my wits about me—Went home and to bed at 1:15 a.m." Fritz Reinert, *Tagebuch 1902–3*, Deutsches Tagebucharchiv, Signatur 1929, 41.

166. Mary Jo Maynes, *Taking the Hard Road: Life Course in French and German Workers' Autobiographies in the Era of Industrialization* (Chapel Hill: University of North Carolina Press, 1995), 140–142; Kelly, *The German Worker*, 31ff.

167. Schulz, *Lebenswelt und Kultur*, 6ff.

168. Louise Tilly, Joan Scott, and Miriam Cohen, "Women's Work and European Fertility Patterns," *Journal of Interdisciplinary History* 6, no. 3 (Winter 1976): 464–465.

169. Quoted in Kelly, *The German Worker*, 255.

170. James Woycke, *Birth Control in Germany, 1871–1933* (London: Routledge, 1988).

171. Ibid., 48.

172. Ibid., 56.

173. Ibid., 53.

174. Ibid., 51.

175. Ibid., 69–70. As Franklin Mendels writes, "The real possibilities of upward social mobility intensified the incentives to adopt effective means of birth control within a few generations." Franklin Mendels, "Proto-industrialization: The First Phase of the Industrialization Process," *Journal of Economic History* 32 (1972): 253.

176. Woycke, *Birth Control in Germany*, 166.

177. On abortion, birth control, and imperial and Weimar Germany, see also Edward Ross Dickinson, "Policing Sex in Germany, 1882–1982: A Preliminary Statistical Analysis," *Journal of the History of Sexuality* 16, no. 2 (2007): 204–250; Dickinson, "Reflections on Feminism and Monism in the Kaiserreich, 1900–1913," *Central European History* 34, no. 2 (2001): 191–230; Cornelie Usborne, *The Politics of the Body in Weimar Germany: Women's Reproductive Rights and Duties* (Ann Arbor: University of Michigan Press, 1992); Atina Grossmann, *Reforming Sex: The German Movement for Birth Control and Abortion Reform, 1920–1950* (Oxford: Oxford University Press, 1995).

178. "Öffentliche Meinung: Liebeserklärung und Heiratsantrag," *Berliner Lokal-Anzeiger*, April 19, 1908, Nr. 200. Cf. Shorter, *Making of the Modern Family*. For a compelling critique of Shorter's thesis, see, for example, Tilly, Scott, and Cohen, "Women's Work."

179. Thanks to a lecture by Timothy Gilfoyle on early twentieth-century American sexuality for this idea.

180. Fritzsche, *Reading Berlin 1900*, 155; "Der Tauentzienstil," *Berliner Zeitung*, November 16, 1911, Nr. 270, quoted in Fritzsche, *Reading Berlin 1900*, 156.

181. Dorothee Goebeler, "Mütter von gestern und Töchter von heute," *Berliner Lokal-Anzeiger*, September 13, 1907, Nr. 466.

182. Dorothee Goebeler, "Männer, die nicht heiraten," *Berliner Lokal-Anzeiger*, June 5, 1912, Nr. 282; Dr. Georg Buschan, *Vom Jüngling zum Mann: Ratschläge zur*

sexuellen Lebensführung (Stuttgart: Verlag von Strecker und Schröder, 1911); A. R. H. Lehmann, *Der Junggsell vom Elternhaus bis zur Heirat* (Schöneberg-Berlin: Hans Klee Verlag, 1909); "Öffentliche Meinung: Eine 'Gewissensfrage,'" *Berliner Lokal-Anzeiger*, May 18, 1902, Nr. 229.

183. "Briefkasten," *Berliner Lokal-Anzeiger*, February 5, 1905, Nr. 61.

184. "Das Publikum: 'Braut' oder 'Verhältnis,'" *Berliner Morgenpost*, January 16, 1910, Nr. 15; Dorothee Goebeler, "Mädchenstolz," *Berliner Lokal-Anzeiger*, November 28, 1909, Nr. 774; "Öffentliche Meinung: Berufsleben der Frau und Frauen-Sehnsucht!," *Berliner Lokal-Anzeiger*, October 27, 1907, Nr. 547; "Öffentliche Meinung: Moderne Anschauung," *Berliner Lokal-Anzeiger*, August 6, 1905, Nr. 382; "Öffentliche Meinung: Moderne Anschauung," *Berliner Lokal-Anzeiger*, August 13, 1905, Nr. 395; "Berliner Beobachter," *Berliner Lokal-Anzeiger*, May 1, 1904, Nr. 203. On Frau Manko, see "Frau Blaubart," *Berliner Morgenpost*, October 21, 1905, Nr. 248.

CHAPTER 3

1. "54000 alte Jungfern," *Berliner Morgenpost*, February 23, 1899, Nr. 46. On so-called old maids, see Catherine Dollard, "The Alte Jungfer as New Deviant: Representation, Sex, and the Single Woman in Imperial Germany," *German Studies Review* 29, no. 1 (2006): 107–126.

2. On the problem of unmarried women in Wilhelmine Germany, see Dollard, "Alte Jungfer as New Deviant"; also Dollard, *The Surplus Woman*. Dollard details the ways in which single women were understood and portrayed not only as deviant, but even as threats to the stability of the German nation.

3. Ilse Müller, his daughter, earned a doctorate and pursued a career as a chemist. Ute Pascher and Petra Stein (eds.), *Akademische Karrieren von Naturwissenschaftlerinnen gestern und heute* (Düsseldorf: Springer, 2013), 72.

4. Statements, Landesarchiv Berlin A Pr. Br. Rep. 030-03, Nr. 1425, Bl. 5–7, 10–12, 29–31.

5. Statement by Antonie Köhler, Landesarchiv Berlin A Pr. Br. Rep. 030-03, Nr. 927, Bl. 115–116.

6. Statements, Landesarchiv Berlin A Pr. Br. Rep. 030-03, Nr. 1425, Bl. 10, 29–31.

7. Statement by Johanna Westphal, Landesarchiv Berlin A Pr. Br. Rep. 030-03, Nr. 1425, Bl. 12.

8. Statements, Landesarchiv Berlin A Pr. Br. Rep. 030-03, Nr. 1425, Bl. 5–7, 11.

9. Letter from Otto Buning to Frieda Kliem, 6 July 1904, Landesarchiv Berlin A Pr. Br. Rep. 030-03, Nr. 1425, Bl. 95.

10. Statement by Emil Freier, Landesarchiv Berlin A Pr. Br. Rep. 030-03, Nr. 1425, Bl. 63–66.

11. Statement by Clara Freier, Landesarchiv Berlin A Pr. Br. Rep. 030-03, Nr. 1425, Bl. 67–70.

12. Statement by Antonie Köhler, Landesarchiv Berlin A Pr. Br. Rep. 030-03, Nr. 1425, Bl. 110–113.

13. Letter from Otto Mewes to police, Landesarchiv Berlin A Pr. Br. Rep. 030-03, Nr. 1425, Bl. 95.

14. Statement by Paul Freier, Landesarchiv Berlin A Pr. Br. Rep. 030-03, Nr. 1425, Bl. 80–81.

15. "Das Publikum: Frau oder Fräulein," *Berliner Morgenpost*, September 30, 1906, Nr. 229. The Society for the Protection of Motherhood (Bund für Muttschutz), Helene Stöcker's prominent women's rights organization, opened this same question up for debate in its journal, *Mutterschutz: Zeitschrift zur Reform der sexuellen Ethik*, and published essay responses from a variety of luminaries from the academy and the women's movement. "Zur 'Frau' oder 'Fräulein'-Frage," *Mutterschutz: Zeitschrift zur Reform der sexuellen Ethik* (1906): 209–210, 247–253, 295–298, 336–338, 383–385.

16. For an excellent overview of the gains of early feminist movements in Germany, see Ute Frevert, *Women in German History: From Bourgeois Emancipation to Sexual Liberation*, trans. Stuart McKinnon-Evans (New York: St. Martin's Press, 1989).

17. On discussions of the "new woman," generally, and specifically vis-à-vis a more assertive female sexuality, see Jill Suzanne Smith, *Berlin Coquette: Prostitution and the New German Woman, 1890–1933* (Ithaca, NY: Cornell University Press, 2013).

18. On the remarkable prevalence of gender debates at the turn of the century, see Barbara Greven-Aschoff, *Die bürgerliche Frauenbewegung in Deutschland, 1894–1933* (Göttingen: Vandenhoeck & Ruprecht, 1981). Dollard refers to this as a time of navel-gazing, "an era in which the elusive goal of national cohesion was pursued and in which debates about the contours of German national identity were widespread." Dollard, *The Surplus Woman*, 6.

19. On women choosing careers over marriage, see Bärbel Kuhn, *Familienstand: ledig. Ehelose Frauen und Männer im Bürgertum (1850–1914)* (Cologne: Böhlau, 2000). Also Ann Taylor Allen, *Feminism and Motherhood in Germany, 1800–1914* (New Brunswick, NJ: Rutgers University Press, 1991); Christoph Sachße, *Mütterlichkeit als Beruf: Sozialarbeit, Sozialreform und Frauenbewegung, 1871–1929* (Frankfurt am Main: Suhrkamp, 1986).

20. Dorothee Goebeler, "Wie Mädchen altern," *Berliner Lokal-Anzeiger*, April 27, 1914, Nr. 211.

21. Dorothee Goebeler, "Aussterbende Frauentypen," *Berliner Lokal-Anzeiger*, November 6, 1906, Nr. 565.

22. Dorothee Goebeler, "Wie Mädchen altern," *Berliner Lokal-Anzeiger*, April 27, 1914, Nr. 211.

23. Dorothee Goebeler, "Aussterbende Frauentypen," *Berliner Lokal-Anzeiger*, November 6, 1906, Nr. 565.

24. Dorothee Goebeler, "Mütter von gestern und Töchter von heute," *Berliner Lokal-Anzeiger*, September 13, 1907, Nr. 466.

25. Heinz Tovote, "Die Berlinerin: Mädchen aus Berlin W.," *Berliner Morgenpost*, December 25, 1909, Nr. 339.

26. Dorothee Goebeler, "Aussterbende Frauentypen," *Berliner Lokal-Anzeiger*, November 6, 1906, Nr. 565.

27. Clara Blüthgen, "Werbende Frauen," *Berliner Lokal-Anzeiger*, April 4, 1914, Nr. 173.

28. Dorothee Goebeler, "Die Frau die nichts zu sagen hat," *Berliner Lokal-Anzeiger*, December 10, 1913, Nr. 627.

29. For example, "Briefkasten," *Berliner Lokal-Anzeiger*, January 17, 1904, Nr. 27.

30. R. C., "Hat Berlin ein Klubleben?," *Berliner Lokal-Anzeiger*, April 18, 1903, Nr. 179.

31. Ad for Manoli Cigaretten, *Berliner Morgenpost*, July 25, 1914, Nr. 201.

32. Dorothee Goebeler, "Die Frau mit dem Innenleben," *Berliner Lokal-Anzeiger*, July 29, 1914, Nr. 380.

33. "Das Heiratsalter moderner Mädchen," *Berliner Lokal-Anzeiger*, January 16, 1902, Nr. 26. Cf. Dollard, *The Surplus Woman*, chapter 3. See also the contemporary statistical work of Robert and Lisbeth Wilbrandt, *Die Deutsche Frau im Beruf*; Friedrich Prinzing, "Die alten Junggesellen und alten Jungfern in den europäischen Staaten jetzt und früher," *Zeitschrift für Sozialwissenschaft* 8 (1905): 615–622, 713–719; Prinzing, "Heiratshäufigkeit."

34. G. Wolft, "Wann die Leute heiraten: Statistische Plauderei," *Berliner Lokal-Anzeiger*, September 3, 1905, Nr. 434.

35. Hans Ostwald, "Die Berlinerin: Die Arbeiterin," *Berliner Morgenpost*, December 25, 1909, Nr. 339.

36. Schulz, *Lebenswelt und Kultur*, 5ff.

37. Heinz Tovote, "Die Berlinerin: Mädchen aus Berlin W.," *Berliner Morgenpost*, December 25, 1909, Nr. 339.

38. A. von Wartenberg, "Der Trost," *Berliner Lokal-Anzeiger*, December 28, 1903, Nr. 303.

39. Julie Jolowicz, "Zwei Briefe," *Berliner Morgenpost*, September 7, 1907, Nr. 210.

40. Gertrud Steinbach, "Liebe," *Berliner Morgenpost*, September 5, 1906, Nr. 207.

41. Q, "Moderne Frauenideale: Emancipation und Mutterschaft," *Berliner Morgenpost*, July 23, 1905, Nr. 171.

42. Eliza Ichenhäuser, "Ehe-Ideale und Ideal-Ehen," *Berliner Lokal-Anzeiger*, November 22, 1905, Nr. 582.

43. On the marital aspirations and calculations of single women in interwar England, see Selina Todd, *Young Women, Work, and Family in England, 1918–1950* (New York: Oxford University Press, 2005), especially 217–223.

44. "Das Heiratsalter moderner Mädchen," *Berliner Lokal-Anzeiger*, January 16, 1902, Nr. 26.

45. Mary Oberberg, "Weibliche Junggesellen," *Berliner Lokal-Anzeiger*, February 14, 1904, Nr. 75; Dorothee Goebeler, "Wenn Mädchen heiraten wollen," *Berliner Lokal-Anzeiger*, February 11, 1914, Nr. 76.

46. Rudolf Lothar, "Eine Liebesszene," *Berliner Lokal-Anzeiger*, December 5, 1910, Nr. 617.

47. Brönner, "Der Kampf," 7; Rudolf Lothar, "Liebe von heute," *Berliner Lokal-Anzeiger*, March 30, 1908, Nr. 165; Anselm Timmler, "Schönheit und Anmut: Wie Frauen gefallen," *Berliner Morgenpost*, January 12, 1908, Nr. 10.

48. S. Wities, "Moderne Frauentypen," *Berliner Lokal-Anzeiger*, January 19, 1913, Nr. 33.

49. Rudolf Lothar, "Die Mode der Unliebenswürdigkeit," *Berliner Lokal-Anzeiger*, April 8, 1910, Nr. 176.

50. Victor Ottmann, "Wovon die jungen Mädchen träumen," *Berliner Lokal-Anzeiger*, October 25, 1903, Nr. 501.

51. Dorothee Goebeler, "Die Frauenbewegung und die Frau," *Berliner Lokal-Anzeiger*, May 7, 1912, Nr. 232.

52. Ibid. Dorothee Goebeler, who, in her choice of topics and viewpoints presented, normally embraced a fairly progressive—one might say "modern"—stance, took a surprisingly conservative course in these debates. Then again, her employer, the *Berliner Lokal-Anzeiger* was, at least in comparison to the *Berliner Morgenpost* (and others, such as the *Berliner Tageblatt* and the *Berliner Zeitung*), one of Berlin's more conservative daily newspapers.

53. J. Lorm, "Frauen-Sehnsucht," *Berliner Lokal-Anzeiger*, October 13, 1907, Nr. 521; S. Wities, "Die Frau ohne Mann," *Berliner Lokal-Anzeiger*, September 12, 1912, Nr. 466; Dorothee Goebeler, "Mädchen, die man heiratet," *Berliner Lokal-Anzeiger*, August 29, 1912, Nr. 440; Dorothee Goebeler, "Wenn Mädchen heiraten wollen," *Berliner Lokal-Anzeiger*, February 11, 1914, Nr. 76.

54. Alfred Holzbock, "Mitten in der Gesellschafts-Saison," *Berliner Lokal-Anzeiger*, January 9, 1906, Nr. 14.

55. A. von Wartenberg, "Moderne Frauen-Typen," *Berliner Lokal-Anzeiger*, January 1, 1907, Nr. 1.

56. *Statistisches Jahrbuch der Stadt Berlin*, 1905, 26.

57. Compare this, for example, with 1884, when 38.6 percent between ages twenty and twenty-five and 31.4 percent between ages twenty-five and thirty were married. *Statistisches Jahrbuch der Stadt Berlin* (Berlin: P. Stankiewicz' Buchdruckerei, 1884), 9.

58. "Unsere Preisfragen," *Die Welt der Frau* 1 (1905): 203–204.

59. "Wie verheirate ich meine Tochter?," *Berliner Lokal-Anzeiger*, April 2, 1905, Nr. 157.

60. Arthur Zapp, "Moderne Mädchen," *Berliner Lokal-Anzeiger*, December 8, 1903, Nr. 287, 2.

61. Ibid.

62. Arthur Zapp, "Moderne Mädchen," *Berliner Lokal-Anzeiger*, December 9, 1903, Nr. 288, 2.

63. Ibid., 3.

64. Dollard, "Alte Jungfer."

65. Arthur Zapp, "Moderne Mädchen," *Berliner Lokal-Anzeiger*, January 14, 1904, Nr. 11, 3.

66. "Von mutigen Männern und Frauen," *Berliner Lokal-Anzeiger*, June 6, 1906, Nr. 281.

67. "Aus Furcht vor der Ehe ins Wasser gesprungen," *Berliner Lokal-Anzeiger*, August 25, 1913, Nr. 429.

68. "Eine Artistenhochzeit," *Berliner Morgenpost*, February 18, 1899, Nr. 42.

69. "Es ist die alte Geschichte . . . Liebeständeleien," *Berliner Morgenpost*, January 26, 1900, Nr. 21.

70. Arthur Brehmer, "Meine Hochzeitsreise im Automobil," *Berliner Morgenpost*, June 30, 1899, Nr. 151.

71. "Ein Reinfall," *Berliner Lokal-Anzeiger*, April 16, 1901, Nr. 175; "Berliner Beobachter," *Berliner Lokal-Anzeiger*, May 5, 1901, Nr. 209; "Öffentliche Meinung: Vom verschwundenen Bräutigam," *Berliner Lokal-Anzeiger*, May 12, 1901, Nr. 221.

72. Albert Frick, "Berühmte Junggesellen," *Berliner Morgenpost*, April 30, 1908, Nr. 101; Gregor, "Die Küche des Junggesellen," *Berliner Morgenpost*, August 12, 1905, Nr. 188; W., "Wenn Junggesellen kochen," *Berliner Morgenpost*, May 8, 1903, Nr. 107; H. N., "Weihnachtsverlobungen: Zur Warnung," *Berliner Morgenpost*, December 23, 1905, Nr. 301.

73. A. Slottko, *Unsere Heirathskandidaten* (Berlin, 1878), in Landesarchiv Berlin A Pr. Br. Rep. 030-05-01, Nr. U4.

74. "Öffentliche Meinung: Am Scheideweg," *Berliner Lokal-Anzeiger*, June 29, 1902, Nr. 299.

75. "Wie verheirate ich meine Tochter?," *Berliner Lokal-Anzeiger*, April 2, 1905, Nr. 157.

76. Hans Ostwald, "Liebe im Rausch," *Berliner Morgenpost*, May 29, 1911, Nr. 146.

77. For example, Paul Oppermann, *Der verheiratete Junggeselle* (Mühlhausen i. Thür: Verlag von G. Danner, 1905); Leo Berthold, "Die Ehescheuen," *Berliner Morgenpost*, February 7, 1899, Nr. 32; "Vor dem Standesamt," *Berliner Morgenpost*, July 5, 1901, Nr. 155; Hermann Heinrich, "Furcht vor der Ehe," *Berliner Morgenpost*, December 12, 1902, Nr. 291; Else Krafft, "Seine Liebe," *Berliner Morgenpost*, February 28, 1908, Nr. 50; Else Krafft, "Männer," *Berliner Lokal-Anzeiger*, July 7, 1912, Nr. 341.

78. Dorothee Goebeler, "Mädchenstolz," *Berliner Lokal-Anzeiger*, November 28, 1909, Nr. 774; Dorothee Goebeler, "Männer, die nicht heiraten," *Berliner Lokal-Anzeiger*, June 5, 1912, Nr. 282.

79. For example, Reinhold Gerling, *Junggesellen-Steuer* (Oranienburg: Orania, 1907); "Das Publikum: Junggesellensteuer," *Berliner Morgenpost*, July 5, 1908, Nr. 156.

80. "Junggesellensteuer," *Berliner Morgenpost*, June 28, 1908, Nr. 150.

81. Berg, *Auf dem Standesamt*; Otto Elster, "Judiths Ehe," *Berliner Lokal-Anzeiger*, October 14, 1910, Nr. 241 (Unterhaltungs-Beilage); "Das frühere Verhältnis," *Berliner Morgenpost*, August 14, 1903, Nr. 189.

82. "Öffentliche Meinung: Männer, die man nicht heiratet," *Berliner Lokal-Anzeiger*, September 22, 1912, Nr. 484.

83. Gustav Kukutsch, "Die alten Junggesellen," *Berliner Lokal-Anzeiger*, January 14, 1906, Nr. 24. Newspapers published a handful of other statistical studies confirming that most men did, indeed, end up married, as, for example, in "Die Heiratslust der Männer," *Berliner Morgenpost*, October 9, 1907, Nr. 237; M. R., "Die Heiratslust steigt," *Berliner Morgenpost*, April 4, 1909, Nr. 80.

84. "Das Publikum: Männliche Ehescheu und weibliche Berufsarbeit," *Berliner Morgenpost*, July 14, 1912, Nr. 191. See also Kuhn, *Familienstand: ledig*.

85. For example, "Briefkasten: Eros 777," *Berliner Lokal-Anzeiger*, May 1, 1904, Nr. 203. Writers, for their part, lampooned men for their concern over the amorous pasts of their potential brides. For example, Alfred Fiedler, "Der Andere," *Berliner Morgenpost*, May 13, 1909, Nr. 116. And women complained that they could not shake the stain of being divorcées. "Das Publikum: Eine geschiedene Frau," *Berliner Morgenpost*, November 8, 1908, Nr. 264.

86. "Berliner Beobachter," *Berliner Lokal-Anzeiger*, November 2, 1902, Nr. 515.

87. "Das Publikum: Der Weg zur Ehe," *Berliner Morgenpost*, August 20, 1911, Nr. 228; "Das Publikum: Folgsame Töchter," *Berliner Morgenpost*, August 28, 1910, Nr. 235.

88. J. Ka., "Die Brautkutsche: Leiden eines Berliner Bräutigams," *Berliner Morgenpost*, January 25, 1913, Nr. 24.

89. "Berliner Beobachter," *Berliner Lokal-Anzeiger*, September 6, 1903, Nr. 417.

90. Dagobert von Gerhardt-Amyntor, "Die modern Ehescheu," *Berliner Lokal-Anzeiger*, November 8, 1908, Nr. 571.

91. Lotte Gubalke, "Im Nebenberuf—Ehefrau," *Berliner Lokal-Anzeiger*, September 17, 1912, Nr. 475.

92. "Die wahre Liebe ist das nicht," *Berliner Morgenpost*, November 29, 1904, Nr. 280; "Öffentliche Meinung: Wie sollen wir für unsere Töchter sorgen?!," *Berliner Lokal-Anzeiger*, December 22, 1907, Nr. 649; "Ohne Geld, keine Heirat," *Berliner Morgenpost*, September 3, 1904, Nr. 207; Alfred Rossig, "Frauengedanken über Männererziehung," *Berliner Lokal-Anzeiger*, January 18, 1907, Nr. 32.

93. The exception here, as Marion Kaplan demonstrates, was Jewish families, who seem consistently to have provided dowries, even if it took the collective effort of the local Jewish community. Kaplan," "For Love or Money," 136.

94. Quite a few stories—real and imagined—played on the idea of a dowry being refused either as a test of real love, out of lack of approval of the daughter's intended spouse, or simply because the family was too poor to provide one. See, for example, "Aus Liebesgram in den Tod gegangen," *Berliner Lokal-Anzeiger*, August 27, 1905, Nr. 421; "Die aufgehobene Verlobung," *Berliner Morgenpost*, June 3, 1899, Nr. 128; "Öffentliche Meinung: Eine Verlobungsgeschichte," *Berliner Lokal-Anzeiger*, June 8, 1902, Nr. 263.

95. J. Lorm, "Ehefragen," *Berliner Lokal-Anzeiger*, August 13, 1905, Nr. 395.

96. Dorothee Goebeler, "Was man zum Heiraten braucht," *Berliner Lokal-Anzeiger*, July 3, 1913, Nr. 331. As Paul Kirstein noted in 1902, men who expressed a desire to get married too soon—in their twenties—were considered fools. Paul A. Kirstein,

"Verlobungen: Auch eine Osterplauderei," *Berliner Morgenpost*, March 30, 1902, Nr. 75.

97. Archiv der Akademie der Künste, Kempowski Bio-Archiv 3623/1, 14.

98. Ibid., 17.

99. Ibid., 19.

100. Ibid., 20–21.

101. Ibid., 21–22.

102. Ibid., 23.

103. Ibid.

104. Ibid., 28–31.

105. "Das Publikum: Das Heiratsalter," *Berliner Morgenpost*, November 29, 1908, Nr. 281.

106. Cf. Schulz, *Lebenswelt und Kultur*.

107. Archiv der Akademie der Künste, Kempowski Bio-Archiv 3623/1, 29.

108. "Öffentliche Meinung: Die moderne Ehescheu," *Berliner Lokal-Anzeiger*, November 22, 1908, Nr. 595. See also Dorothee Goebeler, "Versorgte Frauen," *Berliner Lokal-Anzeiger*, January 28, 1914, Nr. 50.

109. "Öffentliche Meinung: Die moderne Ehescheu," *Berliner Lokal-Anzeiger*, November 22, 1908, Nr. 595.

110. Both Christa Putz and Caroline Arni have written about the ways in which German-speaking Europeans conceived of a crisis with regard to marriage, though both scholars focus primarily on the sexual science and emotional dynamics of marriage and less on the rise of individualism and its conflict with marriage. Christa Putz, *Verordnete Lust: Sexualmedizin, Psychoanalyse und die "Krise der Ehe," 1870–1930* (Bielefeld: transcript Verlag, 2011), chapter 3; Caroline Arni, *Entzweiungen: Die Krise der Ehe um 1900* (Cologne: Böhlau, 2004).

111. Hedwig Dohm, "Ehe Aphorismen," in Helene Stöcker (ed.), *Mutterschutz: Zeitschrift zur Reform der sexuellen Ethik* (1907): 215–217.

112. Rudolf Lothar, "Moderne Eheprobleme," *Berliner Lokal-Anzeiger*, May 30, 1911, Nr. 272.

113. For example, Erna Heinemann-Grautoff, *Möglichkeiten der Liebe* (Berlin: Karl Curtius, 1912); E. M., "Wie man Männer fesselt: Möglichkeiten der Liebe," *Berliner Morgenpost*, December 10, 1911, Nr. 339; Carry Brachvogel, "Elektrische Frauen," *Berliner Morgenpost*, October 21, 1906, Nr. 247; "Berliner Beobachter," *Berliner Lokal-Anzeiger*, June 15, 1902, Nr. 275; S. Wities, "Vorbeigelungene Ehen," *Berliner Lokal-Anzeiger*, October 27, 1912, Nr. 549; Eliza Ichenhaeuser, "Warum das Heiraten unmodern ist," *Berliner Lokal-Anzeiger*, September 9, 1906, Nr. 458.

114. "Die menschliche Ehe," *Berliner Lokal-Anzeiger*, January 8, 1910, Nr. 12.

115. D. A., "Für und gegen die Ehe," *Berliner Lokal-Anzeiger*, November 13, 1911, Nr. 589.

116. J. Lorm, "Ehe-Reformen," *Berliner Lokal-Anzeiger*, March 25, 1906, Nr. 154;

117. "Wie sich Bräute schmücken: Eine Hochzeitsmonatsplauderei," *Berliner Morgenpost*, October 9, 1904, Nr. 238.

118. "Öffentliche Meinung: Ehen auf Zeit," *Berliner Lokal-Anzeiger*, October 30, 1904, Nr. 511; "Öffentliche Meinung: Ehereform?!," *Berliner Lokal-Anzeiger*, October 15, 1905, Nr. 512.

119. On the decline of religiosity in turn-of-the-century Berlin, see McLeod, *Piety and Poverty*; also Tyler Carrington, "Instilling the 'Manly' Faith: Protestant Masculinity and the German *Jünglingsvereine* at the *Fin de Siècle*," *Journal of Men, Masculinities, and Spiritualities* 3, no. 2 (June 2009): 142–154.

120. Siegbert Salter, "Aus dem Standesregister einer Millionstadt: 1. Der Berliner Heiratsmarkt," *Berliner Morgenpost*, March 2, 1906, Nr. 51.

121. "Standesamt, kirchliche Trauung oder freie Liebe," *Berliner Lokal-Anzeiger*, March 23, 1907, Nr. 150.

122. Alexander Elster, "Erikas Hochzeit," *Berliner Morgenpost*, November 3, 1907, Nr. 259.

123. "Briefkasten," *Berliner Lokal-Anzeiger*, April 17, 1904, Nr. 179.

124. On alternative marital arrangements and "radical couples" in England in the late nineteenth century, see Ginger S. Frost, *Living in Sin: Cohabiting as Husband and Wife in Nineteenth-Century England* (Manchester: Manchester University Press, 2008), especially 195–224.

125. Rudolf Lothar, "Revolution der Ehe," *Berliner Lokal-Anzeiger*, April 4, 1908, Nr. 175.

126. "Öffentliche Meinung: Unliebenswürdige Frauen," *Berliner Lokal-Anzeiger*, June 26, 1910, Nr. 318.

127. "Der eifersüchtige Liebhaber," *Berliner Morgenpost*, August 31, 1907, Nr. 204.

128. S. Sborowitz, *Freie Liebe* (Berlin, 1907), in Landesarchiv Berlin A Pr. Br. Rep. 030-05-02, Nr. 3826.

129. Hermann Heisermans, "Liebschaft," *Berliner Morgenpost*, May 3, 1903, Nr. 103.

130. Rudolf Lothar, "Revolution der Ehe," *Berliner Lokal-Anzeiger*, April 4, 1908, Nr. 175.

131. "Bund für Mutterschutz. Ehereform, uneheliche Kinder, Säuglingssterblichkeit," *Berliner Morgenpost*, January 15, 1907, Nr. 12.

132. Reinhold Gerling, *Freie Liebe oder bürgerliche Ehe* (Oranienburg: Orania, 1907), 5.

133. Ibid., 21.

134. Ibid., 21.

135. Ibid., 13.

136. Ibid., 24, 28.

137. Ibid., 3.

138. Ibid., 28.

139. Pascal, "Moderne Eheexperimente," *Berliner Lokal-Anzeiger*, April 11, 1907, Nr. 182.

140. Rudolf Lothar, "Moderne Eheprobleme," *Berliner Lokal-Anzeiger*, May 30, 1911, Nr. 272.

CHAPTER FOUR

1. "Der Frauenmord bei Finkenkrug: Zweiter Verhandlungstag," *Berliner Lokal-Anzeiger*, March 10, 1916, Nr. 129.

2. Letter from Weißenseeer Sparkasse to police, Landesarchiv Berlin A Pr. Br. Rep. 030-03, Nr. 1426.

3. Landesarchiv Berlin A Pr. Br. Rep. 030-03, Nr. 927, Bl. 54–61.

4. "Der Frauenmord bei Finkenkrug: Zweiter Verhandlungstag," *Berliner Lokal-Anzeiger*, March 10, 1916, Nr. 129.

5. Written charge against Paul Kuhnt, Landesarchiv Berlin A Pr. Br. Rep. 030-03, Nr. 927, Bl. 4–7.

6. Police memoranda, Landesarchiv Berlin A Pr. Br. Rep. 030-03, Nr. 1232, Bl. 26–39.

7. "Auf der Spur des Tegeler Frauenmörders," *Berliner Lokal-Anzeiger*, September 3, 1913, Nr. 447. The case was so sensational that at least one Dutch newspaper, the *Rotterdamsch Nieuwsblad*, ran the story of the search for her murderer, as a Google search of the victim and suspect reveals. "De vrouwenmoord te Berlijn," *Rotterdamsch Nieuwsblad*, September 5, 1913, Nr. 617.

8. *Berliner Tageblatt*, June 29, 1914, Nr. 323.

9. Letters to Adolf Mertens, Landesarchiv Berlin A Pr. Br. Rep. 030-03, Nr. 1232, Bl. 26–39.

10. Ibid.

11. Written charge against Paul Kuhnt, Landesarchiv Berlin A Pr. Br. Rep. 030-03, Nr. 927, Bl. 4–7.

12. Statements, Landesarchiv Berlin A Pr. Br. Rep. 030-03, Nr. 1425, Bl. 10–12, 48–49, 101–103.

13. Statement by Antonie Köhler, Landesarchiv Berlin A Pr. Br. Rep. 030-03, Nr. 1425, Bl. 110–113.

14. Statement by Antonie Köhler, Landesarchiv Berlin A Pr. Br. Rep. 030-03, Nr. 1425, Bl. 110–113.

15. *Berliner Lokal-Anzeiger*, June 7, 1914, Nr. 283.

16. Letter to Frieda Kliem, Landesarchiv Berlin A Pr. Br. Rep. 030-03, Nr. 1425, Bl. 40.

17. Cards and letters belonging to Frieda Kliem, Landesarchiv Berlin A Pr. Br. Rep. 030-03, Nr. 1232, Bl. 40.

18. Police memoranda, Landesarchiv Berlin A Pr. Br. Rep. 030-03, Nr. 1232.

19. Written charge against Paul Kuhnt, Landesarchiv Berlin A Pr. Br. Rep. 030-03, Nr. 927, Bl. 4–7.

20. Statements, Landesarchiv Berlin A Pr. Br. Rep. 030-03, Nr. 1425, Bl. 10–12.

21. Letter from Frieda Kliem to Otto Mewes, Landesarchiv Berlin A Pr. Br. Rep. 030-03, Nr. 1425, Bl. 95.

22. Written charge against Paul Kuhnt, Landesarchiv Berlin A Pr. Br. Rep. 030-03, Nr. 927, Bl. 4–7.

23. Letter from Frieda Kliem to Otto Mewes, Landesarchiv Berlin A Pr. Br. Rep. 030-03, Nr. 1425, Bl. 95.

24. Statement by Marie Schönemann, Landesarchiv Berlin A Pr. Br. Rep. 030-03, Nr. 1425, Bl. 10.

25. Statement by Hulda Sello, Landesarchiv Berlin A Pr. Br. Rep. 030-03, Nr. 1425, Bl. 11.

26. Statements, Landesarchiv Berlin A Pr. Br. Rep. 030-03, Nr. 1425, Bl. 106–107, 82.

27. Report, Landesarchiv Berlin A Pr. Br. Rep. 030-03, Nr. 1425, Bl. 4.

28. Ibid.

29. Postcard from Antonie Köhler to Otto Mewes, Landesarchiv Berlin A Pr. Br. Rep. 030-03, Nr. 1425, Bl. 95.

30. Report, Landesarchiv Berlin A Pr. Br. Rep. 030-03, Nr. 1425, Bl. 4.

31. Written charge against Paul Kuhnt, Landesarchiv Berlin A Pr. Br. Rep. 030-03, Nr. 927, Bl. 4–7.

32. Report, Landesarchiv Berlin A Pr. Br. Rep. 030-03, Nr. 1425, Bl. 4.

33. It is interesting that there is no record of the police pursuing charges relating to sexual assault or rape, not least because such "crimes against morality" and "offenses against persons" (among others, assault and rape) were on the rise at the turn of the century (a fact that got the attention of a great many moral reformers). This case, moreover, seemingly had all of the usual elements of sexual crime: a woman lured out into the forest; the personal ad connection of suspect and victim; and the depression in the grass. It seems possible that the investigators' discoveries about Frieda's apparent liasons with a variety of men (information relayed to the police by her neighbors) made them less willing to see Frieda as a sexual victim than as complicit in this part of her sad fate. On sexual crime in imperial Germany, see, among others, Lees, *Cities, Sin, and Sexual Reform*, especially 138, 201; Edward Ross Dickinson, *Sex, Freedom, and Power in Imperial Germany, 1880–1914* (Cambridge: Cambridge University Press, 2015).

34. Postcard from Antonie Köhler to Otto Mewes, Landesarchiv Berlin A Pr. Br. Rep. 030-03, Nr. 1425, Bl. 95.

35. Save for one short-lived gang known as the "Mauerjungen," which had operated in the 1870s and 1880s east of the city center until the city bought up the slums and brothels of this area and effectively ended the group's reign, Berlin had as good as no organized crime. Roth, *Kriminalitätsbekämpfung*, 290.

36. Wehler, *Deutsche Gesellschaftsgeschichte*, 521.

37. "Die Sterblichkeit nach Todesursachen und Altersklassen der Gestorbenen im preußischen Staate während des Jahres 1904," in *Preußische Statistik* 195 (Berlin: Verlag des Königlichen Statistischen Bureaus, 1905), xxiv; "Die tödlichen Verunglückungen und die Selbstmorde nach Provinzen im Jahre 1915," in *Statistisches Jahrbuch für den preußischen Staat* (Berlin: Verlag des Königlichen Statistischen Landsamts, 1917), 33.

38. Backhaus does not include his profession in the letter, but an address book from 1863 lists his name and profession. *Berliner Adressbücher*, 1863. Zentral- und Landesbibliothek Berlin, 14.

39. Letter from Backhaus to police, Landesarchiv Berlin A Pr. Br. Rep. 030, Nr. 16925.

40. Paul A. Kirstein, "Verlobungen: Auch eine Osterplauderei," *Berliner Morgenpost*, March 30, 1902, Nr. 75.

41. K., "Heiratskandidaten," *Berliner Morgenpost*, April 20, 1901, Nr. 92.

42. "Berliner Beobachter," *Berliner Lokal-Anzeiger*, July 27, 1902, Nr. 347.

43. Oscar Pitschil, *Die Heiratsfälle*, in Landesarchiv Berlin A Pr. Br. Rep. 030-05-02, Nr. 3967.

44. J. L., "Die verkaufte Braut," *Berliner Morgenpost*, November 6, 1907, Nr. 261.

45. C. Weßner, "Ein Weiberfeind," *Berliner Morgenpost*, April 7, 1899, Nr. 81.

46. "Briefkasten," *Berliner Lokal-Anzeiger*, August 26, 1903, Nr. 397.

47. For example, "Ein Heiratsschwindler," *Berliner Lokal-Anzeiger*, November 20, 1905, Nr. 578; "Die Geschäftspraktiken eines Heiratsvermittlers," *Berliner Lokal-Anzeiger*, October 23, 1913, Nr. 539; "Ich bin eine Witwe," *Berliner Morgenpost*, October 6, 1903, Nr. 234; "Eine Warnung vor Berliner Heiratsvermittlern," *Berliner Lokal-Anzeiger*, September 9, 1904, Nr. 424.

48. "Der Mann mit den acht Bräuten," *Berliner Lokal-Anzeiger*, October 3, 1901, Nr. 463.

49. "Heiratsschwindel en gros," *Berliner Lokal-Anzeiger*, July 5, 1905, Nr. 322; "Heiratsschwindel Engros," *Berliner Morgenpost*, July 5, 1905, Nr. 155; "Heiratsschwindel Engros," *Berliner Morgenpost*, July 6, 1905, Nr. 156.

50. "Der große Heiratsschwindelprozeß," *Berliner Lokal-Anzeiger*, July 6, 1905, Nr. 324. Just a year and a half later, a woman named Fanni Wenzel received the same prison sentence for an almost identical racket. "Die Liebesbriefe der Heiratsvermittlerin," *Berliner Lokal-Anzeiger*, January 4, 1907, Nr. 5. Later that same year, another man was sentenced to prison for swindling Berliners this way. "'Eine vermögende Dame wünsche sich zu verheiraten': Die 'guten Partien' unter Nachnahme," *Berliner Morgenpost*, November 16, 1907, Nr. 270. Also "Hinter den Kulissen eines Heiratsvermittlungsbureaus," *Berliner Lokal-Anzeiger*, February 16, 1908, Nr. 85.

51. R. Neurich, "Ein 'internationales Heiratsbureau': Skizze aus dem Nordseebad Westerland-Sylt," *Berliner Morgenpost*, August 30, 1903, Nr. 203; Wilhelm Cremer, "Das Heiratscafé," *Berliner Morgenpost*, January 5, 1914, Nr. 4; "Der Photograph als Heiratsvermittler," *Berliner Lokal-Anzeiger*, August 22, 1906, Nr. 425.

52. Hopkins Bar, "Kein Heiraths-Bureau," *Berliner Morgenpost*, February 19, 1899, Nr. 43.

53. Fritz Skowronnek, "Ein seltsamer Ehestifter," *Berliner Morgenpost*, June 24, 1904, Nr. 146.

54. "Briefkasten," *Berliner Lokal-Anzeiger*, August 9, 1903, Nr. 369.

55. The law essentially stated that contracts for marriage with matchmakers were not actionable. "Briefkasten," *Berliner Lokal-Anzeiger*, December 17, 1905, Nr. 627; "Briefkasten," *Berliner Lokal-Anzeiger*, January 1, 1905, Nr. 1.

56. Landesarchiv Berlin A Rep. 342-02-X3, Nr. 47141 (Margarethe Bornstein, Heirats-Vermittlungs-Geschäft).

57. Matchmaking, as Marion Kaplan has shown, was long an important part of Jewish marriage practices—so much so that, for purposes of maintaining respectability, Jewish parents of young men and women who "fell in love" often resorted to elaborate acts of revisionist, arranged staging (e.g. hiring a matchmaker after the fact) such that these love unions might appear in a more respectable light. Kaplan, "For Love or Money," 150. See also Jacob Katz, "Family, Kinship, and Marriage among Ashkenazim in the Sixteenth to Eighteenth Centuries," *Jewish Journal of Sociology* 1 (1959): 3–22;

58. "Heiratsschwindel," *Berliner Lokal-Anzeiger*, January 10, 1901, Nr. 16.

59. Mary Oberberg, "Die Engländerin als Ehestifterin," *Berliner Lokal-Anzeiger*, October 26, 1902, Nr. 503.

60. For that matter, as Marion Kaplan has discovered, even (in this case, Jewish) parents understood the allure of the coincidental meeting, decided to "accommodate to modern sensibilities," and expended considerable effort camouflaging their matchmaking efforts so that they appeared entirely fortuitous. Kaplan rather cleverly calls this "ritual spontaneity." Kaplan, "For Love or Money," 148.

61. Hermann Heinrich, "Furcht vor der Ehe," *Berliner Morgenpost*, December 12, 1902, Nr. 291.

62. "Die Heiratsstifterin," *Berliner Morgenpost*, July 4, 1909, Nr. 166.

63. See, for example, Kaplan, "For Love or Money"; Coontz, *Marriage, a History*; Simmons, *Making Marriage Modern*.

64. Fritz Podszus, "Die gewerbsmäßige Heiratsvermittlung," *Heirats-Zeitung* 29, no. 235 (1913): 1.

65. Hans Ringlau, "Gelegenheiten zur Heirat," *Heirats-Zeitung* 30, no. 238 (1914): 1–2.

66. Dr. H., "Theodors Bekehrung," *Heirats-Zeitung* 30, no. 237 (1914): 1.

67. Joachim Werner, *Die Heirats-Annonce: Studien und Briefe* (Berlin: Verlag Martin Aronhold, 1908), 36–37.

68. Classified ads have received scant treatment by historians. For example, Karin Hausen's article "Die Ehe in Angebot und Nachfrage: Heiratsanzeigen historisch durchmustert," in Ingrid Bauer et al. (eds.), *Liebe und Widerstand: Ambivalenzen historischer Geschlechterbeziehungen* (Vienna: Böhlau, 2005), 428–448, essentially argues that classified ads deserve more attention. Marion Kaplan's essay "For Love or Money" gestures at some of the points made in each chapter of this book, but her concern is primarily the centrality of dowries in Jewish marriages. Two other historians concentrate on classified ads but are interested in the moral outrage they incited: see H. G. Cocks, *Classified: The Secret History of the Personal Column* (London: Random House, 2009); Cocks, "Peril in the Personals: The Dangers and Pleasures of Classified Advertising in Early Twentieth-Century Britain,"

Media History 10, no. 1 (2004): 3–16; and Stephan Lovell, "Finding a Mate in Late Tsarist Russia: The Evidence from Marriage Advertisements," *Cultural and Social History* 4, no. 1 (2007): 51–72. The only other notable work on classifieds comes from contemporary anthropology: see Annegret Braun, *Ehe- und Partnerschafts-vorstellungen von 1948–1996: eine kulturwissenschaftliche Analyse anhand von Heiratsinseraten* (Münster: Waxman, 2001).

69. Letter from Baerwald to police, June 23, 1837, Landesarchiv Berlin A Pr. Br. Rep. 030, Nr. 16925.

70. Newspaper clipping, Landesarchiv Berlin A Pr. Br. Rep. 030, Nr. 16925.

71. Police correspondence, Landesarchiv Berlin A Pr. Br. Rep. 030, Nr. 16925.

72. Newspaper clipping, Landesarchiv Berlin A Pr. Br. Rep. 030, Nr. 16925.

73. Report, Landesarchiv Berlin A Pr. Br. Rep. 030, Nr. 16925.

74. *Berliner Intelligenz-Blatt*, May 7, 1850.

75. F. Bartholomäi's 1874 study of twelve hundred ads in the *Vossische Zeitung* suggests something of this relatively early popularity, but his approach to them is largely dismissive, and two-thirds of the ads he found aimed not at marriage but at recovering debts and resolving other personal matters. Dr. F. Bartholomäi, "Volkspsychologische Spiegelbilder aus Berliner Annoncen," *Berliner Städtisches Jahrbuch für Volkswirthschaft und Statistik* (Berlin: Verlag von Leonhard Simion, 1874), 45.

76. Fritzsche, *Reading Berlin 1900*, 52–53.

77. J. B., "Was sie im Café lesen," *Berliner Morgenpost*, October 25, 1899, Nr. 251.

78. Max Pollaczek, "Wie man die Zeitungen liest," *Berliner Morgenpost*, September 26, 1900, Nr. 225.

79. H. Dt., "Berlin wie sie wird und ist: Die Friedrichstadt," *Berliner Morgenpost*, November 17, 1901, Nr. 271.

80. Maximilian Wolff, "Maskenball der Taubstummen," *Berliner Lokal-Anzeiger*, March 3, 1901, Nr. 105.

81. Max Pollaczek, "Wie man die Zeitungen liest," *Berliner Morgenpost*, September 26, 1900, Nr. 225.

82. "Berliner Beobachter," *Berliner Lokal-Anzeiger*, December 16, 1906, Nr. 638.

83. "Berliner Beobachter," *Berliner Lokal-Anzeiger*, December 18, 1910, Nr. 641.

84. Rudolf Hirschberg-Jura, "Ein Zeitungsausschnitt," *Berliner Morgenpost*, November 15, 1910, Nr. 314.

85. Schwarz, *Liebesleute*, 5.

86. Rudolf Kessler and A. Stein, *Die Heiratsannonce* (Berlin: Verlag von Kühling & Güttner, Theater-Buchhandlung, 1910).

87. Duncker, *Reelles Heiratsgesuch*.

88. Karl Escher, "Die Verlobungseiche," *Berliner Morgenpost*, April 16, 1911, Nr. 105.

89. Rem., "Reelles Heiratsgesuch," *Berliner Morgenpost*, October 19, 1909, Nr. 273.

90. *Berliner Lokal-Anzeiger*, March 11, 1905, Nr. 119. *Berliner Lokal-Anzeiger*, January 11, 1906, Nr. 18.

91. "Das Rendezvous im Café," *Berliner Morgenpost*, January 4, 1907, Nr. 3; "Ein pfiffiger Caféhauswirt," *Berliner Lokal-Anzeiger*, January 3, 1907, Nr. 4.

92. Wilhelm Cremer, "Das Heiratscafé," *Berliner Morgenpost*, January 5, 1914, Nr. 4.

93. *Berliner Lokal-Anzeiger*, August 11, 1901, Nr. 373. Kaplan writes that the same was true of exclusively Jewish publications like the *Israelitisches Monatsblatt*. Kaplan, "For Love or Money," 130.

94. In general, people interested in studying personal ads used one of two methods: either they posted a variety of test ads on their own and then studied the responses, or they responded to real ads and, if granted access, interviewed the authors of those ads about their experiences, successes, and failures. For an example of the first method, see Dr. Leo Perry, *"Auf diesem nicht mehr ungewöhnlichen Wege...": Der Liebesmarkt des Zeitungs-Inserates* (Vienna: Verlag für Kulturforschung, 1927). For the second, see Werner, *Die Heirats-Annonce*. In a third and rather spectacular case, a Berlin author named Karl Theodor Dreste (who published under the pseudonym "Spektator-Jüngster") published a sort of memoir about—as the title goes—*Love-Crazy Women: or What I Experienced When Searching for a Spouse*. Dreste's book, which he published himself, carried the tagline, "A very practical and useful book for every marriage-eligible young woman" and promised a "large number of heart-stopping original letters by normal as well as perverse modern marriage-seekers." Whether or not the ads—and accompanying experiences—were real or fictitious is impossible to know, but Dreste's book nevertheless made for rather sensational reading. Karl Theodor Dreste, *Liebestolle Weiber: oder Was ich auf der Suche nach einer Gattin erlebte* (Berlin: Verlag Karl Theodor Dreste, 1914). A final method—simply studying the many ads plainly available in newspapers—was perhaps most successfully carried out by F. Bartholomäi.

95. Bartholomäi, "Volkspsychologische Spiegelbilder," 37; Werner, *Die Heirats-Annonce*, 10, 12. Interestingly, the average age seems to have been rising, for Bartholomäi's 1874 estimate was that most ads were written by men and women between twenty-five and thirty. Bartholomäi, 38.

96. *Berliner Lokal-Anzeiger*, June 7, 1914, Nr. 283.

97. In this, users of ads seem, over the years, to have grown more adept and confident in penning ads. Bartholomäi's major conclusion was that, other than age and wealth, very few ads listed much of anything in terms of specific traits desired or possessed by the authors. Bartholomäi, "Volkspsychologische Spiegelbilder," 41.

98. Save, of course, for the Jewish Berliners Marion Kaplan analyzes in her study of Jewish marriage practices. Kaplan, "For Love or Money." It is also true that the majority of Berliners were, if anything, at least nominally Protestant and that specifying what was mostly assumed was simply a waste of money in the context of this pay-by-the-word method of looking for love. Intermarriage, especially between Jews and Gentiles, was, at the turn of the century, still somewhat rare and discouraged, and Jewish Berliners seem to have advertised mostly in Jewish-oriented publications like the *Israelitisches Wochenblatt* (note: inasmuch as the

major daily newspapers were put out by Jewish publishing houses—for example, by Rudolf Mosse—few publications were somehow "either" Jewish "or" Gentile; but the *Berliner Tageblatt*, published by Mosse, and the *Israelitisches Wochenblatt* were naturally totally different papers). See, again, Kaplan, "For Love or Money." On intermarriage during this imperial period, see also Eric McKinley, "Intimate Strangers: Intermarriage among Jews, Catholics, and Protestants in Germany, 1875–1935," PhD dissertation, University of Illinois at Urbana-Champaign, 2015.

99. "Öffentliche Meinung: 'Vermögen erwünscht,'" *Berliner Lokal-Anzeiger*, February 16, 1908, Nr. 85.

100. "Öffentliche Meinung: 'Vermögen erwünscht,'" *Berliner Lokal-Anzeiger*, March 22, 1908, Nr. 150.

101. As Bartholomäi put it, women clearly recognized that "when it comes to marriage, women know that money is the *nervus rerum* [*driving force*]." Bartholomäi, "Volkspsychologische Spiegelbilder," 43.

102. Werner, *Die Heirats-Annonce*, 16. This accords with Bartholomäi's study, as well. Bartholomäi, "Volkspsychologische Spiegelbilder," 43–44.

103. Bartholomäi, "Volkspsychologische Spiegelbilder," 44.

104. Dorothee Goebeler, "Die Frau mit dem Innenleben," *Berliner Lokal-Anzeiger*, July 29, 1914, Nr. 380.

105. "Öffentliche Meinung: 'Anonym zwecklos,'" *Berliner Lokal-Anzeiger*, April 5, 1908, Nr. 176.

106. "Briefkasten," *Berliner Lokal-Anzeiger*, March 25, 1905, Nr. 143.

107. "Öffentliche Meinung: Verfehlte Annoncen," *Berliner Lokal-Anzeiger*, December 12, 1909, Nr. 800.

108. In one case, for example, a man who owned a delivery office used his access to ads (and, more importantly, the identity of their authors) to propose to an ad writer (who was desperate to get married) and essentially swindle her of her dowry. "Unerquickliche Heirathsgeschichten," *Berliner Lokal-Anzeiger*, May 8, 1902, Nr. 213.

109. Cases of swindlers using personal ads were at least a weekly occurrence in Berlin. See, for example, "Heirathsschwindel und kein Ende," *Berliner Morgenpost*, October 14, 1900, Nr. 241; "Vom Heirathsschwindler 'Prinzen Antonio, Herzog von Siano,'" *Berliner Lokal-Anzeiger*, September 13, 1901, Nr. 429; "Ein Heirathsschwindler," *Berliner Lokal-Anzeiger*, October 27, 1901, Nr. 505; "Verhaftung eines Heiratsschwindlers," *Berliner Lokal-Anzeiger*, August 31, 1903, Nr. 406.

110. For example, "Der Heiratsagent," *Berliner Lokal-Anzeiger*, January 20, 1904, Nr. 31; "Der Heiratsvermittler vor Gericht," *Berliner Lokal-Anzeiger*, January 4, 1912, Nr. 6.

111. Newspaper clipping, September 9, 1894, Landesarchiv Berlin A Pr Br. Rep. 030, Nr. 16230 (Überwachung Paul v. Hoensbroech, Heiratsvermittlungsprozess, 1891–1915).

112. Newspaper clipping, November 2, 1898, Landesarchiv Berlin A Pr Br. Rep. 030, Nr. 16230 (Überwachung Paul v. Hoensbroech, Heiratsvermittlungsprozess, 1891–1915).

113. Newspaper clippings, December 7, 1898; December 6, 1898, Landesarchiv Berlin A Pr Br. Rep. 030, Nr. 16230 (Überwachung Paul v. Hoensbroech, Heiratsvermittlungsprozess, 1891–1915).

114. Newspaper clipping, October 21, 1899, Landesarchiv Berlin A Pr Br. Rep. 030, Nr. 16230 (Überwachung Paul v. Hoensbroech, Heiratsvermittlungsprozess, 1891–1915).

115. Newspaper clipping, Landesarchiv Berlin A Pr Br. Rep. 030, Nr. 16230 (Überwachung Paul v. Hoensbroech, Heiratsvermittlungsprozess, 1891–1915).

116. Newspaper clipping, March 13, 1902, Landesarchiv Berlin A Pr. Br. Rep. 030, Nr. 16230 (Überwachung Paul v. Hoensbroech, Heiratsvermittlungsprozess, 1891–1915).

117. Margarete Pick, "Ehen auf Erden," *Geschlecht und Gesellschaft* 1, no. 1 (1906): 569.

118. "Das Publikum: Die Heiratsannonce," *Berliner Morgenpost*, April 9, 1911, Nr. 99.

119. "In der Affäre des Heiratsschwindlers Schiemang," *Berliner Lokal-Anzeiger*, January 22, 1904, Nr. 36.

120. Bartholomäi, "Volkspsychologische Spiegelbilder," 37; "Das Publikum: Der Weg zur Ehe," *Berliner Morgenpost*, August 6, 1911, Nr. 214.

121. Helene Kuërs, *Aufzeichnungen aus meinem Leben* (1954) Deutsches Tagebucharchiv, Signatur 11581 II.2, 17.

122. Leipziger, *Der Rettungsball*, 83.

123. Kessler and Stein, *Die Heiratsannonce*, 3.

124. Bartholomäi, "Volkspsychologische Spiegelbilder," 44.

125. Hans Ringlau, "Gelegenheiten zur Heirat," *Heirats-Zeitung* 30, no. 238 (1914): 1–2.

126. Paul Näcke, "Ein Besuch bei den Homosexuellen in Berlin," 171–172; Hirschfeld, "Das Ergebnis der statistischen Untersuchungen," 121; *Das perverse Berlin*, 128–129; *Goodbye to Berlin*, 71; Dobler, *Von andern Ufern*.

127. Magnus Hirschfeld, "Das Ergebnis der statistischen Untersuchungen über den Prozentsatz der Homosexuellen," 121; *Goodbye to Berlin*, 71.

128. Dr. P. Näcke, "Angebot und Nachfrage von Homosexuellen in Zeitungen," *Archiv für Kriminal-Anthropologie und Kriminalistik* 8, nos. 3–4 (1902): 341.

129. Ibid., 344.

130. Ibid., 342–343.

131. Ibid., 340–341.

132. Ibid., 344. Richard von Krafft-Ebing, perhaps the most famous sexologist of all, also notes the prevalence of veiled—but clearly same-sex—ads, in particular, those written by women, in his famous *Psychopathia Sexualis*. See Richard Freiherr von Krafft-Ebing, *Psychopathia Sexualis* 10th ed. (Stuttgart: Verlag von Ferdinant Enke, 1898), 256.

133. Adolf Brand, "Wochenbericht," *Die Gemeinschaft der Eigenen*, January 9, 1904.

134. Beachy, *Gay Berlin.*
135. Näcke, "Angebot und Nachfrage," 341.
136. Ibid., 341, 345; Näcke, "Ein Besuch bei den Homosexuellen in Berlin," 171–172.
137. Based on my preliminary investigations of personal ads after World War I, it seems that gay personal ads may have peaked in the 1920s, where laws governing censorship and sexuality were significantly less restrictive. In fact, other nonhegemonic sexualities—notably transvestitism—are represented in ads in the 1920s, as well.
138. The fact that we even know about Fritz Reinert is, itself, a rather interesting story. Reinert kept a diary during those teenage years when he was preparing to go to Berlin and then did actually spend a year there, but the diary stops as he is about to leave Berlin and return home to the provinces. There is no record of what Reinert did with the diary after that, nor is there any indication that he continued to keep a diary after leaving Berlin. Roughly seventy years later, the tenant of an apartment in Duisburg some 350 miles from Berlin found Fritz's diary in his attic and eventually gave it to the German Diary Archive (Deutsches Tagebucharchiv).
139. Fritz Reinert, *Tagebuch 1902–3*, Deutsches Tagebucharchiv, Signatur 1929, 53.
140. Ibid., 54.
141. Ibid., 55.
142. Ibid.
143. Ibid., 57.
144. Ibid., 59.
145. Ibid., 62.
146. Ibid., 109.
147. K. S., "Die Ehe durch die Zeitung," *Berliner Lokal-Anzeiger*, August 10, 1900, Nr. 371.
148. Werner, *Die Heirats-Annonce*, 7; "Das Publikum: Die Heiratsannonce," *Berliner Morgenpost*, April 9, 1911, Nr. 99.
149. Werner, *Die Heirats-Annonce*, 7–8.
150. In this way, personal ads might even be understood as modernist texts. Marshall Berman famously described the response to modernity—modernism—as the "struggle to make ourselves at home in a constantly changing world." When discussing Baudelaire, specifically, Berman wrote that what made this "first modernist" so insightful about modernism was that he realized—as many in the twentieth century later forgot—that modernism is about, even composed of, the everyday lives of men and women as they "orient [them]selves toward the primary forces of modern life." After all, personal ads were nothing if not the mundane, everyday attempts of modern men and women to make themselves at home in the ultramodern city in which they lived. Personal ads were not solely an expression of what it was like to live in the modern world, but the shape and form of the ads, not to mention the words themselves, were the artistic and textual products of Berliners as they quite self-consciously broke with the past and endeavored to fit their lives to the beats and rhythms of the modern world. Like

Baudelaire's "painter of modern life," who sketches moments and preserves their fleetingness, so too was each personal ad a tiny sketch of its author's life. Ads were snapshots that described not simply the isolated present but also both a past and an imagined future. Berman, *All That Is Solid*, 6, 133–134, 146; Andreas Huyssen, "Modernist Miniatures: Literary Snapshots of Urban Spaces," *PMLA* 122, no. 1 (2007): 27–42.

151. Letter from H. Krämer to police, November 26, 1915, Landesarchiv Berlin A Pr. Br. Rep. 030-03, Nr. 927.

152. K. S., "Die Ehe durch die Zeitung," *Berliner Lokal-Anzeiger*, August 10, 1900, Nr. 371.

153. Newsletter, "Dies ist der Weg," Landesarchiv Berlin A Pr. Br. Rep. 030-03, Nr. 927.

154. "Öffentliche Meinung: Warum Junggeselle bleiben," *Berliner Lokal-Anzeiger*, December 29, 1907, Nr. 659; newsletter, "Dies ist der Weg," Landesarchiv Berlin A Pr. Br. Rep. 030-03, Nr. 927.

155. "Die Heiratsannonce," *Berliner Morgenpost*, December 10, 1908, Nr. 290.

156. Paul A. Kirstein, "Wie sie sich kennen lernen," *Berliner Morgenpost*, November 9, 1902, Nr. 264.

157. "Die Heiratsannonce," *Berliner Morgenpost*, December 10, 1908, Nr. 290; "Öffentliche Meinung: Heiraths-Anzeigen!," *Berliner Lokal-Anzeiger*, November 2, 1902, Nr. 515.

158. "Berliner Beobachter," *Berliner Lokal-Anzeiger*, September 10, 1905, Nr. 447; Dr. M. A., "Eine Heiratsenquete," *Berliner Lokal-Anzeiger*, July 29, 1913, Nr. 380.

159. Letter from S. Stahl to Adolf Mertens, Landesarchiv Berlin A Pr. Br. Rep. 030-03, Nr. 1232.

CHAPTER 5

1. Bahn's father was a judge, and his grandfather was a Berlin district court director and the author of a well-known book on theft.

2. Ismar Lachmann, "Die Größen der Berliner Advokatur," *Das Kriminal-Magazin* 29 (August 1931), accessed via http://www.anwaltsgeschichte.de/kriminal-magazin/kriminal-magazin.html.

3. Ibid.

4. Walter Bahn, *Meine Klienten: Beiträge zur modernen Inquisition*, vol. 42 of *Großstadt-Dokumente*, ed. Hans Ostwald (Berlin: Verlag von Hermann Seemann Nachfolger, 1908), 7.

5. Ibid., 8.

6. Ibid., 7.

7. Ibid., 8.

8. The *Berliner Lokal-Anzeiger* actually printed four short lines of text about the discovery of a woman's body in the forest in its evening edition on June 27, but the

story was cryptic and unconfirmed, at best, and not until the following day did all of the Berlin newspapers run the story of the probable murder. *Berliner Lokal-Anzeiger*, June 27, 1914, Nr. 321.

9. "Auf der Spur eines Frauenmordes," *Berliner Lokal-Anzeiger*, June 28, 1914, Nr. 322; "Kleine Nachrichten," *Berliner Tageblatt*, June 28, 1914, Nr. 322; "Der Frauenmord in der Falkenhagener Forst," *Berliner Lokal-Anzeiger*, June 29, 1914, Nr. 323; "Frauenmord im Falkenhagener Forst: 1000 Mark Belohnung für die Ermittelung des Täters," *Berliner Tageblatt*, June 29, 1914, Nr. 323; "Frauenmord im Falkenhagener Forst," *Berliner Morgenpost*, Nr. 175; "Der Frauenmord bei Falkenhagen," *Berliner Morgenpost*, June 30, 1914, Nr. 176.

10. Letter from Walter Bahn to police, October 18, 1915, Landesarchiv Berlin A Pr. Br. Rep. 030-03, Nr. 927, Bl. 8.

11. Letter from Margarethe Kuhnt to police, October 31, 1915, Landesarchiv Berlin A Pr. Br. Rep. 030-03, Nr. 927, Bl. 13.

12. Letter from Margarethe Kuhnt to Paul Kuhnt, December 9, 1914, Landesarchiv Berlin A Pr. Br. Rep. 030-03, Nr. 927, Bl. 62–63.

13. Letter from Paul Jeserich to police, Landesarchiv Berlin A Pr. Br. Rep. 030-03, Nr. 927, Bl. 36–38.

14. Deposition, Landesarchiv Berlin A Pr. Br. Rep. 030-03, Nr. 927, Bl. 32.

15. Landesarchiv Berlin A Pr. Br. Rep. 030-03, Nr. 927, Bl. 29–30.

16. Letter from Walter Bahn to police, November 23, 1915, Landesarchiv Berlin A Pr. Br. Rep. 030-03, Nr. 927, Bl. 34–35.

17. Letter from Walter Bahn to police, Landesarchiv Berlin A Pr. Br. Rep. 030-03, Nr. 927, Bl. 39.

18. Letter from Walter Bahn to police, November 23, 1915, Landesarchiv Berlin A Pr. Br. Rep. 030-03, Nr. 927, Bl. 34–35.

19. "Mitgliederliste," *Deutsche Entomologische Zeitschrift* 1 (1911): 9; "Vereinsangelegenheiten I," *Berliner Entomologische Zeitschrift* 55 (1910): i.

20. Kuhnt is listed as the librarian on many pages of the journal, as, for example, at Paul Kuhnt, "Aus der entomologischen Welt," *Deutsche Entomologische Zeitschrift* 1 (1911): 109. "P. Kuhnt" is listed as a member of the "Redaktionskommission" on the cover page of the 1911 volume of his entomological society's journal. *Deutsche Entomologische Zeitschrift* 1 (1911): cover page. For Kuhnt's participation in society meetings, see Paul Kuhnt, "Aus den Sitzungen," *Deutsche Entomologische Zeitschrift* 1 (1911): 100. For one of Kuhnt's reviews, see "Rezensionen und Referate," *Deutsche Entomologische Zeitschrift* 1 (1911): 111–112. For one of Kuhnt's articles, see Paul Kuhnt, "Neue *Erotylidae*," *Deutsche Entomologische Zeitschrift* 3 (1910): 219–270. For Kuhnt's (well-reviewed) book, see Paul Kuhnt (ed.), *Illustrierte Bestimmungstabellen der Käfer Deutschlands: ein Handbuch zum genauen und leichten Bestimmen aller in Deutschland vorkommenden Käfer* (Stuttgart: E. Schweizerbart'sche Verlagsbuchhandlung, 1913). An online search for Kuhnt's handbook suggests that seventy-one books and articles cite to it, some as recently

as the 1990s. And in a rather creepy twist, I discovered that my erstwhile "home" library at the University of Illinois owns a copy of the book.

21. Landesarchiv Berlin A Pr. Br. Rep. 030-03, Nr. 927, Bl. 54–61.

22. Ibid.

23. Statement by Marie Schönemann, Landesarchiv Berlin A Pr. Br. Rep. 030-03, Nr. 1425, Bl. 10.

24. Statement by Hulda Sello, Landesarchiv Berlin A Pr. Br. Rep. 030-03, Nr. 1425, Bl. 11.

25. Statement by Johanna Westphal, Landesarchiv Berlin A Pr. Br. Rep. 030-03, Nr. 1425, Bl. 12.

26. Statement by Anna Selka, Landesarchiv Berlin A Pr. Br. Rep. 030-03, Nr. 1425, Bl. 8–9.

27. Statement by Otto Seiffert, Landesarchiv Berlin A Pr. Br. Rep. 030-03, Nr. 1425, Bl. 48–49.

28. Statement by Anna Selka, Landesarchiv Berlin A Pr. Br. Rep. 030-03, Nr. 1425, Bl. 8–9; Report, July 7, 1914, Landesarchiv Berlin A Pr. Br. Rep. 030-03, Nr. 1425, Bl. 101–103.

29. Report, July 7, 1914, Landesarchiv Berlin A Pr. Br. Rep. 030-03, Nr. 1425, Bl. 101–103.

30. Deposition, Landesarchiv Berlin A Pr. Br. Rep. 030-03, Nr. 927, Bl. 144, 151–152.

31. Statement by Anna Selka, Landesarchiv Berlin A Pr. Br. Rep. 030-03, Nr. 1425, Bl. 8–9.

32. Statement by Otto Westphal, Landesarchiv Berlin A Pr. Br. Rep. 030-03, Nr. 1425, Bl. 5–7.

33. Statement by Hermann Selka, Landesarchiv Berlin A Pr. Br. Rep. 030-03, Nr. 1425, Bl. 18–21.

34. Statement by Robert Adam, Landesarchiv Berlin A Pr. Br. Rep. 030-03, Nr. 1425, Bl. 76–77.

35. Report, July 7, 1914, Landesarchiv Berlin A Pr. Br. Rep. 030-03, Nr. 1425, Bl. 101–103.

36. Letter from Otto Mewes to police, Landesarchiv Berlin A Pr. Br. Rep. 030-03, Nr. 1425, Bl. 95.

37. Statement by Otto Westphal, Landesarchiv Berlin A Pr. Br. Rep. 030-03, Nr. 1425, Bl. 5–7; written charge against Paul Kuhnt, Landesarchiv Berlin A Pr. Br. Rep. 030-03, Nr. 927, Bl. 4–7.

38. Föllmer, "Suicide and Crisis."

39. "Der Frauenmord bei Finkenkrug: Die neue Gerichtsverhandlung," *Berliner Lokal-Anzeiger*, March 10, 1916, Nr. 128.

40. Written charge against Paul Kuhnt, Landesarchiv Berlin A Pr. Br. Rep. 030-03, Nr. 927, Bl. 4–7.

41. "Der Frauenmord im Falkenhagener Forst: Ein Rentier unter Anklage," *Berliner Tageblatt*, November 25, 1915, Nr. 603.

42. Letter from Deutsche Apotheker-Verein, November 26, 1915, Landesarchiv Berlin A Pr. Br. Rep. 030-03, Nr. 927, Bl. 119.

43. "Der Frauenmord im Falkenhagener Forst: Ein Rentier unter Anklage," *Berliner Tageblatt*, November 25, 1915, Nr. 603; "Der Frauenmord bei Finkenkrug," *Berliner Lokal-Anzeiger*, March 9, 1916, Nr. 127; letter to police, November 26, 1915, Landesarchiv Berlin A Pr. Br. Rep. 030-03, Nr. 927, Bl. 64.

44. Benjamin Carter Hett, in his history of Berlin's turn-of-the-century criminal justice system, notes that "stories about criminal trials (almost never the much less sensational civil cases) made up a considerable portion of the new mass papers. Most journals ran a regular column headed *Gerichtliches* or *Aus dem Gerichtssaal* ('From the Courtroom'). When a major trial was in progress, these one or two paragraph synopses gave way to full transcripts, which could spread across several closely printed pages." Hett also quotes Franz Hoeniger (a turn-of-the-century lawyer) on the presence of the press at criminal trials: "In front of the [Moabit courthouse] stand a dozen motorcycles of the great Berlin newspapers, which are supposed to carry the fresh reports in sections at rush speed to the editors." Benjamin Carter Hett, *Death in the Tiergarten: Murder and Criminal Justice in the Kaiser's Berlin* (Cambridge, MA: Harvard University Press, 2004), 49.

45. Imperial Germany's judicial system was a unique mixture of adversarial and inquisitorial elements. Hett, *Death in the Tiergarten*, 23ff.

46. "Der Frauenmord im Falkenhagener Forst: Ein Rentier unter Anklage," *Berliner Tageblatt*, November 25, 1915, Nr. 603.

47. "Der Frauenmord im Falkenhagener Forst: Unterbrechung der Schwurgerichtsverhandlung," *Berliner Tageblatt*, November 26, 1915, Nr. 604.

48. "Der Frauenmord im Falkenhagener Forst: Ein Rentier unter Anklage," *Berliner Tageblatt*, November 25, 1915, Nr. 603.

49. Ibid.

50. Ibid.

51. Ibid.

52. Ibid.

53. Ibid.

54. Ibid.

55. Letter from Otto Mewes to police, March 13, 1916, Landesarchiv Berlin A Pr. Br. Rep. 030-03, Nr. 927, Bl. 274.

56. "Der Frauenmord bei Finkenkrug," *Berliner Lokal-Anzeiger*, March 9, 1916, Nr. 127.

57. "Der Frauenmord bei Finkenkrug: Die neue Gerichtsverhandlung," *Berliner Lokal-Anzeiger*, March 10, 1916, Nr. 128.

58. Ibid.; "Das Urteil im Frauenmordprozeß," *Berliner Lokal-Anzeiger*, March 11, 1916, Nr. 130.

59. "Das Urteil im Frauenmordprozeß," *Berliner Lokal-Anzeiger*, March 11, 1916, Nr. 130.

60. On this point, it is interesting to point out that Berlin's so-called Mordkommission (Murder Investigation Unit)—formed in 1902 in response to two straight years of rising homicide numbers)—had, as Andreas Roth explains, a set one-year rotation for those investigating and prosecuting murders. Thus the switch from Fuhrmann to Mix, and thus perhaps also the change in charges the state wanted to make against Kuhnt. Roth, *Kriminalitätsbekämpfung*, 290.

61. Ibid.

62. Ibid., 289. Viewed from a different angle, as Benjamin Carter Hett notes, juries in Berlin's Superior Court I acquitted 30.1 percent of all defendants presented to them as guilty in the 1890s. Hett, *Death in the Tiergarten*, 34.

63. Richard Evans, *The German Underworld: Deviants and Outcasts in German History* (London: Routledge, 1988), 174.

64. Hett, *Death in the Tiergarten*, 34, 180–181.

65. Ibid.

66. Ibid.

67. Paul Braun, "Ein Berliner Apotheker als Entomologe," *Pharmazeutische Zeitung*, July 12, 1950: 413.

68. On the centrality of masks in the modern city (in this case, St. Petersburg), see Steinberg, *Petersburg Fin de Siècle*, chapter 3.

69. Rainer Maria Rilke, *Die Aufzeichnungen des Malte Laurids Brigge* (Stuttgart: Philipp Reclam jun., 1997), 7–8.

70. Rudolf Lothar, "Freundschaft und Gesellligkeit," *Berliner Lokal-Anzeiger*, December 31, 1909, Nr. 834.

71. Georg Simmel, *Über sociale Differenzierung* (Leipzig: Duncker & Humbolt, 1890).

72. Rudolf Lothar, "Die Kunst des Auseinandergehens," *Berliner Lokal-Anzeiger*, January 12, 1911, Nr. 22.

EPILOGUE

1. Peter Fritzsche's excellent—and out-of-print—historical walking tour of Berlin offers a host of fantastic hints for where to look for the Berlin of yesteryear. Peter Fritzsche and Karen Hewitt, *Berlinwalks* (New York: Henry Holt and Company, 1994).

2. Quoted in Fritzsche, *Reading Berlin 1900*, 30. In this way, Fritzsche notes, "Berlin has remained the paradigmatic modern city because its character has been so forcefully determined by the experience of transience." Ibid., 31.

3. Quoted in Fritzsche, "Vagabond," 386.

4. Gertrud Steinbach, "Liebe," *Berliner Morgenpost*, September 5, 1906, Nr. 207.

5. Lees, *Cities Perceived*, 197–198.

6. Ginger Frost makes a similar point with regard to the extent to which bourgeois women "had more to lose" and "hesitated to risk their reputations." Frost, *Living in Sin*, 216.

7. Annemarie Lüning, "Heiraten? Nicht so wichtig," *Parship Magazin*, http://www.parship.de/beziehung/heiraten-nicht-so-wichtig.htm.

8. Dorothee Goebeler, "Männer, die nicht heiraten," *Berliner Lokal-Anzeiger*, June 5, 1912, Nr. 282; A. von Wartenberg, "Moderne Frauen-Typen," *Berliner Lokal-Anzeiger*, January 1, 1907, Nr. 1; Dagobert von Gerhardt-Amyntor, "Die moderne Ehescheu," *Berliner Lokal-Anzeiger*, November 8, 1908, Nr. 571.

9. Ute Frevert's recent work on trust (and the history of emotions, more generally) offers a useful perspective on the relationship between individualism, tradition, and the middle class. Frevert examines that the increasing but yet inchoate robustness of individualism at the turn of the century, which left men and women in the somewhat uncomfortable position of having a greater degree of autonomy (from the strictures of tradition and/or communal values) in their lives and yet also the burden and risk of being solely responsible for their failures. She suggests that trust and trustworthiness, as a sort of intangible interpersonal currency, acquired greater importance as a result, for it eased slightly the risk associated with modern individual decision-making. In this way, she argues, trust allowed individuals a certain space, an ability to develop their independence and structure their lives according to their own subjectivities while maintaining a certain connection to the people they trusted. Trust, put differently, had a "binding" and "linking" effect in love, family, and interpersonal relationships insofar as it created an elective community of values. The rising importance of trust, she concludes, was a "corollary of the individualism that accompanied the development of middle-class society." Ute Frevert, *Vertrauensfragen: Eine Obsession der Moderne* (Munich: C. H. Beck, 2013), 213.

10. In "The Painter of Modern Life," Baudelaire writes that "for the flâneur, for the passionate spectator"—that is, for the consummate urban dweller—"it is an immense joy to set in the midst of the fugitive and the infinite. To be away from home and yet feel oneself everywhere at home." Charles Baudelaire, "The Painter of Modern Life," in ed. Vincent B. Leitsch (ed.), *Norton Anthology of Theory and Criticism* (New York: Norton, 2001), 795.

11. Detlev Peukert, *The Weimar Republic: The Crisis of Classical Modernity*, trans. Richard Deveson (New York: Hill and Wang, 1992), xiv.

12. Eric D. Weitz, *Weimar Germany: Promise and Tragedy* (Princeton, NJ: Princeton University Press, 2007), 298.

13. For further discussion of the upheaval created by World War I, see Martin Geyer, *Verkehrte Welt: Revolution, Inflation, und Moderne: München, 1914–1924* (Göttingen: Vandenhoeck & Ruprecht, 1998).

14. On Weimar sexualities, see, for example, Maria Tartar, *Lustmord: Sexual Murder in Weimar Germany* (Princeton, NJ: Princeton University Press, 1995); Paul Lerner, "Hysterical Cures: Gender and Performance in World War I and Weimar Germany," *History Workshop Journal* 45 (1998): 79–101; also my article on masculinity and fatherhood: Tyler Carrington, "Conflicted Fatherhood: Masculinity and the Modern World in the Life and Work of Thomas Mann," *Snodi: Pubblici*

e privati nella storia contemporanea 7 (Spring 2011): 16–37. For other contexts, see Joanna Bourke, *Dismembering the Male: Men's Bodies, Britain and the Great War* (Chicago: University of Chicago Press, 1996); Leslie Hall, *Hidden Anxieties: Male Sexuality, 1900–1950* (Cambridge: Blackwell, 1991); Ralph LaRossa and Donald C. Reitzes, "Continuity and Change in Middle-Class Fatherhood, 1925–1939: The Culture-Conduct Connection," *Journal of Marriage and the Family* 55 (1993): 455–468. On sexuality in the Third Reich and postwar years, see Josie McLellan, *Love in the Time of Communism: Intimacy and Sexuality in the GDR* (Cambridge: Cambridge University Press, 2011); Dagmar Herzog, *Sex after Fascism: Memory and Morality in Twentieth-Century Germany* (Princeton, NJ: Princeton University Press, 2007); Elizabeth Heineman, *What Difference Does a Husband Make? Women and Marital Status in Nazi and Postwar Germany* (Berkeley: University of California Press, 2003).

15. Of the many books and articles on online and digital dating, Aziz Ansari and Eric Klinenberg's take is perhaps the best (and most enjoyable). Aziz Ansari and Eric Klinenberg, *Modern Romance: An Investigation* (New York: Penguin, 2015).

16. Raymond Carver, *What We Talk about When We Talk about Love* (New York: Knopf, 1981).

References

ARCHIVAL SOURCES AND LIBRARIES

Akademie der Künste

Kempowski Bio-Archiv 69
Kempowski Bio-Archiv 183
Kempowski Bio-Archiv 3623/1
Kempowski Bio-Archiv 3931/1-2
Kempowski Bio-Archiv 995

Deutsches Tagebucharchiv

Else Behrens, *Tagebuch 1898–1903*, Signatur 1314 / I.1—1314 / I.2
Fritz Reinert, *Tagebuch 1902–3*. Signatur 1929
Helene Kuërs, *Aufzeichnungen aus meinem Leben* (1954), Signatur 11581 II.2

Landesarchiv Berlin

A Rep 342-02-X3, Nr. 47141
A Pr. Br. Rep. 030-03, Nr. 927
A Pr. Br. Rep. 030-03, Nr. 1232
A Pr. Br. Rep. 030-03, Nr. 1425
A Pr. Br. Rep. 030-03, Nr. 1426
A Pr. Br. Rep. 030-05-01, Nr. U4
A Pr. Br. Rep. 030-05-02, Nr. 3826
A Pr. Br. Rep. 030-05-02, Nr. 3961
A Pr. Br. Rep. 030-05-02, Nr. 3967
A Pr. Br. Rep. 030-05-02, Nr. 4782
A Pr. Br. Rep. 030-05-02, Nr. 4801
A Pr. Br. Rep. 030-05-02, Nr. 5171
A Pr. Br. Rep. 030-05-02, Nr. 5923

A Pr. Br. Rep. 030, Nr. 16230
A Pr. Br. Rep. 030, Nr. 16925
A Pr. Br. Rep. 030, Nr. 16927
A Pr. Br. Rep. 030, Nr. 18659
A Pr. Br. Rep. 30 Berlin C Titel 74, Nr. 1470
A Pr. Br. Rep. 30 Berlin C Titel 610, Th 3833 Schbg. Th. Nr. 12
F Rep. 290, Nr. 121830
F Rep 290 (01), Nr. O317909
F Rep. 290 (01), Nr. OO72473
F Rep. 290-02-06, Nr. 167/1

Zentral- und Landesbibliothek Berlin

Berliner Adressbücher, 1863, 1902–1904, 1905, 1907

PERIODICALS

Archiv für Kriminal-Anthropologie und Kriminalistik
Berliner Intelligenz-Blatt
Berliner Lokal-Anzeiger
Berliner Morgenpost
Berliner Tageblatt
Berliner Zeitung
Das Geschlecht: Aufklärung über alle Fragen des Geschlechtslebens
Der Eigene
Deutsche Entomologische Zeitschrift
Die Wandlung
Die Welt der Frau
Geschlecht und Gesellschaft
Heirats-Zeitung
Jahrbuch für sexuelle Zwischenstufen mit besonderer Berücksichtigung der Homosexualität
Mutterschutz: Zeitschrift zur Reform der sexuellen Ethik
Preußische Statistik
Simplicissimus
Statistisches Jahrbuch der Stadt Berlin
Statistisches Jahrbuch für den preußischen Staat

PRIMARY SOURCES

"Rezensionen und Referate." *Deutsche Entomologische Zeitschrift* 1 (1911): 111–112.
Anonymous. *Das perverse Berlin*. Berlin: Rich. Eckstein Nachf., 1910.

Anonymous. *Eine männliche Braut. Aufzeichnungen eines Homosexuellen.* Berlin: Janssen Verlag, 1996.

Bab, Edwin. *Die Gleichgeschlechtliche Liebe (Lieblingsminne): Ein Wort ueber ihr Wesen und ihre Bedeutung.* Berlin: Hugo Schildberger, 1903.

Baedeker, Karl. *Berlin and Its Environs.* 5th ed. Leipzig: Karl Baedeker, 1912.

Bahn, Walter. *Meine Klienten: Beiträge zur modernen Inquisition.* Vol. 42 of *Großstadt-Dokumente,* edited by Hans Ostwald. Berlin: Verlag von Hermann Seemann Nachfolger, 1908.

Bartholomäi, F. "Volkspsychologische Spiegelbilder aus Berliner Annoncen." In *Berliner Städtisches Jahrbuch für Volkswirthschaft und Statistik,* 37–53. Berlin: Verlag von Leonhard Simion, 1874.

Baudelaire, Charles. "The Painter of Modern Life." In *Norton Anthology of Theory and Criticism,* edited by Vincent B. Leitsch, 789–802. New York: Norton, 2001.

Benjamin, Walter. *Illuminations.* Edited by Hannah Arendt. Translated by Harry Zohn. New York: Schocken Books, 1968.

Benjamin, Walter. "Paris, die Hauptstadt des XIX. Jahrhunderts." In *Das Passagen-Werk,* vol. 5.1, 45–59. Frankfurt am Main: Suhrkamp, 1982.

Berg, Wilhelm v. *Auf dem Standesamt.* Vol. 76 of *Intime Geschichten.* Berlin: Berliner Roman-Verlag, 1905.

Berg, Wilhelm v. *Die Radler-Marie.* Vol. 71 of *Intime Geschichten.* Berlin: Berliner Roman-Verlag, 1905.

Bertz, Eduard. *Philosophie des Fahrrads.* Dresden: Verlag von Carl Reitzner, 1900.

Braun, Paul. "Ein Berliner Apotheker als Entomologe." *Pharmazeutische Zeitung,* July 12 (1950): 413.

Brönner, Wilhelm. "Der Kampf um die neue Liebe." *Geschlecht und Gesellschaft* 1, no. 1 (1906): 7–14.

Buschan, Georg. *Vom Jüngling zum Mann: Ratschläge zur sexuellen Lebensführung.* Stuttgart: Verlag von Strecker und Schröder, 1911.

Dreste, Karl Theodor. *Liebestolle Weiber: oder Was ich auf der Suche nach einer Gattin erlebte.* Berlin: Verlag Karl Theodor Dreste, 1914.

Duncker, Dora. *Reelles Heiratsgesuch etc.: Inserat Studien.* Stuttgart: Carl Krabbe, 1888.

Edel, Edmund. "Berlin tanzt!" In *Berliner Nächte,* 77–102. Berlin: Conrad Haber's Verlag, 1914.

Frau M. F. "Wie ich es sehe." *Jahrbuch für sexuelle Zwischenstufen mit besonderer Berücksichtigung der Homosexualität* 3, no. 1 (1901): 308–312.

Gerling, Reinhold. *Freie Liebe oder bürgerliche Ehe.* Oranienburg: Orania, 1907.

Gerling, Reinhold. *Junggesellen-Steuer.* Oranienburg: Orania, 1907.

Gerling, Reinhold. *Mädchen, die man nicht heiraten soll: Warnungen und Winke.* Oranienburg: Orania, 1917.

Heinemann-Grautoff, Erna. *Möglichkeiten der Liebe.* Berlin: Karl Curtius, 1912.

Hirschfeld, Magnus. "Das Ergebnis der statistischen Untersuchungen über den Protentsatz der Homosexuellen." *Jahrbuch für sexuelle Zwischenstufen mit besonderer Berücksichtigung der Homosexualität* 6, no. 1 (1904): 109–178.

Hirschfeld, Magnus. "Sind sexuelle Zwischenstufen zur Ehe geeignet?" *Jahrbuch für sexuelle Zwischenstufen mit besonderer Berücksichtigung der Homosexualität* 3, no. 1 (1901): 37–71.

Katte, Max. "Aus dem Leben eines Homosexuellen, Selbstbiographie." *Jahrbuch für sexuelle Zwischenstufen mit besonderer Berücksichtigung der Homosexualität* 2, no. 1 (1900): 295–323.

Kessler, Rudolf and A. Stein. *Die Heiratsannonce.* Berlin: Verlag von Kühling & Güttner, Theater-Buchhandlung, 1910.

Kirstein, Paul. *Verlobung!* Berlin: Kühling & Güttner Theaterbuchhandlung, 1894.

Köhrer, Erich. *Warenhaus Berlin: Ein Roman aus der Weltstadt.* Berlin: Wedekind, 1909.

Krafft-Ebing, Richard Freiherr von. *Psychopathia Sexualis.* 10th ed. Stuttgart: Verlag von Ferdinand Enke, 1898.

Krause, E. "Die Wahrheit über mich: Selbstbiographie einer Konträrsexuellen." *Jahrbuch für sexuelle Zwischenstufen mit besonderer Berücksichtigung der Homosexualität* 3, no. 1 (1901): 292–307.

Kuhnt, Paul. "Aus den Sitzungen." *Deutsche Entomologische Zeitschrift* 1 (1911): 100.

Kuhnt, Paul. "Aus der entomologischen Welt." *Deutsche Entomologische Zeitschrift* 1 (1911): 109.

Kuhnt, Paul, ed. *Illustrierte Bestimmungstabellen der Käfer Deutschlands: ein Handbuch zum genauen und leichten Bestimmen aller in Deutschland vorkommenden Käfer.* Stuttgart: E. Schweizerbart'sche Verlagsbuchhandlung, 1913.

Kuhnt, Paul. "Neue Erotylidae." *Deutsche Entomologische Zeitschrift* 3 (1910): 219–270.

Lachmann, Ismar. "Die Größen der Berliner Advokatur." *Das Kriminal-Magazin* 29 (August 1931). http://www.anwaltsgeschichte.de/kriminal-magazin/kriminal-magazin.html.

Lange, Helene and Gertrud Bäumer, eds. *Handbuch der Frauenbewegung.* Berlin: W. Moeser, 1902.

Lehmann, A. R. H. *Der Junggsell vom Elternhaus bis zur Heirat.* Schöneberg-Berlin: Hans Klee Verlag, 1909.

Lehnhard, Paul. *Die Liebe im Kontor: Posse mit Gesang in einem Akt.* Mühlhausen i. Thür: Druck und Verlag von G. Danner, 1899.

Leipziger, Leo. *Der Rettungsball.* Berlin: Roland von Berlin, 1912.

Levitus, Hans. *Von Stufe zu Stufe.* Vol. 80 of *Intime Geschichten.* Berlin: Metropol-Verlag, 1905.

Lomer, Georg. *Liebe und Psychose.* Wiesbaden: Bergmann, 1907.

Mimosa. "Die weib-weibliche Liebe." *Das Geschlecht: Aufklärung über alle Fragen des Geschlechtlebens* 1 (1904): 3–5.

Moll, Albert. "Wie erkennen und verständigen sich die Homosexuellen unter einander?" *Archiv für Kriminal-Anthropologie und Kriminalistik* 9, nos. 2–3 (1902): 157–160.

Näcke, Paul. "Angebot und Nachfrage von Homosexuellen in Zeitungen." *Archiv für Kriminal-Anthropologie und Kriminalistik* 8, nos. 3–4 (1902): 339–350.

Näcke, Paul. "Ein Besuch bei den Homosexuellen in Berlin." In Magnus Hirschfeld, *Berlins Drittes Geschlecht* (1904), edited by Manfred Herzer. Berlin: Verlag rosa Winkel, 1991.

Oppermann, Paul. *Der verheiratete Junggeselle.* Mühlhausen i. Thür: Verlag von G. Danner, 1905.

Ostwald, Hans. "Dunkle Winkel und Menschen." In *Berliner Nächte*, 1–24. Berlin: Conrad Haber's Verlag, 1914.

Ostwald, Hans. "Notlage oder Trieb? Eine Erwiderung." *Die Neue Zeit* 1, no. 2 (1906–1907): 74–77.

Perry, Leo. *"Auf diesem nicht mehr ungewöhnlichen Wege . . .": Der Liebesmarkt des Zeitungs-Inserates.* Vienna: Verlag für Kulturforschung, 1927.

Prinzing, Friedrich. "Die alten Junggesellen und alten Jungfern in den europäischen Staaten jetzt und früher." *Zeitschrift für Sozialwissenschaft* 8 (1905): 615–622.

Prinzing, Friedrich. "Die Wandlungen der Heirathshäufigkeit und des mittleren Heiratsalters." *Zeitschrift für Sozialwissenschaft* 5 (1902): 656–674.

Prinzing, Friedrich. "Heirathshäufigkeit und Heiratsalter nach Stand und Beruf." *Zeitschrift für Sozialwissenschaft* 6 (1903): 546–559.

Ranzow, Fr. "Radelnde Damen." *Die Welt der Frau* 26 (1905): 411–413.

Rilke, Rainer Maria. *Die Aufzeichnungen des Malte Laurids Brigge.* Stuttgart: Philipp Reclam jun., 1997.

Schwabe, Hermann. *Betrachtungen über die Volksseele von Berlin.* Berlin: Guttentag, 1870.

Scott, Franz. *Die Tanzfee: Das Drama der Treue.* Vol. 78 of *Intime Geschichten.* Berlin: Berliner Roman-Verlag, 1905.

Simmel, Georg. "The Metropolis and Mental Life." In *The Blackwell City Reader*, edited by Gary Bridge and Sophie Watson, 11–19. Oxford: Wiley-Blackwell, 2002.

Simmel, Georg. *On Women, Sexuality, and Love.* Translated by Guy Oakes. New Haven: Yale University Press, 1984.

Simmel, Georg. *Über sociale Differenzierung.* Leipzig: Duncker & Humbolt, 1890.

Steiner, Olga. *Heiratskandidatinnen; oder: Wie junge Mädchen lieben: Lustspiel in einem Akt.* Berlin: Theater-Buchhandlung Eduard Bloch, 1896.

Südekum, Albert. *Großstädtisches Wohnungselend.* Vol. 45 of *Großstadt-Dokumente*, edited by Hans Ostwald. Berlin, 1908.

Trojan, Johannes. *Berliner Bilder: Hundert Momentaufnahmen.* Berlin: Grote, 1903.

Twain, Mark. "The Chicago of Europe." *Chicago Daily Tribune*, April 3, 1892.

Weber, Marianne. *Die Frauen und die Liebe.* Königstein im Taunus: Karl Robert Langewiesche Verlag, 1935.

Werner, Joachim. *Die Heirats-Annonce: Studien und Briefe.* Berlin: Verlag Martin Aronhold, 1908.

Wilbrandt, Robert and Lisbeth Wilbrandt. *Die Deutsche Frau im Beruf.* Vol. 4. *Handbuch der Frauenbewegung*, edited by Helene Lange und Getrud Bäumer. Berlin: Moeser, 1902.

Zweig, Stefan. *The World of Yesterday: An Autobiography.* Translated by Harry Zohn. Lincoln: University of Nebraska Press, 1964.

SECONDARY SOURCES

Abraham, Julie. *Metropolitan Lovers: The Homosexuality of Cities.* Minneapolis: University of Minnesota Press, 2008.

Allen, Ann Taylor. *Feminism and Motherhood in Germany, 1800–1914.* New Brunswick, NJ: Rutgers University Press, 1991.

Anderson, Michael. *Family Structure in Nineteenth-Century Lancashire.* Cambridge: Cambridge University Press, 1971.

Ansari, Aziz, and Eric Klinenberg. *Modern Romance: An Investigation.* New York: Penguin, 2015.

Arni, Caroline. *Entzweiungen: Die Krise der Ehe um 1900.* Cologne: Böhlau, 2004.

Augustine, Dolores L. "Arriving in the Upper Class: The Wealthy Business Elite of Wilhelmine Germany." In *The German Bourgeoisie*, edited by David Blackbourn and Richard Evans, 46–86. New York: Routledge, 1991.

Bajohr, Stefan. "Partnerinnenwahl im Braunschweiger Arbeitermilieu, 1900–1933." *Jahrbuch für Forschungen zur Geschichte der Arbeiterbewegung* 2, no. 3 (2003): 83–98.

Beachy, Robert. *Gay Berlin: Birthplace of a Modern Identity.* New York: Knopf, 2014.

Beck, Ulrich. *Risk Society: Towards a New Modernity.* Translated by Mark Ritter. London: Sage, 1992.

Beck, Ulrich and Elisabeth Beck-Gernsheim. *The Normal Chaos of Love.* Translated by Mark Ritter and Jane Wiebel. Cambridge: Polity Press, 1995.

Beck, Ulrich and Elisabeth Beck-Gernsheim. "Passage to Hope: Marriage, Migration, and the Need for a Cosmopolitan Turn in Family Research." *Journal of Family Theory & Review* 2 (December 2010): 401–414.

Bergero, Adriana. *Intersecting Tango: Cultural Geographies of Buenos Aires, 1900–1930.* Pittsburgh: University of Pittsburgh Press, 2008.

Berman, Marshall. *All That Is Solid Melts into Air: The Experience of Modernity.* New York: Penguin, 1982.

Borscheid, Peter. "Romantic Love or Material Interest: Choosing Partners in Nineteenth-Century Germany." *Journal of Family History* 11, no. 2 (1986): 157–168.

Bourke, Joanna. *Dismembering the Male: Men's Bodies, Britain and the Great War.* Chicago: University of Chicago Press, 1996.

Braun, Annegret. *Ehe- und Partnerschafts-vorstellungen von 1948– 1996: eine kulturwissenschaftliche Analyse anhand von Heiratsinseraten.* Münster: Waxman, 2001.

Bushnell, George D. "When Chicago Was Wheel Crazy." *Chicago History* 4, no. 3 (Fall 1975): 167–175.

Carrington, Tyler. "Conflicted Fatherhood: Masculinity and the Modern World in the Life and Work of Thomas Mann." *Snodi: Pubblici e privati nella storia contemporanea* 7 (Spring 2011): 16–37.

Carrington, Tyler. "Instilling the 'Manly' Faith: Protestant Masculinity and the German *Jünglingsvereine* at the *Fin de Siècle.*" *Journal of Men, Masculinities, and Spiritualities* 3, no. 2 (June 2009): 142–154.

Carver, Raymond. *What We Talk about When We Talk about Love.* New York: Knopf, 1981.

Champion, Tony and Graeme Hugo, eds. *New Forms of Urbanization: Beyond the Urban-Rural Dichotomy.* Aldershot: Ashgate, 2003.

Chauncey, George. *Gay New York: Gender, Urban Culture, and the Making of the Gay Male World, 1890–1940.* New York: Basic Books, 1994.

Cherlin, Andrew J. *The Marriage-Go-Round: The State of Marriage and the Family in America Today.* New York: Knopf, 2009.

Cocks, H. G. *Classified: The Secret History of the Personal Column.* London: Random House, 2009.

Cocks, H. G. "Peril in the Personals: The Dangers and Pleasures of Classified Advertising in Early Twentieth-Century Britain." *Media History* 10, no. 1 (2004): 3–16.

Collins, Marcus. *Modern Love: An Intimate History of Men and Women in Twentieth-Century Britain.* London: Atlantic Books, 2003.

Connell, R. W. *Masculinities.* 2nd ed. Berkeley: University of California Press, 2005.

Connell, R. W. "A Very Straight Gay: Masculinity, Homosexual Experience, and the Dynamics of Gender." *American Sociological Review* 57, no. 6 (1992): 735–751.

Coontz, Stephanie. *Marriage, a History: From Obedience to Intimacy, or How Love Conquered Marriage.* New York: Viking, 2005.

Cronon, William. *Nature's Metropolis: Chicago and the Great West.* New York: Norton, 1991.

Crowley, David. "Castles, Cabarets, and Cartoons: Claims on Polishness in Kraków around 1905." In *The City in Central Europe: Culture and Society from 1800 to the Present,* edited by Malcolm Gee, Tim Kirk, and Jill Steward, 101–117. Brookfield, VT: Ashgate, 1999.

Dasey, Robyn. "Women's Work and the Family: German Garment Workers in Berlin and Hamburg before the First World War." In *The German Family: Essays on the Social history of the Family in Nineteenth- and Twentieth-Century Germany,* edited by Richard Evans and W. R. Lee, 221–255, London: Croom Helm, 1981.

Deutsche Bundesbank. "Kaufkraftäquivalente historischer Beträge in deutschen Währungen." https://www.bundesbank.de.

Dickinson, Edward Ross. "'A Dark, Impenetrable Wall of Complete Incomprehension': The Impossibility of Heterosexual Love in Imperial Germany." *Central European History* 40 (2007): 467–497.

Dickinson, Edward Ross. "Policing Sex in Germany, 1882–1982: A Preliminary Statistical Analysis." *Journal of the History of Sexuality* 16, no. 2 (2007): 204–250.

Dickinson, Edward Ross. "Reflections on Feminism and Monism in the Kaiserreich, 1900–1913." *Central European History* 34, no. 2 (2001): 191–230.

Dickinson, Edward Ross. *Sex, Freedom, and Power in Imperial Germany, 1880–1914.* Cambridge: Cambridge University Press, 2015.

Dießenbacher, Hartmut. "Soziale Umbrüche und sozialpolitische Antworten: Entwicklungslinien vom 19. ins frühe 20. Jahrhundert." In *Hinterhof,*

Keller und Mansarde: Einblicke in Berliner Wohnungselend, 1901–1920, edited by Gesine Asmus, 10–31. Hamburg: Rowohlt, 1982.

Dobler, Jens. *Von andern Ufern: Geschichte der Berliner Lesben und Schwulen in Kreuzberg und Friedrichshain*. Berlin: Bruno Gmünder Verlag, 2003.

Dollard, Catherine. "The Alte Jungfer as New Deviant: Representation, Sex, and the Single Woman in Imperial Germany." *German Studies Review* 29, no. 1 (2006): 107–126.

Dollard, Catherine. *The Surplus Woman: Unmarried in Imperial Germany, 1871–1918*. New York: Berghahn Books, 2009.

Evans, Richard. *The German Underworld: Deviants and Outcasts in German History*. London: Routledge, 1988.

Finn, Margot. "Sex and the City: Metropolitan Modernities in English History." *Victorian Studies* 44 (2001): 25–32.

Flemming, Jens. "'. . . von Jahr zu Jahr ein Sorgen und Bangen ohne Ende': Einkommen, Lohn, Lebensstandard." In *Die Arbeiter: Lebensformen, Alltag und Kultur von der Frühindustrialisierung bis zum "Wirtschaftswunder,"* edited by Wolfgang Ruppert, 137–145. Munich: C. H. Beck, 1986.

Föllmer, Moritz. *Individuality and Modernity in Berlin: Self and Society from Weimar to the Wall*. Cambridge: Cambridge University Press, 2013.

Föllmer, Moritz. "Suicide and Crisis in Weimar Berlin." *Central European History* 42 (2009): 195–221.

Frevert, Ute, ed. *Bürgerinnen und Bürger: Geschlechterverhältnisse im 19. Jahrhundert. Zwölf Beiträge*. Göttingen: Vandenhoeck & Ruprecht, 1988.

Frevert, Ute. "Bürgerliche Familie und Geschlechterrollen: Modell und Wirklichkeit." In *Bürgerliche Gesellschaft in Deutschland: Historische Einblicke, Fragen, Perspektiven*, edited by Lutz Niethammer et al., 90–98. Frankfurt am Main: Fischer-Taschenbuch-Verlag, 1990.

Frevert, Ute. *Men of Honour: A Social and Cultural History of the Duel*. Cambridge: Polity Press, 1995.

Frevert, Ute. *Vertrauensfragen: Eine Obsession der Moderne*. Munich: C.H. Beck, 2013.

Frevert, Ute. *Women in German History: From Bourgeois Emancipation to Sexual Liberation*. Translated by Stuart McKinnon-Evans. New York: St. Martin's Press, 1989.

Frisby, David. *Fragments of Modernity: Theories of Modernity in the Work of Simmel, Kracauer, and Benjamin*. Cambridge: Polity Press, 1985.

Fritzsche, Peter. *Reading Berlin 1900*. Cambridge, MA: Harvard University Press, 1996.

Fritzsche, Peter. "Vagabond in the Fugitive City: Hans Ostwald, Imperial Berlin and the Grossstadt-Dokumente." *Journal of Contemporary History* 29, no. 3 (1994): 385–402.

Fritzsche, Peter and Karen Hewitt. *Berlinwalks*. New York: Henry Holt, 1994.

Frost, Ginger S. *Living in Sin: Cohabitating as Husband and Wife in Nineteenth-Century England*. Manchester: Manchester University Press, 2008.

Gall, Lothar. "'. . . Ich wünschte ein Bürger zu sein': Zum Selbstverständnis des deutschen Bürgertums im 19. Jahrhundert." *Historische Zeitschrift* 245, no. 3 (December 1987): 601–623.

Garvey, Ellen Gruber. "Reframing the Bicycle: Advertising-Supported Magazines and Scorching Women." *American Quarterly* 47, no. 1 (1995): 66–101.

Gay, Peter. *The Bourgeois Experience: Victoria to Freud*. Vol. 2: *The Tender Passion*. New York: Oxford University Press, 1986.

Geary, Dick. "The Industrial Bourgeoisie and Labour Relations in Germany, 1871–1933." In *The German Bourgeoisie*, edited by David Blackbourn and Richard Evans, 140–161. New York: Routledge, 1991.

Gehrmann, Rolf. "German Towns on the Eve of Industrialization: Household Formation and the Part of the Elderly." *History of the Family* 19, no. 1 (2004): 13–28.

Gestrich, Andreas. *Geschichte der Familie im 19. und 20. Jahrhundert*. Munich: Oldenbourg, 1999.

Geyer, Martin. *Verkehrte Welt: Revolution, Inflation, und Moderne. München, 1914–1924*. Göttingen: Vandenhoeck & Ruprecht, 1998.

Ginsburg, Norton, Bruce Koppel, and T. G. McGee, eds. *The Extended Metropolis: Settlement Transition in Asia*. Honolulu: University of Hawaii Press, 1991.

Goodbye to Berlin: 100 Jahre Schwulenbewegung. Eine Ausstellung des Schwulen Museums und der Akademie der Künste, 17. Mai bis 17. August 1997. Berlin: Verlag rosa Winkel, 1997.

Greven-Aschoff, Barbara. *Die bürgerliche Frauenbewegung in Deutschland, 1894–1933*. Göttingen: Vandenhoeck & Ruprecht, 1981.

Grossmann, Atina. *Reforming Sex: The German Movement for Birth Control and Abortion Reform, 1920–1950*. Oxford: Oxford University Press, 1995.

Hall, Leslie. *Hidden Anxieties: Male Sexuality, 1900–1950*. Cambridge: Blackwell, 1991.

Hall, Thomas. *Planning Europe's Capital Cities: Aspects of Nineteenth-Century Urban Development*. London: Spon, 2005.

Hammerton, James. "Victorian Marriage and the Law of Matrimonial Cruelty." *Victorian Studies* 33, no. 2 (Winter 1990): 269–292.

Harvey, David. *Paris: Capital of Modernity*. New York: Routledge, 2003.

Hausen, Karin. "Die Ehe in Angebot und Nachfrage: Heiratsanzeigen historisch durchmustert." In *Liebe und Widerstand: Ambivalenzen historischer Geschlechterbeziehungen*, edited by Ingrid Bauer et al., 428–448. Vienna: Böhlau, 2005.

Hausen, Karin. *Geschlechtergeschichte als Gesellschaftsgeschichte*. Göttingen: Vandenhoeck & Ruprecht, 2012.

Heineman, Elizabeth. *What Difference Does a Husband Make? Women and Marital Status in Nazi and Postwar Germany*. Berkeley: University of California Press, 2003.

Henning, Hansjoachim. "Soziale Verflechtungen der Unternehmer in Westfalen, 1860–1914." *Zeitschrift für Unternehmensgeschichte* 23 (1978): 1–30.

Henning, Hansjoachim. *Das westdeutsche Bürgertum in der Epoche der Hochindustrialisierung, 1860–1914*. Wiesbaden: F. Steiner, 1973.

Herzog, Dagmar. *Sex after Fascism: Memory and Morality in Twentieth-Century Germany*. Princeton, NJ: Princeton University Press, 2007.

Hett, Benjamin Carter. *Death in the Tiergarten: Murder and Criminal Justice in the Kaiser's Berlin*. Cambridge, MA: Harvard University Press, 2004.

Hettling, Manfred and Stefan-Ludwig Hoffmann, eds. *Der bürgerliche Wertehimmel: Innenansichten des 19. Jahrhunderts*. Göttingen: Vandenhoeck & Ruprecht, 2000.

Hoffman, Alexander von. *Local Attachments: The Making of an American Urban Neighborhood, 1850–1920*. Baltimore: Johns Hopkins University Press, 1994.

Homburg, Heidrun. *Rationalisierung und Industriearbeit: Arbeitsmarkt—Management—Arbeiterschaft im Siemens Konzern Berlin 1900–1939*. Berlin: Haude und Spener Verlag, 1991.

Huyssen, Andreas. "Modernist Miniatures: Literary Snapshots of Urban Spaces." *PMLA* 122, no. 1 (2007): 27–42.

Kaelble, Hartmut. "Wie feudal waren die deutschen Unternehmer im Kaiserreich?" In *Beiträge zur quantitativen vergleichenden Unternehmensgeschichte*, edited by Richard Tilly, 148–171. Stuttgart: Klett-Cotta, 1985.

Kaplan, Marion. "For Love or Money: The Marriage Strategies of Jews in Imperial Germany." *Women & History* 10 (1985): 121–164.

Katz, Jacob. "Family, Kinship, and Marriage among Ashkenazim in the Sixteenth to Eighteenth Centuries." *Jewish Journal of Sociology* 1 (1959): 3–22.

Kaudelka-Hanisch, Karin. "The Titled Businessman: Prussian Commercial Councillors in the Rhineland and Westphalia during the Nineteenth Century." In *The German Bourgeoisie*, edited by David Blackbourn and Richard Evans, 87–114. New York: Routledge, 1991.

Kelly, Alfred. *The German Worker: Working-Class Autobiographies from the Age of Industrialism*. Berkeley: University of California Press, 1987.

Kertzer, David and Dennis Hogan. "On the Move: Migration in an Italian Community, 1865–1921." *Social Science History* 9, no. 1 (Winter 1985): 1–23.

Kiesow, Marion. *Berlin tanzt in Clärchens Ballhaus: 100 Jahre Vergnügen—eine Kulturgeschichte*. Berlin: Nicolai, 2013.

Knodel, John and Mary Jo Maynes. "Urban and Rural Marriage in Imperial Germany." *Journal of Family History* 1 (1976): 129–168.

Kocka, Jürgen, et al. *Familie und Soziale Plazierung: Studien zum Verhältnis von Familie, sozialer Mobilität und Heiratsverhalten am westfälischen Beispielen im späten 18. und 19. Jahrhundert. Forschungsbericht des Landes Nordrhein-Westfalen*. Opladen: Westdeutscher Verlag, 1980.

Korff, Gottfried. "Mentalität und Kommunikation in der Großstadt: Berliner Notizen zur 'inneren' Urbanisierung." In *Großstadt. Aspekte empirischer Kulturforschung*, edited by Theodor Kohlmann and Hermann Bausinger, 343–361. Berlin: Staatliche Museen Preussischer Kulturbesitz, 1985.

Kracauer, Siegfried. *Die Angestellten: Aus dem neuesten Deutschland*. Frankfurt am Main: Frankfurter Societätsdruckerei, 1930.

Kuhn, Bärbel. *Familienstand: ledig: Ehelose Frauen und Männer im Bürgertum (1850–1914)*. Cologne: Böhlau, 2000.

Ladenbauer, Werner. "'Blut ist dicker als Wasser'—Die Wiener Familie Ladenbauer." In *Bürgerliche Familien: Lebenswege im 19. und 20. Jahrhundert*, edited by Hannes Stekl, 75–108. Vienna: Böhlau, 2000.

LaRossa, Ralph and Donald C. Reitzes. "Continuity and Change in Middle-Class Fatherhood, 1925–1939: The Culture-Conduct Connection." *Journal of Marriage and the Family* 55 (1993): 455–468.

Lee, Leo Ou-fan. *Shanghai Modern: The Flowering of a New Urban Culture in China, 1930–1945*. Cambridge, MA: Harvard University Press, 1999.

Lees, Andrew. *Cities, Sin, and Social Reform in Imperial Germany*. Ann Arbor: University of Michigan Press, 2002.

Lees, Andrew. *Cities Perceived: Urban Society in European and American Thought*. New York: Columbia University Press, 1985.

Lenger, Friedrich. "Grossstadtmenschen." In *Der Mensch des 19. Jahrhunderts*, edited by Ute Frevert and Heinz-Gerhard Haupt, 261–291. Frankfurt am Main: Campus-Verlag, 1999.

Lenskyj, Helen. *Out of Bounds: Women, Sport and Sexuality*. Toronto: Women's Press, 1986.

Lerner, Paul. "Hysterical Cures: Gender and Performance in World War I and Weimar Germany." *History Workshop Journal* 45 (1998): 79–101.

Lesger, Clé, Leo Lucassen, and Marlou Schrover. "Is There Life outside the Migrant Network? German Migrants in XIXth Century Netherlands and the Need for a More Balanced Migration Typology." *Annales de Démographie Historique* 2 (2002): 29–50.

Lipp, Carola. "Sexualität und Heirat." In *Die Arbeiter: Lebensformen, Alltag und Kultur von der Frühindustrialisierung bis zum "Wirtschaftswunder,"* edited by Wolfgang Ruppert, 186–197. Munich: C. H. Beck, 1986.

Lovell, Stephan. "Finding a Mate in Late Tsarist Russia: The Evidence from Marriage Advertisements." *Cultural and Social History* 4, no. 1 (2007): 51–72.

Lüning, Annemarie. "Heiraten? Nicht so wichtig." Parship Magazin. http://www.parship.de/beziehung/heiraten-nicht-so-wichtig.htm.

Lynch, Katherine. "The European Marriage Pattern in the Cities: Variations on a Theme by Hajnal." *Journal of Family History* 16 (1991): 79–95.

Ma, Zhao. "Down the Alleyway: Courtyard Tenements and Women's Networks in Early Twentieth-Century Beijing." *Journal of Urban History* 36 (2010): 151–172.

Maase, Kaspar. *Die Kinder der Massenkultur: Kontroversen um Schmutz und Schund seit dem Kaiserreich*. Frankfurt am Main: Campus, 2012.

Maierhof, Gudrun and Katinka Schröder. *Sie radeln wie ein Mann, Madame: wie die Frauen das Rad eroberten*. Zurich: Unionsverlag, 1992.

Mainardi, Patricia. *Husbands, Wives, and Lovers: Marriage and Its Discontents in Nineteenth-Century France*. New Haven: Yale University Press, 2003.

Mangan, J. A. and Roberta J. Park, eds. *From "Fair Sex" to Feminism: Sport and the Socialization of Women in the Industrial and Post-industrial Eras*. London: Frank Cass, 1987.

Marcus, Sharon. *Apartment Stories: City and Home in Nineteenth-Century Paris and London*. Berkeley: University of California Press, 1999.

Maynes, Mary Jo. *Taking the Hard Road: Life Course in French and German Workers' Autobiographies in the Era of Industrialization*. Chapel Hill, NC: University of North Carolina Press, 1995.

McCrone, Kathleen. *Playing the Game: Sport and the Physical Emancipation of English Women, 1870–1914*. Lexington: University of Kentucky Press, 1988.

McElligott, Anthony. *The German Urban Experience 1900–1945: Modernity and Chaos*. London: Routledge, 2001.

McLellan, Josie. *Love in the Time of Communism: Intimacy and Sexuality in the GDR*. Cambridge: Cambridge University Press, 2011.

McLeod, Hugh. *Piety and Poverty: Working-Class Religion in Berlin, London, and New York*. New York: Holmes & Meier, 1996.

McKinley, Eric. "Intimate Strangers: Intermarriage among Jews, Catholics, and Protestants in Germany, 1875–1935." PhD dissertation, University of Illinois at Urbana-Champaign, 2015.

Mendels, Franklin. "Proto-industrialization: The First Phase of the Industrialization Process." *Journal of Economic History* 32 (1972): 241–261.

Moch, Leslie Page. *Moving Europeans. Migration in Western Europe since 1650*. Bloomington: Indiana University Press, 2003.

Mooser, Josef. *Arbeiterleben in Deutschland, 1900–1970: Klassenlagen, Kultur und Politik*. Frankfurt am Main: Suhrkamp, 1984.

Muellner, Beth. "The Photographic Enactment of the Early New Woman in 1890s German Women's Bicycling Magazines." *Women in German Yearbook* 22 (2006): 167–188.

Niethammer, Lutz and Franz Brüggemeier. "Wie wohnten Arbeiter im Kaiserreich?" *Archiv für Sozialgeschichte* 16 (1976): 61–134.

Norcliffe, Glen. *The Ride of Modernity: The Bicycle in Canada, 1869–1900*. Toronto: University of Toronto Press, 2001.

Okin, Susan M. "Women and the Making of the Sentimental Family." *Philosophy and Public Affairs* 11 (1982): 65–88.

Oris, Michel. "The Age at Marriage of Migrants during the Industrial Revolution in the Region of Liège." *History of the Family* 5 (2000): 391–413.

Pascher, Ute and Petra Stein, eds. *Akademische Karrieren von Naturwissenschaftlerinnen gestern und heute*. Düsseldorf: Springer, 2013.

Passerini, Luisa. *Europe in Love, Love in Europe*. New York: New York University Press, 1999.

Peiss, Kathy. *Cheap Amusements: Working Women and Leisure in Turn-of-the-Century New York*. Philadelphia: Temple University Press, 1986.

Peukert, Detlev. *The Weimar Republic: The Crisis of Classical Modernity*. Translated by Richard Deveson. New York: Hill and Wang, 1992.

Pooley, Colin and Jean Turnbull. *Migration and Mobility in Britain since the 18th Century*. London: Routledge, 1997.

Porter, Jeremy and Frank Howell. "On the 'Urbanness' of Metropolitan Areas: Testing the Homogeneity Assumption, 1970–2000." *Population Research and Policy Review* 28, no. 5 (2009): 589–613.

Puschmann, Paul, Per-Olof Grönberg, Reto Schumacher, and Koen Matthijs. "Access to Marriage and Reproduction among Migrants in Antwerp and Stockholm: A Longitudinal Approach to Processes of Social Inclusion and Exclusion, 1846–1926." *History of the Family* 19, no. 1 (2004): 29–52.

Puschmann, Paul and Arne Solli. "Household and Family during Urbanization and Industrialization: Efforts to Shed New Light on an Old Debate." *History of the Family* 19, no. 1 (2004):1–12.

Putz, Christa. *Verordnete Lust: Sexualmedizin, Psychoanalyse und die "Krise der Ehe," 1870–1930*. Bielefeld: transcript Verlag, 2011.

Pütz, Peter. "Die Kiosk ist die Schule der Nation: Trivialliteratur und Demokratie." *Gießener Universitätsblätter* 7, no. 2 (1974): 56–69.

Roth, Andreas. *Kriminalitätsbekämpfung in deutschen Großstädten, 1850–1914: Ein Beitrag zur Geschichte des strafrechtlichen Ermittlungsverfahrens*. Berlin: Erich Schmidt Verlag, 1997.

Ruggles, Steven. *Prolongued Connections: The Rise of the Extended Family in Nineteenth-Century England and America*. Madison: University of Wisconsin Press, 1987.

Sabean, David. "Household Formation and Geographical Mobility: A Family Register Study for a Württemberg Village, 1760–1900." *Annales de démographie historique* (1970): 275–294.

Sachße, Christoph. *Mütterlichkeit als Beruf: Sozialarbeit, Sozialreform und Frauenbewegung, 1871–1929*. Frankfurt am Main: Suhrkamp, 1986.

Salomon, Eleonore. "Aus den Anfängen des bürgerlichen Frauenradsports in Deutschland." *Theorie und Praxis der Körperkultur* 14, no. 3 (March 1965): 199–206.

Schenkel, Elmar. "Cyclomanie: Fahrrad und Literatur um 1900." *Literaturwissenschaftliches Jahrbuch* 37 (1996): 211–228.

Schlör, Joachim. *Nights in the Big City: Paris, Berlin, London, 1840–1930*. Translated by Pierre Gottfried Imhof and Dafydd Rees Roberts. London: Reaktion Books, 1998.

Schnurr, Eva-Maria. "Teenage Angst: Berlin's Turn of the Century Growing Pains." *Spiegel Online International*. November 22, 2012. http://www.spiegel.de/ international/germany/the-late-19th-century-saw-the-birth-of-modern-berlin-a-866321.html.

Schorske, Carl. *Fin-de-Siècle Vienna: Politics and Culture*. New York: Knopf, 1980.

Schraut, Sylvia. *Bürgerinnen im Kaiserreich: Biografie eines Lebensstils*. Stuttgart: W. Kohlhammer, 2013.

Schulz, Andreas. *Lebenswelt und Kultur des Bürgertums im 19. und 20. Jahrhundert*. Munich: Oldenbourg, 2005.

Scott, Joan. "Gender: A Useful Category of Historical Analysis." *American Historical Review* 91, no. 5 (1986): 1053–1075.

Shih, Shu-mei. *The Lure of the Modern: Writing Modernism in Semicolonial Shanghai, 1917–1937.* Berkeley: University of California Press, 2001.

Shorter, Edward. *The Making of the Modern Family.* London: Collins, 1976.

Showalter, Elaine. *Sexual Anarchy: Gender and Culture at the Fin de Siècle.* New York: Viking, 1990.

Simmons, Christina. *Making Marriage Modern: Women's Sexuality from the Progressive Era to World War II.* New York: Oxford University Press, 2009.

Simmons, Sherwin. "Ernst Kirchner's Streetwalkers: Art, Luxury, and Immortality in Berlin, 1913–1916." *Art Bulletin* 82 (2000): 117–148.

Smith, Jill Suzanne. *Berlin Coquette: Prostitution and the New German Woman, 1890–1933.* Ithaca, NY: Cornell University Press, 2013.

Smith, Jill Suzanne. "Working Girls: White-Collar Workers and Prostitutes in Late Weimar Fiction." *German Quarterly* 81, no. 4 (2008): 449–470.

Spector, Scott. *Prague Territories: National Conflict and Cultural Innovation in Franz Kafka's Fin de Siècle.* Berkeley: University of California Press, 2000.

Steinberg, Mark D. *Petersburg Fin de Siècle.* New Haven: Yale University Press, 2011.

Stewart, Charles T., Jr. "The Urban-Rural Dichotomy: Concepts and Uses." *American Journal of Sociology* 64, no. 2 (1958): 152–158.

Stone, Lawrence. *The Family, Sex, and Marriage in England, 1500–1800.* New York: Harper Torchbooks, 1979.

Tamagne, Florence. *A History of Homosexuality in Europe: Berlin, London, Paris, 1919–1939.* New York: Algora, 2006.

Tartar, Maria. *Lustmord: Sexual Murder in Weimar Germany.* Princeton, NJ: Princeton University Press, 1995.

Tenfelde, Klaus. "Urbanization and the Spread of Urban Culture." In *Towards an Urban Nation: Germany since 1780*, edited by Friedrich Lenger, 13–42. Oxford: Berg, 2002.

Thießen, Gabriele. *"Da verstehe ich die Liebe doch anders und besser": Liebeskonzepte der Münchener Boheme um 1900.* Nordhausen: Verlag Traugott Bautz, 2015.

Tilly, Louise, Joan Scott, and Miriam Cohen. "Women's Work and European Fertility Patterns." *Journal of Interdisciplinary History* 6, no. 3 (Winter 1976): 447–476.

Todd, Selina. *Young Women, Work, and Family in England, 1918–1950.* New York: Oxford University Press, 2005.

Usborne, Cornelie. *The Politics of the Body in Weimar Germany: Women's Reproductive Rights and Duties.* Ann Arbor: University of Michigan Press, 1992.

Walkowitz, Judith. *City of Dreadful Delight: Narratives of Sexual Danger in Late-Victorian London.* Chicago: University of Chicago Press, 1992.

Wehler, Hans-Ulrich. *Deutsche Gesellschaftsgeschichte.* 5 vols. Munich: C. H. Beck, 1987–2008.

Weitz, Eric D. *Weimar Germany: Promise and Tragedy.* Princeton, NJ: Princeton University Press, 2007.

Whyte, Iain Boyd and David Frisby, eds. *Metropolis Berlin, 1880–1940*. Berkeley: University of California Press, 2012.

Woycke, James. *Birth Control in Germany, 1871–1933*. London: Routledge, 1988.

You've Got Mail. DVD. Directed by Nora Ephron. Burbank, CA: Warner Home Video, 2001.

Index